1993

GEN 780.
Tawa, Nicholas E.
Mainstream music of early twen

3 0301 00083485 9

Mainstream Music
of
Early Twentieth
Century
America

**Recent Titles in
Contributions to
the Study of Music and Dance**

Mozart in Person: His Character and Health
Peter J. Davies

Music for the Dance: Reflections on a Collaborative Art
Katherine Teck

From Sibelius to Sallinen: Finnish Nationalism and the Music of Finland
Lisa de Gorog with the collaboration of Ralph de Gorog

From Chords to Simultaneities: Chordal Indeterminancy and the Failure of
Serialism
Nachum Schoffman

20th-Century Microtonal Notation
Gardner Read

Movement to Music: Musicians in the Dance Studio
Katherine Teck

The Coming of Age of American Art Music: New England's Classical
Romanticists
Nicholas E. Tawa

Theological Music: Introduction to Theomusicology
Jon Michael Spencer

Philosophy and the Analysis of Music: Bridges to Musical Sound, Form, and
Reference
Lawrence Ferrara

Alfred Einstein on Music: Selected Music Criticisms
Catherine Dower

Salsiology: Afro-Cuban Music and the Evolution of Salsa in New York City
Vernon W. Boggs

Dancing Till Dawn: A Century of Exhibition Ballroom Dance
Julie Malnig

Mainstream Music
of
Early Twentieth
Century
America

THE COMPOSERS, THEIR TIMES, AND THEIR WORKS

NICHOLAS E. TAWA

Contributions to the Study of Music and Dance,
Number 28

GREENWOOD PRESS
Westport, Connecticut • London

LIBRARY
College of St. Francis
JOLIET, ILL.

Library of Congress Cataloging-in-Publication Data

Tawa, Nicholas E.
    Mainstream music of early twentieth century America : the
composers, their times, and their works / Nicholas E. Tawa.
        p.   cm. — (Contributions to the study of music and dance,
ISSN 0193–9041 ; no. 28)
    Includes bibliographical references and index.
    ISBN 0–313–28563–2
    1. Music—United States—20th century—History and criticism.
2. Composers—United States. I. Title. II. Series.
ML200.5.T35   1992
780′.973′09041—dc20   92–10676

British Library Cataloguing in Publication Data is available.

Copyright © 1992 by Nicholas E. Tawa

All rights reserved. No portion of this book may be
reproduced, by any process or technique, without the
express written consent of the publisher.

Library of Congress Catalog Card Number: 92–10676
ISBN: 0–313–28563–2
ISSN: 0193–9041

First published in 1992

Greenwood Press, 88 Post Road West, Westport, CT 06881
An imprint of Greenwood Publishing Group, Inc.

Printed in the United States of America

The paper used in this book complies with the
Permanent Paper Standard issued by the National
Information Standards Organization (Z39.48–1984).

10 9 8 7 6 5 4 3 2 1

780.973
T 233

Contents

149,730

Preface

The following pages propose to examine the most prominent American composers active in the earliest years of the twentieth century and the music they wrote: Kelley, Converse, Mason, Hill, Daniels, Hadley, Taylor, Cadman, Gilbert, Farwell, Powell, Shepherd, Joplin, Griffes, Bauer, and Carpenter. Some years ago, I set out to learn what these composers had accomplished, not what latter-day critics claim they had the obligation to have accomplished. Immediately, it became obvious that the agenda of the former was not that of the latter. Nor was I convinced that the normally temperate music of these composers was necessarily inferior because it is not infused with unfamiliar, unproven, and innovational techniques. I was also interested in finding out what was feasible for these composers to achieve, after considering their era, their place in contemporary society, and their own predilections. Lastly, I wondered how trustworthy was the prevalent notion of today that these composers were a mere footnote to our cultural history and that their works are inconsequential. Such a devastating evaluation seemed unfair to apply to honest artists who devoted so much of their creative lives to producing a body of musical literature that they hoped would represent the best in them.

The first thing that struck me was that these musicians were active during a time when tremendous changes were taking place in American society. Industrial expansion and urban growth were rapidly building up a mass of rootless wage earners. Young people were deserting the farms and villages for the cities and their promise of economic betterment. Millions of immigrants had recently arrived and continued to arrive, not from the congenial North European countries but from Eastern Europe, the Mediterranean basin, and the Far East. The immigrants were not Protestant Christians, were usually darker complexioned, conducted their lives differently and had taste preferences that seemed strange, and—what was more dismaying—most of them were poor, uneducated, and ignorant. The longstanding American way of life, based on Protestant ethics, rural and small-town values, and the cohesive outlook of a homogeneous people, was rapidly being altered. Since almost all of these composers came from old-American stock, they presumably felt disquieted about the changes taking place. They surely noticed the deplorable aftereffects of contemporary urban living—corruption, violence, human degradation, and loss of the moral anchor that had reliably supported the America they cherished. Some felt that time-tested American principles, as they understood them to be, should continue to be a force in resolving the confusions of the present. Several of them did experience the need to reassert musically what they saw as valuable in their own heritage. One or two became largely cultural conservators rather than transformers. This was particularly true of Daniel Gregory Mason and John Powell. It was also true, but to a lesser extent, of Frederick Shepherd Converse, Mabel Daniels, and Edward Burlingame Hill. I do not mean that nothing new entered their thinking and music. I do mean that whatever was new that did enter was tempered by the inheritance they held dear.

Secondly, I found the composers living in a time when the United States was changing from an insular nation to a great economic, political, and colonial power—a shift accelerated by World War I. Commerce with transoceanic countries increased dramatically. Diplomatic relations with other nations took on major importance. Our sphere of political control was extended to islands of the Pacific Ocean and Caribbean Sea, and to Central America. Our sphere of influence embraced all of the Americas. World fairs in Chicago, Philadelphia, and St. Louis celebrated our attainment of national maturity. Goods and ideas freely traveled back and forth across the Atlantic as never before. The composers took notice of the fairs and looked abroad for fresh concepts to incorporate into their works, so long as the novelties were compatible with their viewpoint. Henry Gilbert discovered the national music of Russia and other non-German countries at the Chicago Fair of 1893, and soon was stimulated to seek out America's own national music. During his creative life, Charles Tomlinson Griffes looked for guidance from the music of Germany, then of France, and lastly of Asia. The compositions of national composers, like Dvořák, Mussorgsky, and Grieg, and composers at the cutting-edge of music, like Debussy, Ravel, and Stravinsky, contributed to the stylistic alterations.

I found most fascinating of all the quest for an American musical identity. Was it enough just to live and work in the United States without consciously seeking out an American identity, as Griffes did? Was an Anglo-Celtic musical direction the true expression of what America was about, as was the claim of Powell? Was it an intense identification with one region as was apparent in Edward Burlingame Hill's *Lilacs*, which delineated New England, and Arthur Shepherd's *Horizons* on the American West? Were Amerindian-inspired works representative of the best in America, as Arthur Farwell maintained? What about the African-American music favored by Gilbert, or the contemporary popular-music styles that identified important compositions of John Alden Carpenter? Was Henry Hadley right to go his own way, never debating what it meant to compose an *American* music, never doubting the tried-and-true compositional methods he employed, and writing to please himself and his audiences? The issue of cultural Americanism was predominant during the early years of the century. What is most fascinating is how each composer arrived at his own answer.

Lastly, I faced the question: did I as a listener honestly like the music? The answer was an emphatic yes! Not all of it, to be sure, but certainly more than just a few works. Nor was my enjoyment limited to one style. Compositions as diverse in sound and concept as Converse's *Mystic Trumpeter*, Carpenter's *Skyscrapers*, Griffes's Piano Sonata, Hadley's Second Symphony, and Deems Taylor's *Through the Looking Glass* proved soundly envisioned, skillfully crafted, and expressively meaningful. Compositions such as these are designed to stir the emotions and, at the same time, stimulate the imagination. If the listener does not reject romantic music out of hand, he will find delight in the logically articulated forms, fine invention within an assimilable idiom, and wealth of appealing melody.

Mainstream Music of
of
Early Twentieth
Century
America

Chapter One

Themes and Viewpoints

The first prominent native-born American composers emerged during the last third of the nineteenth century. Among the most outstanding of them were John Knowles Paine, George Chadwick, Edward Mac-Dowell, Horatio Parker, Arthur Foote, and Amy Beach—all related to New England in one way or another. Loosely, they made up what can be called a New England-oriented group. They had achieved international reputations through compositions exhibiting high craftsmanship, mastery of a classical-romantic musical idiom, and content at once substantial, convincing, and agreeable. Their contributions to American culture included songs, characteristic pieces and sonatas for piano, chamber music, symphonies, concertos, symphonic poems, sacred masses, oratorios, and operas.

Their teachers had been Germans, or Americans with a Germanic outlook. Their admiration had gone principally to German composers, at first to Beethoven, Schubert, Mendelssohn, Schumann, and Brahms, and later also to Liszt and Wagner. As one might expect, their own styles had grown out of a Germanic context. Nevertheless, none of their compositions slavishly followed German models and the music of at least one of them, Chadwick, breathed an American sound and spirit before Antonín Dvořák was supposed to have shown the way.[1]

Then a younger generation of American composers came along, born in the 1870s and early 1880s, whose main creative years spanned the first third of the twentieth century. A majority of them had a connection with New England, whether by birth, education, or residence. Among the most well-known in their time were Frederick Shepherd Converse, Edward Burlingame Hill, Daniel Gregory Mason, Henry Gilbert, Henry

Hadley, Arthur Farwell, John Alden Carpenter, Arthur Shepherd, Charles Wakefield Cadman, John Powell, Charles Tomlinson Griffes, and Deems Taylor. To this list one should add Edgar Stillman Kelley. Although born in 1857, Kelley lived on to 1944, composed most of his major works during the twentieth century, and figured prominently in the move away from abstract compositions and towards program music.

Most of their early works, like those of the just mentioned New England group, also rested on Germanic roots. Their styles, however, increasingly felt the influence of either Richard Strauss, Piotr Ilyich Tchaikovsky, Modest Mussorgsky, contemporary French composers (d'Indy, Debussy, Ravel), or one or more American musical dialects (minstrel, British-American folk, American Indian, African-American, and contemporary rag and jazz music). Here and there a work reveals a hint of Alexander Scriabin, Igor Stravinsky, or even Arthur Schoenberg. Farwell, in 1914, saw his generation of composers working in a "transitional period," poised between emulation of older styles and probing for something new, "both in quality and application."[2] By the early 1930s, his generation would be largely supplanted by a new wave of composers who desired to go well beyond the confines of tradition. In 1933, Marion Bauer reported: "To many, the present day music seems to break completely with the past, to have no logical connection with former accepted methods. . . . It must be acknowledged that we are in a stage of transitional upheaval. . . ."[3]

As should be clear, the mainstream composers created their compositions during a period of diverse stylistic explorations. Although they continued to cultivate the genres favored by the older New England group, most of them deemphasized chamber music and concentrated more on opera, tone poems, and other types of descriptive music. Their works evidenced a passage from the Germanic-based classical-romanticism of the older New Englanders, through a couple of decades when a variety of musical styles could exist simultaneously in a state of balance, to a dominant posttriadic "modern" phase which deemphasized accepted cultural values and abandoned conventional musical standards. This last stage would be represented by composers like Carl Ruggles, Wallingford Riegger, Edgar Varèse, Roger Sessions, Henry Cowell, George Antheil, and Aaron Copland. Except for Ruggles and possibly Riegger, most of the composers intent on innovation would be younger than the mainstream composers. Charles Ives, born in 1874, was certainly an innovator. However, he would not have a forceful influence on American music until after World War II.

It should be pointed out that many modernists would also show some allegiance to one or more traditional procedures in several of their significant works, especially those created after the early 1930s and through the 1940s. This allegiance, to be sure, would be much less than that of the mainstream composers and would be manifested in more unique ways. Moreover, throughout the twentieth century, American composers would come along who would adhere to the principles of romanticism and the usages of the common-practice period.[4]

THE CHANGING WORLD OF MUSIC

The first real upsurge in American art music took place in the last third of the nineteenth century, and it came after decades when little of an artistic nature had been composed. Some Moravian compositions, the piano works of Louis Moreau Gottschalk, the mostly church-centered music of Dudley Buck, and the tentative compositional attempts of William Fry and George Bristow constituted a large part of what had been written. After the Civil War, the production and quality of native compositions would increase. Before long, experiments with the American musical vernacular would begin to take place.

Prior to 1870, the chamber-music performance of American compositions had been rare, orchestral performance even more rare, and operatic performance almost unknown. Scarcely a wealthy individual, and certainly no governmental body, federal, state or local, was ready to encourage the creation of native string quartets, symphonies, and operas. What music was heard almost invariably came from Europe. The height of achievement in the American musical world comprised the mounting of an Italian opera, a Central European symphony, or a Handel oratorio. Moreover, thorough musical instruction at an American conservatory of music or college department of music was scarcely to be had. Nor was music a morally sanctionable or useful study. To become a professional musician was to betray a flippant attitude toward life.

Matters changed for the better after the Civil War. Many of the immigrants to America, especially those from Germany, enjoyed art music and fostered its performances. Among them were well-trained musicians, who immediately set about establishing and performing in a variety of musical groups, and who offered proficient instruction in all phases of music-making. Concert tours by highly competent European performers, like Jenny Lind and Ole Bull, romanticized the pursuit of art music. In addition, many young Americans were going to Europe to further their educations, academic and cultural. American men and women grew more sophisticated in their tastes and began to appreciate artists and artistic productions as never before.

Conservatories of music and college music departments came to exist. Capable-performing ensembles increased. Talented Americans, determined to become completely trained composers, began their studies at home, then traveled to Germany to obtain an exhaustive grounding in their art. They returned to the United States not only to create their own works but to train a host of younger composers.

Prominent among these pioneers was John Knowles Paine. He initiated musical instruction at Harvard University and wrote several outstanding compositions, including a sacred mass, an oratorio, an opera, and two symphonies. Another pioneer, George Chadwick, headed the New England Conservatory of Music in Boston, and wrote highly polished symphonic and chamber compositions, cantatas, and operas. Not a little of the American vernacular found its way into his music. Edward MacDowell, a consummate pianist and composer for piano, taught at Columbia University after a Boston sojourn. His two piano concertos, four piano sonatas, numerous poetic pieces for piano, and *Indian* Suite for orchestra won him the high regard of American and European music lovers. Horatio Parker found his way from Boston to a professorship at Yale University. His specialty was vocal music; his oratorio *Hora Novissima* and opera *Mona* were peak achievements in the American culture of his time. Arthur Foote, Amy Beach, and Edgar Stillman Kelley also made estimable contributions to American musical literature.

All of this accomplishment notwithstanding, Rupert Hughes still had to observe in 1900: "Aside from occasional attentions evoked by chance performances, it may be said in general that the growth of our music has been unloved and unheeded by anybody except a few plodding composers, their wives, and a retainer or two." He explained his reason for writing *Contemporary American Composers* as follows: "The only thing that inclines me to invade the privacy of the American composer and publish his secrets is my hearty belief . . . that some of the best music in the world is being written here at home, and that it only needs the light to win its meed of praise."[5]

The possibilities for performance did increase after that. More and more capable ensembles came to exist both because their membership consisted of well-trained European musicians, who were arriving in large numbers, and because they found financial sponsors and ready audiences in the burgeoning urban centers. For example, the New York Philharmonic, the Boston Symphony, and the Chicago Symphony had commenced life in the nineteenth century; their instrumentalists were largely German-born. Now these three ensembles were followed by the establishment of symphony orchestras in Philadelphia (1900), Minneapolis (1903), Cincinnati (1909), Detroit (1914), Baltimore (1916), and Cleveland and Los Angeles (1918). A composer like Frederick Shepherd Converse or John Alden Carpenter could anticipate performances not only from his local Boston Symphony or Chicago Symphony but from orchestras scattered throughout the United States. If fortunate, a European orchestra or two might give him a hearing.

Nevertheless, the native composers found that after an initial performance or within a few years of a premiere, the composition was set aside and forgotten. Composers had to contend with first, foreign-born conductors and musicians who favored the music of their countrymen; second, with impresarios and managers who discovered greater profit in scheduling European works; and third, with Europophilic boards of trustees, patrons, and writers on music for whom most things American were by definition second rate and unprestigious.

To give an instance, *Musical America* writer "E. C. S.," in January 1914, reported on a lecture sponsored by the University of Pittsburgh that Thomas Whitney Surette had delivered. Surette had declared that there was "no purely American music and no real American composers." The condition of music was similar to that of literature in the time of Washington Irving. Americans were copying "from the German and French schools." Nothing they wrote expressed their own country. Surette had contended "that America is still too young and too cosmopolitan, too full of clash and barbarism to produce great music. There are too many kinds of Americans. The exploitation of Indian tunes is not . . . likely to have lasting influence." John C. Freund, editor of *Musical America*, became incensed, later that year, with critics like Surette, "who have squarely set their faces against everything American in music. To them the very idea that there was such a thing as an American composer was cause for hilarity." He cited Henry E. Krehbiel of the *New York Tribune* as an influential critic contemptuous of all American musicians and composers and preferring all foreigners, even those not first-rate.[6]

In addition, although one or two or their works might have some success abroad, these native composers saw none of their music become a lasting addition to the international repertoire. Yet, they were aware that solid acceptance in the United States would only take place after Europeans regarded their creative efforts as distinctive and worth producing. Mabel Daniels testified in 1905 to the disturbing ignorance of and incuriosity about American music that she discovered in Germany, stating: "It is a sad but true fact that American music has, as yet, won no footing in Germany." Carl Engel speaks of Alfredo Casella writing about American musical life in *La Critica Musicale* and praising only jazz; Engel then observes: "In regrettable, though characteristic, silence he passes over our serious composers, and not with a syllable does he betray whether or not he ever heard of Messrs. Chadwick, Loeffler or Gilbert." Aaron Copland mentioned that all sorts of excellent composers had been active in America but were ignored in Europe; he said: "I myself lose patience with the European music lover who wants our music to be all new, brand-new, absolutely different."[7]

Assuredly, the majority of the mainstream composers put great value on the past and allowed it to guide their present. Nevertheless, when thinking about any musician's past, we must keep in mind that the grasp of it differs significantly from person to person. One musician may be shaky about even recent developments and muddle the connection between the tiny fractions of memory that remain with him. His writing, whether good or bad, rests on misinterpretation. It may embrace epochs for another composer, whose mind wanders back to the Middle Ages and who remembers the centuries as logically consistent and ordered. He anticipates a gradual evolution from one state of the art to another, consonant with the past but looking forward to the future. (Almost all composers in this study believed in this gradual evolution.) Still another composer cherishes everything from yesteryear, lingering on former times to the exclusion of everything taking place around him. He is the true reactionary, rejecting even the most deliberate evolvement of musical speech. None of the composers studied here fit into this last category.

Taken as a group, the artists with whom we are concerned had a special sensitivity to the past. They relied upon it to steady them when confronted by the accelerated social, scientific, and cultural transformations going on in their own time. They evinced an acute appreciation of what was handed down to them, letting it supply them with a semblance of personal unity in a disorderly and worldly era and probed it for possible artistic refurbishing, each in his own way.

Because the mainstream composers were likely to build on, rather than repudiate, their inheritance (and this includes even dedicated nationalists like Henry Gilbert and Arthur Farwell), they were beset by a further problem: the hostility of various modernists inclined to reject most works that drew from the musical common practices and tonal-triadic conventions of the time. Bitter over the reception of his and like-minded composers' music, a disturbed Farwell complained:

The attitude of the world of musical "culture" in America is still cold toward the native producer; this narrow-American "culture" world pays for the maintenance of fashionable foreign standards and resents any interference with this course. Concert singers are seldom heard in American songs worthy of their artistry, and orchestral conductors seldom give, on their own initiative, successful native orchestral works, an isolated performance of which has been arduously procured elsewhere. . . . The pathway of true creativity, of healthy growth and achievement for the composer in America to-day, lies in abandoning the competition with European sensationalists and ultra-modernists in the narrow arena of the concert halls of 'culture' and turning to the fulfillment of national needs in the broadest and deepest sense.[8]

The competition from American "ultra-modernists" for a place in the sun intensified as the years rolled by. Too many composers, however they defined themselves, were chasing too few opportunities for performance, for funds to subsidize their activities, and for teaching positions to provide a livelihood. And modernism was very much in the air after 1900. Strong reactions to the clashing, dehumanizing aspects of the emerging industrial society helped give it birth. Its adherents multiplied after World War I, whose attendant horrors and accelerated dissolution of long-standing societal bonds had a lasting effect. It represented an international trend in literature, painting, architecture, and music. It took hold in an America where the customary restraints of church and class had weakened and individuality had strengthened; where cultural Teutonisms met with growing disfavor; where things French were gaining favor; where art music still had a shallow hold on the populace; where the cultural focus was shifting away from New England to New York and other parts of the country; and where composers were no longer inescapably Yankee or Christian.

Modernism's impact on the mainstream composers was twofold. First, while none succumbed completely to any of its manifestations, all were influenced by the fresh modes of expression it made available, some slightly, others to a greater extent. Second, because these musicians refused to embrace fully its artistic precepts, they underwent sustained attack from critics in the several up-to-date camps. The result would be the eventual elimination of their works from serious consideration as musical literature worthy of interest. The avant-gardists would consider them irrelevant to the new American society, that is to say, their subject matter, structures, and substance were deemed to falsify the contemporary world they were expected to represent.[9] Gertrude Stein, around whom several of the young future-looking American musicians clustered in Paris, insisted that tremendous events like World War I served to speed up change in artistic experiences. Frederick Hoffman says that, to her: "The 'pastness' of people and events was not so important as their relevance, and this relevance was tested in the light of its applicability to the present." He continues:

It led to the *isolation* of historical figures and happenings from their original context and to the evaluation of each in terms of contemporary relevance. The *nature* of that relevance was, of course, individualized with each writer who surveyed or selected from the past.[10]

From this perspective, we can understand Carl Van Vechten's attack on all American composers from or loyal to the past, beginning with Paine and including Gilbert, Farwell, Carpenter, and John Powell. He asserted that every one of them lacked inspiration. They represented the genteel bourgeoisie—the affluent upper class and high-ranking clergy—for whom they composed music that was well-bred, maudlin, and disappointingly facile and effortless to fathom. Their music lacked the vitality of popular music, ragtime, and jazz. For these reasons, Van

Vechten had "no warm regard" for Gilbert's *Dance in Place Congo, Negro Rhapsody*, and *Comedy Overture*. Powell's *Rhapsodie Négre* and Carpenter's *Krazy Kat* were not as good as Gershwin's *Rhapsody in Blue*. He confessed that Henry Mencken had "pointed out to" him that it was his

duty to write a book about the American composers, exposing their flaccid opera bar by bar. It was in vain that I urged that this would be but a sleeveless errand, arguing that I could not fight men of straw, that these our composers had no real standing in the concert halls and that pushing them over would be an easy exercise for a child of ten. On the contrary, he retorted, they belonged to the academies; a great many persons believed they were important; it was necessary to dislodge this belief [!].[11]

Van Vechten was indifferent to the premises on which these composers based the legitimacy of their works. Artistic validity was as he and Henry Mencken, not they, defined it.

Again and again the mainstream composers and later traditional composers like Samuel Barber were dismissed because their works were said to lack contemporaneity. Unfortunately for them, the validity of an artistic work, whether in literature, painting, or music, was verified by relevance to if not the mirroring of a "real" contemporary world. It was a concept that took hold at the beginning of the twentieth century and persisted in the decades that followed. Nonetheless, the concept has continuously come under fire. Looking back to the early 1900s, the novelist Ellen Glasgow said:

The modern adventurers who imagine they know love because they have known sex may be wiser than our less enlightened generation. But I am not of their period. I should have found wholly inadequate the mere physical sensation, which the youth of today seek so blithely. . . . I am so constituted that the life of the mind is reality, and love without romantic illumination is a spiritless matter.[12]

John Livingston Lowes, writing about poetry at the end of the second decade, insisted that art interpreted and did not reproduce reality, that instead it admitted a person to "an enchanted ground" beyond mere reality.[13] Etienne Gilson, talking about painting, declared in 1959 that the artist tried to create things that did not exist "ready-made" in reality and that gave him pleasure.[14] Roy McMullen, in 1968, went even further in distinguishing art from reality, saying that a work of art had validity simply because it was not a slice of reality but something willed and given shape by the artist.[15] Finally, toward the end of the century, Charles Newman surveyed the modern scene turning into post-modern and wrote that "first-order" art was not a byproduct or reflection of reality, or a matter of relevance, but a quality achieved only "by a vivid and intensely personal experience of life."[16]

In the brave new world of the twentieth century one came upon a rejection of authority, a revolt against convention, antiromanticism, cultural fragmentation, technical experimentation, and new theories about what it was that art communicated. Novel aesthetic doctrines emanating from Europe were given names like naturalism, symbolism, impressionism, surrealism, futurism, fauvism, Dada, neoclassicism, and expressionism. To most future-looking artists, originality headed the criteria for judging an artistic work. The artist was to cultivate individuality and spurn all external controls as impositions stemming either from sterile reactionism, psychological and sexual repression, or outmoded moral codes. Edith Wharton writes that there was a "dread of doing what has been done before;" a "fear of being unoriginal" that threatened to lead "to pure anarchy."[17]

Musical modernism threatened to uproot the usual guideposts that had made interpretation intelligible and appreciation possible for music lovers. The resultant ambiguity, the simultaneous perception of two or more connotations in a sound or progression of sounds, could produce the effect of anarchy, although the aim was depth and subtlety of meaning, and a cultivation of the unanticipated for the sake of freshness. Traditional ambiguities in music (like swift changes in tonality, chords pointing in several tonal directions, unusual resolutions of dissonance, deceptive cadences, hemiola rhythms, surprising deflections of a melodic phrase) had normally grown out of what was usually anticipated. Modern ambiguities in music (bitonality to atonality, polychordal to posttriadic harmony, constant dissonance, vague meter and uneven rhythms, avoidance of melodic repetition and of sectional recapitulation) made it difficult to anticipate anything in the music and thus might make an entire piece unintelligible.

Because the typical mainstream composer did not believe in revolution, his task was to probe into the pile of assorted modernisms, selecting what was congenial to him and reconciling it with practices from the past within viable musical compositions. He was not a reactionary, one who opposed all innovation and tried to backtrack to some earlier directive or to adamantly maintain the status quo. Some of the new possibilities in music that modernism prospected did excite him.

For example, several American composers testify to the weakening hold of Central Europe and the new attention paid to France, a change accelerated by World War I. César Franck and Vincent d'Indy; Claude Debussy and Maurice Ravel—each suggested a different way of looking at music. Earlier, Chadwick and Foote, and later, Daniel Gregory Mason, Farwell, Converse, Edward Burlingame Hill, Carpenter, Charles Griffes, and, still later, Virgil Thomson felt the fresh cultural winds blowing out of Paris in particular.[18]

On the other hand, the typical mainstream composer did not believe that the acceptability of a composition should hinge on the unusual or iconoclastic. It was clear that artistic postulates were continuously altered; aims and practices were constantly modified. At the same time, he believed that genuine change was effected only slowly. While valuing tradition, he also recognized that "the process of tradition" was "a process of selection." It was inevitable that "parts of the traditional stock drift downward into obscurity so that they are known only to a few persons or conceivably to none at all." Change was common to all periods in history, but total rebellion against the past was a modern cultural phenomenon heretofore unknown to mankind.[19]

The same composer was also anxious to communicate with the American audience, sending out his personal humors, sensibilities, and ideas to his listeners. He believed that music's call was to the natural emotions and aspirations immutable in every person. His creative presentations had a social character; that is to say, they were organized as culturally recognizable gestures, not as singular and provocative displays.[20] If the devices employed were too novel and these too prominently featured, they might strike listeners as grotesque. If they were too well-known, they might prove tedious. He somehow had to reconcile innovation with what was customary. He would certainly have agreed with John Lowes's statement: "Our most permanent aesthetic satisfaction arises as a rule from things familiar enough to give the pleasure of recognition, yet not so trite as to rob us of the other pleasure of surprise. We are keen for the new, but we insist that it establish some connection with what is friendly and our own."[21] Nevertheless, the composer tried not to make the mistake of completely equating a composition's value with its effect on an audience. Even while aware of this relationship, he also was concerned that every work maintain its own integrity as an object separate from the impact it had on listeners.

A very conservative composer like Mason did scarcely any probing into the new; an enterprising one like Griffes or Carpenter did a great deal. All of the mainstream composers sound different from, and musically more adventurous than, the composers that had gone before.

BELIEFS AND VALUES

What most mainstreamers adhered to was a perception of commonly-held tenets. They desired an orderly system with which to back their creative efforts. In order to achieve this, they were willing to admit to some outside rule and restraints. Their convictions upheld their fight against the insistence on up-to-datedness in musical works. Somehow, they found the strength to resist those unsympathetic critics whose subjective reviews belittled their artistic worth. Such critics, they felt, aired opinions that had little relation to artistic values as highly respected thinkers of the past had understood them to be. These hostile writers failed to deal with the intrinsic merits of a work or its ability to communicate importantly to the public. Their test was to discover if the matter of the composition had been handled within recent time, while only superficially pondering, in impartial language, the merit of the handling.[22]

The mainstream composers were certain that their compositions were meaningful to their contemporaries. Giving significance to their music was the serious thought directed toward establishing a body of musical literature founded on obligation to their listeners, and on refinement of the inherited means for expression. The programs they mapped out promised an island of orderliness to a music public repulsed by the growing number of uncompromising and unlovable compositions presented to them. These rejected works dispensed with consonance, lyricism, and tonal direction, and seemed a result of the unruliness in modern artistic life—feverish, apparently aimless, and empty of hope.

The mainstream composers offered what they hoped would be taken as a feasible alternative to all of this. Unlike many modernists, they had no desire to lunge out at their musical predecessors—whose creative existence had been sufficiently arduous without this further aggravation—or at their predecessors' compositions, from which they had benefited greatly. They themselves coupled excellent craftsmanship to musical talent. They did redefine features of musical common practice in what might be considered basic fashion, albeit circumspectly, but always with a sensed duty to speak lucidly to their auditors. Assuredly, the composers would have agreed with Henry Canby's assertion: "I believe that the world is not half so incoherent as the minds of some of the expressionists who write about it. There is plenty of sense in experience if sensible people look for it; and if good art means something it is because life means something also."[23]

In short, these composers proposed their own aesthetic synthesis of current civilization. To offer their synthesis, art had to be lucid, graspable, gratifying to the mind and senses, and held together by configurations of technique, feeling, and thought both methodical and clear. Taken altogether, the successful synthesis produced an "experience of the beautiful which whispers to us that it *is* beautiful and not merely handsomely assembled."[24] To be sure, beauty was not an approved term among modernists; to them, the idea of beauty, like that of God, was so indistinct as to be meaningless. Yet, great artists from every era, and those who enjoyed the works of these same artists, felt they knew what beauty was, though admittedly no two people perceived it in exactly the same way. Thus, it was absurd to claim that they were mistaken. A person who felt music contained beauty sensed that it emanated from the essential character of the artistic work and that it called forth a reciprocating feeling of recognition, pleasure, and gratitude within him. This, too, was the contention of these composers. In reading their commentaries about the musical scene, one is also aware that, save for Mason, they were usually willing to put up with the modernists so long as they were accorded the same courtesy. The courtesy was not always reciprocated.

MUSICAL RECONCILIATIONS

The composers with whom we are concerned were genuine eclectics, selecting what seemed congenial from various musical styles and techniques and incorporating them into their own. Already mentioned was the French overlay to their Germanic base. In addition, there was the input of music from the Slavic world, the Anglo-Celtic American tradition, African-Americans, Amerindians, the Far East, Spain, Latin America, and American popular music. Back in 1900, Rupert Hughes was claiming it was inconceivable that the United States was ready to produce a national musical style that was generally acceptable. His remarks paralleled those by Thomas Whitney Surette cited earlier. Hughes, however, voiced a more encouraging opinion. We were an enormous mix of peoples and cultures not yet assimilated, he said. It would take years to produce a native musical language. It could not come from African-American or Amerindian music alone, however beautiful that music was. Such a core was too limited in scope. He doubted that any strikingly individual composer would arise to give us a national direction based upon his own traits. America's one hope, he said, was to develop a style founded on what he called cosmopolitanism, which contained ingredients from all the world, and yet, when integrated by Americans, was different from any one source. Thus, although American music borrowed from everywhere, the result would ultimately be an assimilated, individual, and instinctive style.[25]

Even the cantankerous and highly conservative Mason acknowledged that it was neither feasible nor healthy for American music to be all of one type, for instance, American-English. It already had embraced American-German, American-French, American-Jewish, Amerindian, and African-American music by 1928. "May it not be," he said, "that we are necessarily polyglot, and that to speak American, in any comprehensible sense" is impossible? Like Hughes, he felt that individual composers had to carve out their own style and accept the cosmopolitanism of American culture.[26]

Carpenter would have agreed with both Hughes and Mason. He was irked with people demanding an "American" attribute in American music. It led to self-consciousness and the extinction of any bona fide creative stimulus, to sterile music. The content of music was by far more important than the affixing of a national label. The American composer should look around and draw his inspiration from whatever point of origin that is most compatible, therefore most stimulating, to him. When stimuli and one's innermost apprehension of human existence fused in a work by a composer living in America, then an American spirit could not help but shine forth. Carpenter concluded: "The American composer is going to be 'American' enough to suit our most fastidious patriots, because in the final analysis he can't, thank God, be anything else."[27]

Each composer showed his eclecticism in a different way. Even when two composers exhibited the same influences, their personalities were so distinct that their compositions cannot be grouped together. Gilbert's rough-and-ready African-American music differs from that of Powell's suaver black Virginians; Farwell's rugged translations from the music of American Indians differ from Charles Wakefield Cadman's sweet-sounding Indianisms. Hill's, Griffes's and Carpenter's interpretations of French impressionism could never be confused with each other or, for that matter, with the music of Debussy or Ravel. Philosophical and symbolic concepts permeate Converse's descriptive music; picturesqueness and vivid colors, Henry Hadley's. Carpenter's mix of Spanish-, Broadway-, jazz-, and blues-related sound within a French-fashioned receptacle are peculiarly his own. Mason and Taylor adhere staunchly to the musical conventions, but in vastly different ways and genres.

In addition, no composer maintained an allegiance to only one manner of utterance. Converse, for example, wrote classically structured non-programmatic symphonies and string quartets; freely episodic tone poems of high romantic content; and pictorial symphonic discourses on the Ford automobile, on California, on America in general, that utilized all sorts of popular and traditional musics representative of America's diverse ethnic groups.

Each composer was a creative entity who shared in and found himself to be a busy proclaimer of some distinctive American style of his age. Autonomy varied from composer to composer, each one determining what freedoms he would allow himself after surveying the multitudinous national modes of expression that were then available. Personal styles do begin to emerge after some investigation of the music, especially if the investigator has sympathy for the manner of setting forth sound and if he subdues the expectations deriving from modernism.

On balance, the mainstream composers also showed certain similarities in their styles. They did adhere to a controlling tonality in most compositions, although an occasional work showed a progressive tonality (as in Carpenter's Concertino for Piano and Orchestra). Some works, especially those employing traditional tunes, may remain diatonic and modulate discreetly, as in Powell's *Natchez-on-the-Hill*. Others indulge in distantly related key centers, extended modulations briefly producing a sense of tonal drift, and splurges of chromaticism that undermine awareness of a definite key. Griffes's *Pleasure Dome of Kubla Khan* and Carpenter's *Sea Drift* provide examples of this. Sometimes, keys that are far apart immediately succeed each other, without pretence of modulation, or, rarely, two keys may sound simultaneously. Bitonal passages, however, are normally short. Tonal ambiguousness may also occur through the use of ecclesiastical modes, a not uncommon practice. Not genuinely modal, this usage does elicit an aura of times long since past, as in Converse's oratorio *Job*.

Harmonies are usually triadic, interdependent, and functional—that is to say, employed so as to contribute to the articulation of a larger structure. Functionality may be suspended if a composer resorts to the harmonic staticism and parallel chordal streams characteristic of French impressionism. Tones added to conventional triadic harmonies, especially the added sixth, are frequently come upon. Almost as frequent are chords of the seventh to the thirteenth and others that are chromatically altered. When especially adventurous, a composer may write a bichordal passage, where different harmonies of the same tonality or from two different tonalities sound together. Obviously, dissonances then may loom large and can resonate without preparation and without resolution to consonances. At times the composer may abandon triadicism and construct chords based on intervals of the fourth or fifth, or on divergent intervallic mixtures. On occasion, harmonies not conforming to any ordinary pattern result from the operation of non-conventional scales—Dorian or Phrygian modes, whole-tone or some kind of gapped scale, and exotic or even invented scales (Griffes's Piano Sonata, for example).

Rhythm inclines to solidness and often exhibits a great deal of vitality. Even the dreamiest and most impressionistic works of Griffes show a firm rhythmic underpinning. The pulsations of American traditional and currently popular song and dance, marches, ragtime, and jazz enrich American rhythm. Strong accents, incisiveness in rhythmic design, and syncopations, especially of the Scotch-snap type (sixteenth note on the beat followed by a dotted eighth note, or followed by an eighth note and a sixteenth note), characterize it. These are especially the attributes of the music written by Gilbert, Carpenter, Shepherd, and Powell.

Melody as a pleasurable sequence of tones, often vocal and lyric in nature, predominates over angular horizontal movement and rhythmically governed chant, except in certain country-fiddle or jazz-oriented works. It may appear expansive and fluid in phraseology after the late-Romantic German fashion (see Mason's Sonata for Clarinet and Piano), or extend itself in short clipped phrases in accord with American dance (see Cadman's *American Suite*). Some readily perceived rationale guides the laying out of melodic phrases and strains. Tunes are usually kept plain, warmhearted, and explicitly congenial to the ear. They incline toward diatonicism even when harmony is chromatic. If a traditional tune is used, whether British-American, African-American, or Amerindian, its arrangement may derive from a gapped scale, seventh tone missing or fourth and seventh tone missing, or from a modal framework, normally exhibiting a lowered seventh. As a case in point, Hadley's Symphony No. 2, *The Four Seasons*, includes a second movement whose tune, à la British-American folksong, neglects the fourth and seventh, and a third movement whose tune, à la Amerindian music, sounds modal with a lowered seventh and missing sixth tone.

From what has just been said, it is evident that a great deal of flexibility prevailed in the composers' use of musical conventions and in their judicious exploitation of modern devices. On the one hand, they continued to alter the ever-malleable tonal system they had inherited; on the other, they were quite willing to displace any convention that they thought overworked with a constructive alternative. Both activities had their proper niche, because both represented the bifurcated tendencies of the age, or of any age.

These musicians did not see themselves as writing transient compositions, possibly suitable for their time but soon to be completely outdated. For the most part, their contributions were serious ones, their music not transitory curiosities. They wished to capture all facets of existence and humanity in their sound, sometimes the earthy, but more often the essential, fixed, or durable, conditions. Every one of them thought they had composed music worthy of rehearing and hoped at least some of their compositions would be cherished as superb contributions to America's musical literature. Among these contributions one can cite Mason's *A Lincoln Symphony*, Hadley's *Four Seasons* Symphony, Converse's *Mystic Trumpeter*, Hill's two *Stevensoniana* Suites, Taylor's *Through the Looking Glass* Suite, Gilbert's *Dance in Place Congo*, Griffes's *Pleasure Dome of Kubla Khan* and Piano Sonata, Carpenter's *Skyscrapers* and *Sea Drift*, and Shepherd's *Horizons* Symphony.

As a final observation, this chapter has underlined the fact that chroniclers and interpreters of American music's past have infrequently presented a dispassionate representation of what has occurred. Critics have written on more than one occasion about what they believed and desired to have occurred. This author has wondered about their analyses, which inevitably bore the impress of their convictions, convictions not often sympathetic to the composers and music to be examined in this study— when they were mentioned at all! The pages that follow attempt first to give information about the composers; second, to try to hear their music with fresh ears; and third, to reassess their compositions and, if need be, to rectify the imbalances in past judgments. The observations that will be made include the composers' views of themselves: what their convictions were and what they were trying to do. The assessments of the music by contemporary music critics and audiences will also be examined. One hopes that the conclusions reached will reflect a greater responsiveness to the cultural needs of a former time and to the musical expression of these needs. They may also suggest that at least some of this music can prove rewarding to listen to today.

NOTES

1. For a study of this New England group of composers see Nicholas E. Tawa, *The Coming-of-Age of American Art Music* (Westport, Connecticut: Greenwood, 1991).

2. "Introduction," to Arthur Farwell and W. Dermot Darby, eds., *Music in America*, The Art of Music 4 (New York: National Society of Music, 1915), p. vii.

3. Marion Bauer, "Author's Foreword," *Twentieth Century Music* (New York: Putnam's Sons, 1933), p. ix.

4. Nicholas E. Tawa, *A Most Wondrous Babble* (Westport, Connecticut: Greenwood, 1987), pp. 183–232.

5. Rupert Hughes, Foreword to *Contemporary American Composers* (Boston: Page, 1900), pp. viii-ix.

6. See the news report by E. C. S. in *Musical America* (3 January 1914), p. 18; also, John C. Freund, "The Young American Artist and the Critic," *Musical America* (17 October 1914), p. 60.

7. Mabel Wheeler Daniels, *An American Girl in Munich: Impressions of a Music Student* (Boston: Little, Brown, 1905), p. 47; Carl Engel, "Views and Reviews," *Musical Quarterly* 9 (1923), p. 149; Aaron Copland, *Music and Imagination* (New York: Mentor, 1959), p. 101.

8. "Introduction," *Music in America*, p. xix.

9. See Allen Tate, *Reason in Madness* (1941, reprint Freeport, New York: Books for Libraries, 1968), pp. 13–14, 153.

10. Frederick J. Hoffman, *The Twenties* (New York: Free Press, 1962), pp. 157–59.

11. Carl Van Vechten, *Red: Papers on Musical Subjects* (New York: Knopf, 1925), pp. 27n, 32.

12. Ellen Glasgow, *The Woman Within* (London: Eyre & Spottiswoode, 1955), p. 163.

13. John Livingston Lowes, *Convention and Revolt in Poetry* (Boston: Houghton Mifflin, 1930), pp. 33, 46.

14. Etienne Gilson, *Painting and Reality* (Cleveland: World, 1959), p. 172.

15. Roy McMullen, *Art, Influence, and Alienation* (New York: Praeger, 1968), p. 9.

16. Charles Newman, *The Post-Modern Era* (Evanston, Illinois: Northwestern University Press, 1985), p. 12.

17. Edith Wharton, *The Writing of Fiction* (New York: Scribner's Sons, 1925), pp. 14, 17.

18. Arthur Foote, "A Bostonian Remembers," *Musical Quarterly* 23 (1937), p. 37ff; Daniel Gregory Mason, *The Dilemma of American Music* (New York: Macmillan, 1928), pp. 5–6; Farwell, "Introduction," *Music in America*, p. xvii; Virgil Thomson, *American Music Since 1910* (New York: Holt, Rinehart & Winston, 1971), p. 5. When Hugo Leichtentritt cites Edward Burlingame Hill, Deems Taylor, John Alden Carpenter, and Frederick Shepherd Converse as being influenced by French Impressionism, we realize that no transitional composer was left untouched; see Hugo Leichtentritt, *Serge Koussevitsky. The Boston Symphony Orchestra and the New American Music* (Cambridge, Massachuetts: Harvard University Press, 1946), p. 45.

19. Douglas Moore concurs with these observations; see *From Madrigal to Modern Music* (New York: Norton, 1942), pp. 254–56. The quotations come from Edward Shils, *Tradition* (Chicago: University of Chicago Press, 1981), p. 26.

20. See Robert Grudin, *The Grace of Great Things* (New York: Ticknor & Fields, 1990), p. 6.

21. Lowes, p. 97.

22. On this point, see John U. Nef, *The United States and Civilization* (Chicago: University of Chicago Press, 1967), p. 275.

23. Henry Seidel Canby, *Definitions: Essays in Contemporary Criticism* (New York: Harcourt, Brace, 1922), p. 21.

24. Ibid., p. 169.

25. Hughes, *Contemporary American Composers*, pp. 13, 22–24.

26. Mason, *The Dilemma of American Music*, p. 18.

27. Carpenter is quoted in Karl Krueger, *The Musical Heritage of the United States: The Unknown Portion* (New York: Society for the Preservation of the American Musical Heritage, 1973), p. 48.

Chapter Two

Kelley and Converse

Both Edgar Stillman Kelley (1857-1944) and Frederick Shepherd Converse (1871-1940) wrote music that at first derived from German academic precepts. Each applied these precepts in his own particular way and thus preserved his own individual identity. Each, in his own characteristic fashion, tried to devise thematic material, chordal combinations, and structural designs based on what he thought were sound and tested principles. They spent a great deal of time deliberating on how to best bring out and make understood the subjects—narrative, pictorial, affective, meditative, or philosophical—upon which they ruminated. They shared an interest in shaping compositions abounding in non-musical references. In this regard, they moved away from the restrictions of the conservative musical world in which they lived and toward the freedoms in sound, structure, and orchestral colorings characteristic of the more forward-looking composers of the turn of the century. In sum, their works display learning, craftsmanship, inventiveness, and unique or fanciful touches that add interest to their otherwise orthodox procedures.

A perusal of the music they produced over their lifetimes establishes their kinship in spirit with George Chadwick, of the New England group, who also had ventured beyond the limits recommended by influential pundits like John Sullivan Dwight. They shared his fondness for discreet musical experimentation, ultra-musical references, inquisitiveness about Americana, and even his inclination toward humor. Moreover, Converse studied composition under Chadwick.

EDGAR STILLMAN KELLEY

Although born in Sparta, Wisconsin, Kelley was descended from New England progenitors. He studied organ playing and music theory in Chicago (under the Massachusetts-born organist Clarence Eddy) and music composition in Stuttgart, Germany (under Max Seifriz). From 1880 to 1886, and 1892 to 1896, he lived in San Francisco, teaching, playing piano and organ, and writing newspaper commentaries on local music activities. From 1886 to 1892, and 1896 to 1900, he was in New York City, conducting an operetta company and teaching at New York College of Music and New York University (for one year he filled in for Horatio Parker, who was on leave, at Yale University). His operetta *Puritania*, completed in 1892, was first performed in Boston in the same year, where around one hundred performances took place. Further successes came when it toured other cities.

Then, until 1910, Kelley was in Berlin, where he conducted and taught. Among his students was the future American composer Wallingford Reigger. He returned to join the faculty at Western College for Women, in Ohio. He remained there until he retired. In later life he would be honored by the formation of the Edgar Stillman Kelley Society, dedicated to sponsoring the publication of American music.

In a few important respects, Kelley shared in the beliefs of the New England group of composers. Like them, he thought that long and widely recognized artistic truths had to come first and guide everything a composer did. Forced nationalism was bound to fail, although he himself was glad if he could use native music to capture the vital force and feelings representative of America. Whatever the governing theme of a composition, be it nationalistic or otherwise, it could only come alive if it attracted and fired the imagination of the composer. To him, originality could not help but reflect an artist's beliefs and values, those inherited and those peculiar to his American circumstances. Remarking on compositions like his Symphony No. 2, *New England*, Kelley said: "The American composer should apply the universal principles of his art to the local and special elements of the subject-matter as they appeal to him, and then, consciously or unconsciously, manifest his individuality, which will involve the expression of mental traits and moral tendencies peculiar to his European ancestry, as we find them modified by the new American environment."[1]

Because he went to live in San Francisco, where he was fascinated by the music in Chinatown, his *Aladdin*, a Chinese suite for orchestra, came to exist. Composed between 1887 and 1893, the suite received its first complete performance in New York City, in 1896. He wanted to saturate the four movements with Chinese musical ideas and the typical sounds of Chinese instruments. The employment of the pentatonic scale and a few traditional Chinese melodies aided his recreation of far-away scenes. The first movement, "At the Wedding of Aladdin and the Princess," calls for the impression of a slack-bowed Chinese fiddle, the exotic strum of mandolins, the flicker of *pizzicato* strings, and the careful placement of muted trumpets and muttering oboes to produce the desired effect of a Far-Eastern celebration.

The second movement, "In the Palace Garden—Serenade," is a delicate piece of Orientalism. Meter alternates between duple and triple time. Lean harmonies are orchestrated adroitly, giving the sensation of music that is both polished and fragile. The sound is at once insubstantial, fetching, spicy, and alluring. This movement is followed by "The Flight of the Genie with the Palace," and "The Return—Feast of Lanterns."

In a letter sent to Kelley in 1915, Edward Burlingame Hill praised *Aladdin* and congratulated Kelley on "the novel features of the instrumentation, and how far they were in advance, as regards independence, not only of current American procedure but of everything in Europe save the Neo-Russians."[2] The composition was indeed novel, even bizarre, for its day, and did manage to win considerable approval. When the score is reexamined today, one can still appreciate the picturesque sounds and clever effects that grow out of an essentially German academic foundation.

Another early work that won him contemporary acclaim was the incidental music he wrote for the New York production of *Ben Hur*, in 1899. The production then traveled through all of the English speaking countries and saw at least 5,000 performances. Like that of *Aladdin*, the music, with its reproduction of Greek and Arabian scales and use of descending parallel-fourth progressions, seemed novel and quite modern to contemporary American ears.[3]

In 1907, Kelley published his two most important contributions to chamber-music literature, the Quintet for Piano and Strings, opus 20, and the Quartet for Strings, opus 25. Arthur Shepherd has praised both works for their solid musical merits and evidence of technical mastery; he also commended their inherent charm, sincerely-felt poetics, and judicious balancing of instruments in the part-writing.[4]

The Symphony No. 2 in B-flat Minor, *New England*, was premiered at the Norfolk, Connecticut, Festival of the Litchfield County Choral Union on 3 June 1913. It soon had many performances throughout the United States. At the time, it was lauded as one of America's most distinguished symphonies, showing imagination, inventiveness, a thorough command of orchestration, a mastery of large structures, and the solid textures attributable to a German grounding.[5] In the preface to the score, Kelley said that he wished to express the thoughts and sentiments of the New England pioneers. Quotations from the Log Book of the Mayflower, a book later extended into the History of Plymouth Colony, prefix the movements and refer to the experiences of those who arrived in Plymouth in 1620. Governor William Bradford, an ancestor of the composer, wrote both books.[6]

The first movement is meant to depict the great difficulties faced by the Pilgrims and the courage shown in overcoming them. A dignified slow introduction precedes a sonata-form *Allegro*, with sections designed to sound passionate, tranquil, agitated, mysterious, and, at the end, resolute. Here, as in so many other examples of his music, original themes seem to derive from a harmonic context and have few distinct features of their own. No really memorable melody emerges. One admires the workmanship, but hears little that is truly passionate and agitated. The pleasant second movement makes reference to birds pleasantly singing in the woods, and, in fact, freely treated bird motives do occur. The third movement, captioned "Great lamentations and heaviness," is presented as a theme and five variations, utilizing the beautiful old New England hymn of Timothy Swan, "Why do we mourn departing friends." Stately solemnity rather than melancholy pervades the movement. The final movement honors and laments the dead and exhorts the living to work together and be true to each other. One hears in it a reworking of first-movement motives, an American Indian-inspired section, an animated version of Swan's hymn, and a coda that recapitulates the main melody of the first movement.

Whatever the attempt to picture New England, the symphony sounds Germanic. The music is mostly ruminative in effect and dwells on the same few ideas. Commenting on the work, Daniel Gregory Mason finds it technically competent but "German to the backbone." Scarcely anything of New England, he says, is actually captured in the music. Mason adds that in a symphony like this, "the dominance of a foreign model seems to paralyse personal feeling."[7] Despite this criticism, the expression sounds sincere. The music is worth reviving.

Kelley went on to compose an oratorio, *The Pilgrim's Progress* (1917), based on Paul Bunyan; the suite *Alice in Wonderland*, a series of pantomime pictures for orchestra (1919), based on Lewis Carroll; a symphonic poem *The Pit and the Pendulum* (1925), based on Edgar Alan Poe; and a programmatic *Gulliver* Symphony (started in 1883, completed in 1936), based on Jonathan Swift. Interestingly, *Alice in Wonderland* was composed about the same time that Deems Taylor was working on his suite *Through the Looking Glass*.

The oratorio and symphonic poem are stylistically similar to the *New England* Symphony. More attractive are the suite's concise portraits, each neatly sketching an event and capturing a mood, of "Alice on her way to Wonderland," "The white rabbit is late," "The Cheshire Cat," "The Caucus Race," "The forest of forgetfulness," and "The Red Queen's banquet." Equally fine is the symphony on Gulliver: first ruminating on Gulliver's voyage and shipwreck; next, on his dreams as he sleeps; next, on the Lilliputians, who tie up Gulliver, playing their national anthem, which is presented as a fugue; and last, Gulliver's rescue and homeward journey to the tune of a hornpipe. Kelley's forte in both compositions lies in the humor and quaint charm of the music and the deftness of the orchestration.

Kelley did compose some pleasurable works, all of them making non-musical references. His importance to American music rests in his early exploration of program music in suites, incidental music to plays, and symphonies. Never himself able to cleanly break away from his musical antecedents, he did make it less difficult for the mainstream composers to lose some of their inhibitions, do a little experimentation, and pursue pathways their mentors had never thoroughly investigated.

FREDERICK SHEPHERD CONVERSE

Student and Tone Poet

There is no question that Converse was a far better composer than Kelley, having a superior talent, imagination, and ability to translate thoughts and feelings into sound. During the first two decades of the twentieth century the art-music public regarded him as one of the foremost composers the United States had yet produced. The few times his works saw performance abroad, they won the respect, however grudging, of European audiences and critics. Beyond any doubt, he added vitally to America's musical literature, and is an important figure in America's cultural past. Several of his compositions continue to be admirable and worthy of a permanent place in the repertoire.

He was born in Newton, Massachusetts, a town just over the line from Boston. Neither his Yankee ancestry nor his immediate background can account for his early interest in music. Yet, his parents seem to have abetted his musical pursuits. Converse explained: "My passion has been music, and all my tastes and surroundings were calculated to stimulate and encourage this passion. I began to study music when yet a mere boy, and my preferences were toward composition."[8]

He studied music at Harvard College, under John Knowles Paine, whom he found to be a gracious and considerate teacher and friend, and took his B.A. with highest honors, in 1893. Although he had shown considerable musical aptitude, he was pressed into a business career by his merchant-father. However, he quickly learned that commerce was not his métier and gave himself totally to music. As Louis Elson wrote: "A few months of a commercial career convinced the young Converse that he was unsuited to business, and he then decided to make music his profession."[9] Chadwick in Boston and (after Converse's marriage) Joseph Rheinberger in Munich furthered his education in music composition. Whether in Boston or Munich, prominent musicians lauded his musical gifts and expected much from him.

Converse taught at the New England Conservatory from 1900 through 1902, and at Harvard from 1903 through 1907. He then resigned from the Harvard faculty in order to dedicate himself to musical composition alone. Fortunately for him, he had an independent income with which to support his musical activities and his large family (five girls and two boys, both of whom died in childhood). The year of his resignation from Harvard also saw him, along with Eben Jordan, working to found the Boston Opera Company, whose vice-president he became in 1909, when the opera company first opened its doors. (George Chadwick and Charles Martin Loeffler were on the board, and Henry Hadley held some of its shares.) After five years the opera company found itself insolvent and ceased existence.[10] In 1920, Converse returned to the New England Conservatory, becoming its dean of faculty in 1931, and continued there until 1938, two years before he died. Converse, the mature artist, fulfilled the expectations of his mentors; he was admired both as a person and creative artist by the composers of his generation. Hadley enthusiastically advanced his name before the American Academy of Arts and Letters, to which body Converse was elected in 1937.

Contemporaries described him as unpretentious, sociable with acquaintances, kind to students, and modest about his artistic worth. On the evidence of Ruth Severance, he was a successful teacher. She wrote: "As one of his former pupils I can speak of his character and ability as a teacher. He is clear and thorough in the presentation of his subject, and has the faculty of making it interesting and attractive. He always encourages and stimulates the development of originality in his pupils."[11]

An interview was granted an unnamed reporter from the *Christian Science Monitor* in 1910, when Converse was at the height of his creative vigor and fame. He stated a belief close to that of Kelley when he admitted: "I do not believe in nationality in music, but I do believe in good music. I think that we will eventually infuse a new freshness and vitality into music in America; that we will not be hampered by traditions that the European writers have to cope with; that music will grow simpler— we will go back to less complex forms, to more originality."[12] His style at that time was fairly restrained when compared to that of the European mavericks—Scriabin, Schoenberg, and Stravinsky—although showing some willingness to try out one or two of the innovations proposed by these more daring experimenters.

As if to belie his words, several later works would utilize a greater amount of musical modernities and/or explore one or another national vein. Not least of these compositions would be *Flivver Ten Million* (1926), *California* (1927), and the *American Sketches* (1928). Assuredly, his musical practices did not remain rigid. By 1930, he was calling himself conservatively modern; yet, toward the end of the decade, he was declaring: "I am through with the extravagant elements of modern music. No more experimentation of that sort for me. It is already old-fashioned. What we need is deeper spiritual and emotional significance in our music. Given that, all the rest will take care of itself."[13]

One can safely say that he always spurned the construction of cool cerebral edifices in favor of stirring formats that revealed a disciplined romanticism, touches of mysticism, clear and personal poetic speech, and recourse to the values of Yankee America for inspiration. His works stressed orderly beauty, but also looked inward, and now and again disclosed a wistful yearning. Several significant compositions were meditations on human life and on the permanencies that philosophy and religion tried to express. One or two were high-spirited larks, which were in their own way meditations on human life.

In the final analysis, the significance of his music depends on its convincing explication of what is quintessentially human, regardless of style and genre. On one level, it did entertain and give pleasure to contemporary audiences. But that was not all that he wanted to accomplish. He also aspired to signify deeper levels of meaning. He would have said that he wished each of his compositions to vindicate itself, over and above the elements of divertissement and agreeableness, by increasing the experience of and insight into the fabric of life itself.

His student works show him mastering his craft and assimilating time-honored usages. Engaging music is found in the Sonata for Violin and Piano in A Major and the Symphony No. 1 in D Minor. The former piece, his Harvard honors thesis, received public performance at a commencement concert, given 12 June 1893. Seventeen years later, Converse would say: "Today it seems very young, yet it has enthusiasm and freshness, but of course I had not arrived at any degree of originality. . . . Now I consider the sonata pretty bad, but it is still played a little."[14]

The sonata never sounds original or daring. It does demonstrate emotional restraint, stylistic consistency, pleasing moments, and hints of the freshness that Converse mentions. A genial sonata-allegro is succeeded by a temperate romance, then an animated minuet, and an exuberant rondo-finale.[15] Many years after it was written, Arthur Shepherd acclaimed the sonata for its "mastery of sonata form together with an unaffected simplicity which gives throughout a feeling of spontaneity."[16]

The symphony was composed in 1898, under the guidance of Rheinberger, and had its first movement premiered in July 1898. The occasion was the commencement concert of the Munich Academy, from which Converse was graduated with the highest honors. A few months later,

147,730

College of St. Francis Library
Joliet, Illinois

the Boston Symphony under Wilhelm Gericke did the piece. Some years after Chadwick had conducted the symphony at the Worcester Festival, he said: "It would have been hardly possible for any work which showed a radical departure from recognized forms and methods to be considered for performance in the Munich School, and this symphony is not the only American work which has been affected by such conservatism."[17]

Nevertheless, more individuality in thematic invention and greater technical security is apparent here than in the sonata. An orthodox handling of structure applies to all four movements. The orchestration seems cautiously done but with some attempt at diverseness in instrumental coloration. With this symphony, Converse closed off the flow of severely academic works.

On his return from Germany, Chadwick says, Converse heeded the dictates of his "imaginative and poetic nature" and his "vigorous mind." An intense study of modern scores, heretofore forbidden him in Munich, resulted in his "radical departure" into the world of the symphonic poem embracing a program of some sort.[18] A series of these musical poems came out: *The Festival of Pan, Endymion's Narrative, Night and Day, The Mystic Trumpeter, Ormazd, Ave Atque Vale, Song of the Sea, The Elegiac Poem*, to name eight. Orchestration grows more sonorous and varied, the harmony less predictable and more complex. The structure fluently responds to the exigencies of the programmatic intent, whether a succession of scenes, events, emotions, or deliberations. Unlike Kelley, he disfavored a preoccupation with anything that was preponderantly picturesque or a progression of events. He preferred the expression of a sequence of dramatic moods and subtle shifts in feeling, the delineation of changing character in an individual, and the interpretation of those universal forces and ideals that drive humanity. One should also keep in mind that Converse was an intensely religious person who would seek expression for his beliefs in several of his works.

His breakaway composition was the *Festival of Pan*, a "Romance for Orchestra," completed in 1899 and performed by Gericke and the Boston Symphony in December 1900.[19] Converse drew inspiration from Keats's poem *Endymion* (1818). The resultant work owed nothing to Debussy's composition on a somewhat similar subject, *Prélude à l'Après-midi d'un faune*. On the other hand, Converse did take a little direction from the orchestral music of Hector Berlioz, Richard Wagner, and Richard Strauss. It was not long, however, before he would admire the music of Debussy and Sibelius. The composer did not claim his was true program music and did not indicate what sections of the poem inspired him. He did feature the contrast between Endymion's dejection and the exhilarating splendor of the festival itself in several loosely connected episodes.[20]

Philip Hale, reviewing the work in the *Boston Journal*, notes a marked advance in color, feeling, and imagination over the symphony. Although

Converse did not go out of his way to sound strikingly original, his music proved he had plenty of his own to say. Moreover, Hale is surprised that this youthful work had so few reminiscences of other composers. The older critic William Apthorp, writing in the *Boston Evening Transcript*, finds the music "thoroughly modern—even ultra-modern—in feeling and expression." While he commended its lack of artifice, its spontaneity, and its fertile melodic inventiveness, he felt the orchestration was so rich, sensuous, and gorgeous in coloring that it attracted attention to itself and hindered a grasp of the work as a whole. Other newspaper writers in Boston, New York, and London, praise the work in words similar to those of Hale.[21]

Converse composed his second "Romance for Orchestra," entitled *Endymion's Narrative*, in 1901, scoring it for a large orchestra. The Boston Symphony gave the premier performance on 11 April 1903. Again, Converse drew on Keats's *Endymion*. In a letter to Hale, the composer wrote that he wanted the work to be judged as music, so had omitted quotations from the poem. The contents of his composition were "suggested" by certain scenes from the poem. Listeners would find no detailed illustration of the text; only reference to its emotional aspects. He had in mind the downhearted Endymion's withdrawal from the festival of Pan; and his sister Peona leading him away, soothing him, and trying to learn the reason for his despair. Converse continued: "He then related to her what seems to me the spiritual essence of the whole poem, the struggle of a mind possessed of an ideal beyond the common view, and yet bound by affection and devotion to conditions which confine and stifle its surging internal impulses,—one of the most painful spiritual struggles to which man is subject. . . . "[22]

A slow introduction has the cello expressively render the melancholic Endymion theme, twice interrupted by glimpses of the "ideal" theme in the oboe. This is followed by a constantly accelerating and increasingly fervid passage. The rest of the movement comes through as rondo-like recurrences of the Endymion theme that punctuate eight episodes of differing tempi and emotional content. The piece had begun gloomily and uneasily. Then one hears alternating depictions of the sister's love (first as a solo-violin melody accompanied by harp, next as a clarinet melody) and the questioning Endymion's tormented but mesmeric fixation on the ideal. At the end, the ideal vanquishes doubt; bliss takes over as well as a resolve to hold on to the ideal.[23]

This second "Romance" is an improvement over the first. His craftsmanship is of a higher order; his discourse, more assured and persuasive; his grasp on fantasy, firmer. Intense feeling permeates the music. Critic after critic of the time applauded the work's telling orchestration and expressive potency.[24]

In 1902, Converse had completed *La Belle Dame Sans Merci*, after the

Keat's poem (1820), subtitling it a "Ballade for Baritone Solo and Orchestra." Converse thought the results comprised "a symphonic poem with voice part," and with "extended orchestral interludes expressive of the moods of the text."[25] The composer's gifts are apparent in the music. Nevertheless, the style is more secure in the purely instrumental portions. The music allotted to the singer seems secondary. The total musical structure does not coalesce into a persuasive entity.

At the same level of excellence as *Endymion's Narration* is *Night and Day*, "Two Poems for Pianoforte and Orchestra," completed in 1904, first performed in January 1905 by the Boston Symphony Orchestra, and published in score in 1906.[26] The piano is integrated into the orchestra and not given the prominence of a solo instrument in a concerto. An unnamed interviewer of Converse reported, in 1910, that the composer was now noted for his "symbolic musical poems," and that *Night and Day*, when compared with earlier compositions, disclosed a maturer artist with a "more awakened individuality." He then quoted Converse himself about the work:

It seems curious that I wrote this work first for a small group of stringed instruments, five or six, and piano, but I found that these were inadequate to express what I felt from the text that inspired me, and the text? Well, it was not exactly Whitman, although I afterward added mottoes from the poet—such as, "This is thy hour, O soul, thy flight into the wordless" [to preface *Night*], and "Day, full-blown and splendid—day of the immense sun, action, ambition and laughter" [to preface *Day*], but these excerpts do not really express the essence of my music, as I intended it. I treated night as the ideal—the things we dream of—vaguely, reverently. Day is reality—or the sterner side which presents itself—yet there are moments of supreme joy. The one is a meditative, personal mood—the other indicates things as they are.

During the same interview, Converse also said that he composed music for four or five hours daily and tried to feel strongly what he was creating: "Very often while writing I seem to become an actual part of the expression itself—and then it is I know that I have felt real emotion."[27]

Walt Whitman (1819-1892) was receiving wide recognition as one of America's foremost poets after the turn of the century. He was considered a nonconformist, a transcendent thinker, an audacious innovator in poetic procedures, and a champion of American democracy. Other poets ingested his musings and studied his manner of speaking, among them Vachel Lindsay, Carl Sandburg, Edgar Lee Masters, and Stephen Vincent Benét.[28] Many composers were inspired by his words or set his verses, not only Converse but other Americans—Arthur Farwell, John Alden Carpenter, Howard Hanson, Roy Harris, and William Schuman. Whitman inspired European composers as well—Charles Stanford, Frederick Delius, Hamilton Harty, Ralph Vaughan Williams, and Paul Hindemith.

One should note, however, Converse's warning that *Night and Day* is "not exactly Whitman," and the admission that he added the Whitman mottoes afterward. Thus "R.R.G." in the *Christian Science Monitor* for 22 January 1905 is wrong in accusing Converse of not capturing Whitman's breadth and grandeur. Nor is the music indebted to the theater composition of similar title, *Le Jour et la Nuit* (1881), of Alexandre Charles Lecocq.[29]

The first movement, *Night*, is cast as a nocturne and a prelude to the next movement. This warmhearted, delicately orchestrated contemplation of night, an *Andante molto sostenuto e tranquillo*, strikes the ear as more introspective than dynamic or imposing. A clarinet outlines the main motive, accompanied by the piano and two horns. Other instruments expand on the theme. In the middle of the movement, a *più mosso*, based on a variant of the motive, is heard in diminution. It leads to an expansion of the motive in the full orchestra. Later, tranquility again rules, with a reorchestrated return of the opening, and the music ends quietly. The second movement, *Allegro con fuoco*, features a spirited first theme and a diffident, slower second idea. The movement unfolds episodically, with marked diversity from section to section. It introduces three climaxes, the last being the most powerful, at which point the main theme returns, then gives way to a long animated coda. The composer leaves it to the listener's imagination to make the connection between the Whitman motto and the music.

Next came one of Converse's undoubtedly finest works, *The Mystic Trumpeter*, an "Orchestral Fantasy (after the Poem by Walt Whitman)."[30] Completed in 1904, it received its premiere with the Philadelphia Orchestra on 3 March 1905. Interestingly, the English composer Sir Hamilton Harty would have his *Mystic Trumpeter*, for baritone solo, mixed chorus, and orchestra, introduced at the Leeds Festival in 1913. Nevertheless, no musical likenesses exist between the two works. (Whitman had published his poem in 1872.)

Converse omitted consideration of the first episode of the poem, which referred to medieval pageantry, because he wanted, in his own words, "only to use the elemental phrases of the poem: mystery and peace, love, war or struggle, humiliation, and finally joy. So I divided the poem into five parts and my music follows this division. Each section is introduced or rather tied to the preceding one by characteristic phrases for trumpet."[31]

The work is best thought of as a cycle of imaginary scenes giving expression to universal human feelings. The five divisions are fitted together and made into a coherent whole by means of the recurring trumpet song and its development. The song is first heard sounding meditatively, yet with an aura of cryptic questioning, in the opening measures of the piece. The caption prefacing the beginning tells of hearing a trumpeter whose "song expands my numb'd, imbonded spirit." (One wonders if Charles Ives had this work at all in mind when he composed *The Unanswered Question*, in 1908.) Later, the violins, in octaves, give it a resonant reading. Section two discourses on "Love, that is pulse of all—the sustenance and the pang," first with a dreamlike melody in the strings; then the woodwinds joining in. At the end, Converse releases the full power of the orchestra in an eloquent paean to an affection suggestive more of agape than of eros. "War's wild alarms," in the third section, is appropriately characterized by the sound of brass instruments and marching tunes, one of which refers to "Marching Through Georgia." A *meno mosso* in the middle of the movement displays a sorrowful English horn solo, possibly mourning those slain in battle. The caption to the fourth section, "I see the enslaved, the overthrown, the hurt, the oppressed of the whole earth," is translated into a exalted lamentation, first in the bass clarinet alone, next in the strings, and eventually in the brasses. The last section, "Vouchsafe a higher strain than any yet; Sing to my soul—renew its languishing faith and hope," sums up the entire piece by recycling snatches of themes from all previous sections but focusing mainly on the trumpeter's song. The imposing peroration by the full orchestra provides a exultant culmination to the entire work.

Most critics praised the work highly. Edward Burlingame Hill remarks on its advanced constructive technique and psychological discourse, concluding that in its interpretation of inner human ambiences and capture of poignant expression, *The Mystic Trumpeter* surpassed all of Converse's previous works.[32] One can still listen to it with enjoyment and profit.

The symphonic poem *Ormazd* was completed in 1911 and premiered the next year in St. Louis. Again, Converse reveals his predilections in program music. Ormazd is the God of Light in Persian mythology. In this symphonic poem, he and his hosts contend with and eventually prevail over Ahriman, the God of Darkness, and his forces. The Ormazd motive is introduced as the defenders of light gather: shadowy trumpet fanfares sound; the music becomes more pronounced in expression; soon blazingly militant music illustrates the advance of the troops. The audience next hears the diaphanous music of the blessed Fravashis, the Souls of the Good, in praise of Ormazd. As if from an abyss, the Ahriman motive emerges alongside the sullen cries of lost souls. The composition heats up as a battle ensues, with motives of Ormazd and Ahriman vying for dominance. A series of vehement climaxes are achieved until Ormazd, and his motive, gain victory. At the end there is joyful music and a return of the song of the blessed Fravashis.

Converse, in *Ormazd*, has modified his style toward greater chromaticism, expanded use of altered chords, some employment of the wholetone scale, and increased dissonance. No false Eastern exoticisms mar the score. One 'does hear passages of considerable emotional eloquence or of robust, even virile, statement.[33]

After *Ormazd*, a falloff in inspiration appears in Converse's symphonic poems. *Ave Atque Vale* (1916), "a subjective expression of the feelings of one who bids farewell at the call of duty to all that is infinitely loved and cherished,"[34] is overly bleak in mood. *Song of the Sea*, a musical imaging of "On the Beach at Night" from Whitman's *Sea Drift*, opens mournfully and mysteriously but offers consolation and affirmation at its close. The music is not about the sea, as it will be in Carpenter's *Sea Drift*. The piece begins with a child bemoaning the brief vanishing of the stars and eventually culminates on the reassurance that all things are immortal. There are moments of exalted loveliness. Nevertheless, while fluency is always evident, the aliveness of the earlier symphonic poems is missing.

On the occasion of the performance of *Song of the Sea*, in April 1924, The Boston Symphony also presented Ernest Schelling's *A Victory Ball*, which had had its premier in Philadelphia the year before. (This symphonic poem was based on a poem by Alfred Noyes that described a ball in praise of Armistice Day and the overthrow of the German army, while phantom apparitions of the human casualties of war haunt the scene.) Army bugle calls precede the ball itself. Various dances are heard (like the fox trot, tango, and waltz), interrupted by martial trumpet calls. A phrase of the *Dies Irae* sounds; then an echo of bagpipes playing; next, the tread of marching feet; and then "Taps" concludes the fantasy. It captured the mood of the contemporary music public. As a result, *Song of the Sea* was overshadowed by *A Victory Ball*, which became the celebrated composition of the hour.

The most engaging attribute of Converse's *The Elegiac Poem* (1925) is its folklike musical character. Otherwise, the sound of sorrow, however poignant and elegant, parallels music already heard in Converse's other works. *Prophecy*, a symphonic poem for soprano and orchestra (1932) involves a text from *Isaiah*, "Come near, ye nations, to hear. . . . For the indignation of the Lord is upon all nations, and his fury upon all their armies." Of large scope, the work proceeds with a grand seriousness. It has melodiousness and imaginative touches, but seems too somber. Converse himself said: "I recognize inspiration in this work and am convinced of divine assistance."[35]

One other work needs mention here, although not a symphonic poem: the *Jeanne d'Arc*, "Dramatic Scenes for Orchestra." It originally comprised an overture and incidental music for a play by Percy MacKaye, which was mounted in Philadelphia, in 1906. Converse extracted a suite from this music, orchestrated it for a large ensemble, and heard its premier performance in 1907 at the New England Conservatory's Jordan Hall. He then revised the score, which version the Boston Symphony performed in 1908.

The first scene, "In Domrémy," serves as a prelude to the whole work. It describes Jeanne d'Arc's early life through music of blithe innocence, though not without hints at the conflict in the future. Converse knits together ideas depicting the Vespers service and the dreams of the young maid, a portrayal of the Ladies of Lorraine via the French traditional song "Derrière chez mon père," and the love theme of Jeanne's bucolic wooer. The second scene, "Pastoral Reverie," extends the pastoral image, with artless piping adding to the atmosphere. "Battle Hymn," the third scene, sets the stage for conflict to the sound of the ancient hymn "Veni, Creator," and the onslaught begins. After much strife comes victory; the hymn returns, exultantly shouted out by the trumpets. Next, "Night Vision," centers on the sleeping Jeanne's vision of St. Michael. Finally, "The Maid of God" reviews her life-mission with a return of the several motives in previous movements plus additional medieval chants, and closes with her pathetic death and ascension to heaven.

The total effect is dramatic. The suite has an abundance of excellent tunes, most of them his own. Unusual harmonies and harmonic progressions, several of them bold for Converse, are exploited for some striking effects. The manipulation of orchestral color is masterly. It reveals Converse at the height of his powers.

All in all, some of Converse's most satisfying music is found in his programmatic compositions. In addition, works like *Endymion's Narrative* and *The Mystic Trumpeter* deserve a place among the most outstanding musical contributions to American culture.

Converse's Abstract Chamber and Orchestral Works

Converse had written a first string quartet while a student taking direction from Chadwick. A second string quartet came out in 1904, about the time of *The Mystic Trumpeter*. Skillfully made and likable, its three slight movements do not represent a sizable creative venture on the part of the composer. Absent is any ambitious working out of ideas; absent is that emphasis on contrapuntal play between instruments which adds vitality to a chamber format; absent is anything more than an occasional flash of something exceptional that would intrigue a sophisticated listener. Yet, it strikes the ear as a sincere offering of the composer. The lively first movement, with its interesting rhythmic variety, is quickly over. When the *molto vivace* tempo breaks down to *molto meno mosso*, the violin introduces a fetchingly lyric second subject. The slow second movement contains an articulate main melody, contrasted with a faster theme whose shifting tonalities and tentative quality make the reorchestrated return of the initial idea welcome. The perky last movement, in ternary form, has more instrumental interplay and a greater willingness to experiment than have the previous movements. The slower and affable middle section unfolds with an especially appealing lilt.[36]

For the most part, his later chamber pieces share the same strengths and drawbacks as the quartet. The two movements of the Sonata for Cello and Piano, of 1922, exhibit greater romantic ardor and sensitivity to instrumental colorations, but are otherwise cut from the same cloth. The same is true of the Piano Trio, of 1932, and the String Quartet, of 1935. Both works benefit from the composer's by-now greater expertise in composing chamber music. Polyphony is definitely to the fore, as is the commitment to elaborate thoroughly on his ideas. However, for all the attractiveness of these and other of his chamber works, Converse's efforts in this genre are of much lesser import than his orchestral and larger vocal compositions.

The composer's Symphony in C Minor, his second, received its initial performance by the Boston Symphony, under Pierre Monteux, on 30 January 1920. Converse outlined no program for the music. He admitted, however, that the composition tried to express the moods and emotions related to the recently concluded world war. He advised the listener: "The point-of-view is subjective and human, rather than impersonal and epic," and added: "I have used the Symphonic form because it suited my needs of expression; not from my especial desire to write a conventional symphony." He means the two main themes of the fast opening movement to suggest the fortitude of the men and the compassionate feelings of the women on the home front. A brief *adagio misterioso* introduction "crystallizes into a stern and determined mood which dominates the whole movement, except for the contrasting feminine quality of the second theme." The slow movement that follows is a peaceful, serene nocturne involving moonlight on a lake's waters, with one episode suggesting the meeting of lovers. The *scherzando* third movement delineates happy and insouciant youth. Nevertheless, an interruption occurs in order to indicate pathos and foreboding. The last movement is warlike in character, suggesting conflict, interrupted by a passage of solemn, almost religious mood. It concludes with a jubilant commemoration of the reunion of the men with their loved ones.[37]

The symphony's reception was generally enthusiastic. Reviewers detected an upsurging creative stimulus that inspired the composer. Praised as singularly beautiful were the mysterious start of the first movement, the imaginatively realized nocturnal atmosphere of the second movement, and the opposition of feelings in the concise and vibrant third movement. H. T. Parker writes of his keen pleasure "in the misty

... beginning in which the music as from spiritual contemplation flames into lusty vigor; in the soft and silvery lustres, the gentle undulation of not a little of the slow movement in the quick and novel turns of the beginning and the end of the Scherzo... [which] stings with high musical spirits at once robust and fanciful."[38]

Fellow composer Hill applaudes the music's vitality, so much like "the immeasurable outpouring of energy which this country brought to bear on entering the war." The composer is a "spokesman of his country's heart. It [the symphony] is a concrete expression of 'the American spirit' from a new angle, which as far as I know has not been approached in this country.... [Mr. Converse] has become more universal but none the less eloquent...."[39] The complaints were few and involved the prolixity of the piece, the at times dense textures, and the overly-frequent climactic passages.[40]

The next symphony, in E Minor, came out in 1922 and was also well-liked, but was found to lack striking individuality and was slightly too conservative for the times. At the time of its premier, Converse gave an unassuming appraisal of the work, saying it had no program and was a succession of universal moods—those of suffering, defiance, consolation, hope, and joy. He cut down the percussion instruments to kettledrums only, "because I am tired of the cheap, conventional effects obtained by their use."[41]

The music has virtues. Melodies are plentiful and engaging; harmonies, natural and never farfetched; orchestrations, lavish in their rich detail; structures, under firm control. The first movement, in sonata form, is mostly agitated Sturm und Drang, yet exits on measures of tranquil charm. The warm melody of the slow movement, in ternary form, is interrupted by a *scherzo* that impresses the ear as spontaneous, ear-catching, and possibly related to Amerindian music.[42] The rondo-like Finale has a steady flow of musical ideas, all of them carefully integrated into an organic whole.

In 1922 Converse also finished a Fantasy for Piano and Orchestra, which was performed at the New England Conservatory's Jordan Hall. Certainly not a major effort, this sunny, sometimes tender, work gains significance as it reveals the composer making judicious use of jazz-influenced rhythms and melodies for the first time. Ten years later, a Concertino for Piano and Orchestra saw the light and received a rather inadequate performance by Lucille Monaghan and the New England Conservatory Orchestra. By the 1930s the mainstream composers, including Converse, were being dismissed out of hand, their music evicted from the repertoire of leading performance groups. The year before his death, in August 1939, the piece remained unpublished, and the composer complained that it had never received a "first rate performance," though "it is one of my best pieces."[43]

His Symphony No. 4, in F Major, completed in 1934, waited until the end of 1936 for a first performance at a concert, not of the Boston Symphony Orchestra, but of a W.P.A.-sponsored ensemble, the Massachusetts State Symphony Orchestra. Whatever the modernistic experimentation he had made in previous works, he remains conservative here. One does hear intimations of American popular song and African-American music, and even of jazz. The work is intended to gratify, not to astonish, the music public; therefore its openhearted, direct, homespun character and its resort to assimilable melody, harmony, and rhythm.[44]

Just before he died Converse completed a last symphony, in F minor, which Fabien Sevitz premiered in Indianapolis at the end of the same year. Pleasantly tuneful, the work reaches for no great heights. It seems more an casual assemblage of miscellaneous movements than a formal symphony.

His second and third symphonies remain Converse's most compelling abstract works. In workmanship and appeal to the senses, though not in innovation, they can challenge most other symphonies of their era. Still and all, they demonstrate as well that Converse hit on his happiest musical ideas when stimulated by some non-musical concept.

OPERA AND ORATORIO

One of the most arresting events in the history of American art music was the performance of Converse's opera *The Pipe of Desire* by the Metropolitan Opera Company in New York, the first American opera ever mounted by that company.

The history of opera in the United States during the nineteenth century had consisted mostly of the performance of foreign operas in their original languages, by foreign singers, usually in New Orleans and New York City. The Manuel Garcia company, including Garcia's daughter Maria Malibran, had given Americans their first real taste of Italian opera during a visit to these shores in 1825-26. Their brief sojourn registered the first indisputable attempt to establish this musical genre in the United States. Edward and Anne Seguin arrived in New York in 1838, formed an English Opera Troupe, and traveled the country in order to present English and Italian operas sung in the English language, until Luigi Arditi's opera company arrived in New York in 1847. These were among several failed attempts to put opera on a permanent basis in America. The first permanent, and most important, opera company in the United States, the Metropolitan, commenced operations on 22 October 1883. It mounted European operas exclusively and featured imported "star" vocalists.

The Philadelphia composer William Fry had offered his grand opera

Leonora to the public in 1845, and George Bristow had done the same with his *Rip Van Winkle* in 1855. Flaws in the music and librettos and lack of interest among the music-loving public had doomed both to failure. Moreover, the American as a composer of operas was as yet a strange beast to most Americans. John Knowles Paine had completed his *Azara* in 1900, and Chadwick his *Judith* in 1901, but commendable as these operas were, no major performance of either had ensued.

Converse's *The Pipe of Desire*, "Romantic Grand Opera in One Act,"[45] was composed in 1904-05, to a libretto by George Edward Burton, a Boston architect. Wallace Goodrich, 50 players from the Boston Symphony, and a chorus from the New England Conservatory of Music premiered it on 31 January 1906. Then, amazingly enough, the Metropolitan Opera Company produced the work on 18 March 1910. According to a report in the *Boston Evening Transcript*, 10 October 1908, it was Gustave Mahler, the great Viennese composer and conductor, who was responsible for the selection of this opera over those of other Americans.

Romantic symbolism, of a sort congenial to Converse, abounds in this stage work. Two days after the first Metropolitan presentation, Converse was interviewed as saying that he considered the English language excellent for musical setting, and in this regard superior to the German language. He observed that too many contemporary operas dwelt mainly on the sexual emotions. These feelings had their place (he said that he admired Strauss's *Salome* and *Elektra*), but there were other emotions to delineate, and some of importance, that he felt music should idealize.[46]

Iolan, the protagonist, represents common man. He is portrayed as benighted, heedful only of his own appetites, and without thought for the consequences of his actions. He challenges a fundamental principle affecting all humanity, prevails for an instant, but ultimately brings the sentence of death on his beloved, Naoia, and himself. The plot would have pleased Nathaniel Hawthorne. The prelude begins mysteriously on a series of dominant sevenths and ninths. The cellos play a brief *legato* melody, quietly and gently. The music grows animated; then an expansive *molto largamente* coincides with the rise of the curtain. The audience views a mountain glade in springtime and hears the singing of a chorus of elves. A water nymph (a soprano) sings a pretty, quasi-scherzando ditty, "An old bullfrog down by the rock" that goes from minor to major key. Next, a gnome (a baritone) sings "I found the great oak still asleeping," to an beguiling melody. The Old One enters with the Pipe, to the motive associated with him, which continues to reappear as he warns the elves about showing themselves to mortals. However, they have allowed Iolan to see them, and he has invited them to his wedding to Naoia. The solemn dignity of the Old One's presentation in a solemn minor mode makes a marked contrast to the cheerful Iolan who proclaims his joyous feelings in disjunct motion and major mode.

The elves insist that the Pipe be played for dancing. An attractive dance scene ensues as forest and water creatures celebrate springtime to the Old One's playing of the Pipe. Its lawful use apparently brings happiness.

When Iolan jeers at the Pipe's power, the Old One makes him dance to its sound. Suddenly, Iolan snatches the Pipe away from the Old One and refuses to return it. The Old One cautions him not to try to play on it. A long and very fine discourse of the Old One begins "It is the Pipe God gave to Lilith," which grows more melodic on the words "Let thy tune, now sad, now merry, wax and wane with ev'ry breath." Iolan, heedless of the warning, plays on the Pipe. He sounds a lengthy and magnificently realized monologue: "It is the strain I heard within my soul." Modulation is constant as he grows more excited by the vision he sees and finally, he calls out in impassioned tones for his beloved Naoia to come to him. She arrives fatally ill. An affecting dialogue with some really lovely music follows, although the scene is perhaps overly long. Naoia dies, then the despairing Iolan also. The Old One utters the opera's moral:

> There is a God whose laws unchanging,
> No one may hope to disobey:
> Man's own desires forced upon the ordained way.
> He for a moment triumphs,
> He has his will:
> He pays the penalty.

The opera closes on haunting music that lingers in one's consciousness after the last measure is completed.

Leading motives and their transformations are the significant conveyors of symbolic expression. They are never lackluster, always poetic. Their permutations are enriched by the composer's inventiveness; one moment vehement, another rhapsodic, still another lightly tuneful, and so forth. An extraordinary amount of chromaticism invests the score.

Unfortunately, Burton's libretto employs stilted language and stifles the potentially dramatic moments with excess verbiage and inactivity. Although Converse writes genuinely ingratiating melodies and makes subtle use of harmony, modulation, and orchestral color, he is denied the opportunity for writing scene-length music of conflict and strong contrast. Nevertheless, he makes fine use of the opportunities he is given, coming through now with a powerful climax, now with a vocal phrase that elucidates character, now with a sensitive orchestral painting of a touching episode. In short, the music is far superior to the libretto. The critics of the time complained that the libretto failed to feature realistic detail and action. In addition, they found the singers' diction so poor that the words could not be understood.

Most of them, on the other hand, laud the music. Hale, for example, finds the libretto undramatic, unreal, without recognizable connection to actual men and women, while the music showed a bona fide feel for the theater: "The human interest and the dramatic life of this opera are wholly in the music." The imaginative music "broadens, enlarges, italicizes the text; it gives character to the inherently characterless. It is written in the ultra-modern manner." Speech receives a natural setting. Clever orchestral tricks are absent. Converse admirably suggests the sportiveness of the wood-dwellers. The dance music is delightful. The scene where Iolan expresses his longing, another where Naoia describes her peaceful cottage life, and that delineating the pathos of Naoia's death are sustained adroitly. Without question, Philip Hale concludes, Converse has sincerely felt the emotions he portrays.[47]

Converse tried again with another opera, *The Sacrifice*, in three acts, which was premiered by the Boston Opera Company on 3 March 1911. This time the composer wrote his own libretto, based on Henry Wise's "Dolores" from Wise's book of memoirs, *Los Gringos* (1849). He tried to stay within operatic tradition and insure himself scenes with color, movement, drama, and contrast. In addition, he allowed himself plenty of opportunity for featuring the voice as a lyrical instrument. Thus he avoided the kind of innovation, music intended for philosophic symbolization, that characterized *The Pipe of Desire*.

The setting is southern California in 1846. Chonita and Bernal, both Mexican-Americans, love each other. Burton, an officer in the United States Army, loves Chonita. Hating Burton because he is part of a foreign army of occupation and also because he dares to love Chonita, Bernal assaults him. Chonita rushes to separate the two men and receives a serious wound. The stricken Chonita begs Burton to save Bernal's life. This the noble Burton does at the expense of his own, during a clash between his men and the Mexicans.

Leading motives are again employed to represent the various characters but do not dominate the music. Instead ample room is made for set pieces emphasizing complete melodies. Among the characters is Tomasa, an Indian of heroic size, who represents her patiently enduring people. She grieves over the former grandeur of her race with music that is both dignified and fervent in its description of tragedy. The first act contains a fine love duet. The second act has swaggering soldiers' music, a winsome song from a flower girl, and Chonita's innocent and affecting prayer. In the last act, Bernal and Chonita pledge themselves to each other with music of great warmth, and Burton's sacrifice is given a worthy musical rendition. Like a master chef, Converse flavors the score with a variety of contrasting tunes—Amerindian chants, Spanish-American dances, Catholic religious hymns, Gypsy music, hints of the "Star Spangled Banner" and "Yankee Doodle." All in all, *The Sacrifice* is a well-realized musical drama. Contemporary critics reviewed it favorably. Unfortunately, no other opera company took it up and the Boston Opera Company was soon no more.

Converse tried again with a third opera, *The Immigrant*, possibly influenced by George Chadwick's *The Padrone*, which Chadwick composed in 1912-13. Meant for production by the Boston Opera Company, *The Immigrant* on its completion, in 1914, found the opera company defunct. It was shelved, as was another Converse opera, *Sinbad, the Sailor*.

The famous American prima donna Louise Homer gave an interview to Sylvester Rawlings of the *New York Evening World*, in March 1910, in order to talk about Converse's *The Pipe of Desire*. Her statement is applicable to all American composers laboring, as was Converse, to write operas acceptable to critics and audiences as well as to themselves. She said:

If native composers are to be encouraged we must enlarge our vision and become more lenient in our vision and become more lenient in our judgment. Musically, whatever foreigners think of us, we are a spoiled people. We set the highest standards of artistic excellence. A composer must be a Beethoven, or a Mozart, or a Wagner. . . . Do you think if such were the attitude of the people of France or of Italy, there would have been founded the new schools represented by Debussy and D'Indy, or by Puccini and Mascagni? Why not give the native genius a chance to find itself in whatever direction it may take?

In literature we are far more broad. While we may not have developed a Shakespeare, we are producing, because of our larger tolerance, a school of writers, graphic, realistic, distinct and characteristically American. Give our composers a chance to be heard. Let their fancy find flight in any direction. Schools of music are not made by the scores that are never printed [and never performed].[48]

One final vocal work needs mention, the oratorio *Job*, for solo voices, chorus, and orchestra, commissioned by the Worcester (Massachusetts) Musical Association, and premiered at the Worcester Music Festival, on 12 October 1907. John Hays Gardner assisted Converse in readying a Latin text taken from the "Job" and "Psalms" books of the Old Testament, and John Albert Macy prepared an English version. Converse explained that he was attempting a new departure by turning to a distinctive compositional method and form, neither theatrical like opera, nor discontinuous like oratorio. *Job* to him was an attempt more at an epic than an oratorio, with the emotions and atmospheres of the different sections ultimately prescribing the overall approach and framework. He had also pruned down the Job narration of the *Bible* for the sake of a more penetrating portrayal and a more arresting performance.[49]

The troubled *Job* comes through as a flesh-and-blood Everyman striving to approach and apprehend divinity. The principal moods are contemplative. Realistic depictions à la Strauss or Puccini are absent. Job is a tenor; Jehovah, a bass or a few basses singing in unison. The chorus normally engages in prayer to, or in reverential adoration of, Jehovah. Converse's melodic resourcefulness is sure. On the one hand, up-to-date chromaticisms appear with some frequency; on the other, ancient modes and plainsong inform many of the measures. He attempts no "authentic" use of medieval devices. Church melodies, like "Veni Creator" (which he had also employed in *Jeanne d'Arc*), are inserted into a contemporary musical context. More than a few of the harmonic effects seem novel. The evolution of melodic lines and harmonic progressions continues confident and cogent from beginning to end. The orchestra is an equal partner with the voices in the advancement of the drama. On occasion, the music hints at another composer's style; on occasion, it fails to capture completely the sentiment of the words.[50] Notice of the posttertiary developments in musical composition is little evident. These commentaries notwithstanding, the music can sound vital and fresh to a listener sympathetic to the contrivances of turn-of-the century romanticism. It deserves revival.

THE PICTURIZATION OF AMERICA

Most of the works already discussed have a direct relation to what New England thinkers, if not most thoughtful Americans, considered intrinsically worthwhile, embodying ideals toward which humans should aspire. In this regard, Converse was American in spirit. However, three conspicuous compositions, among others, relate directly to an American setting and are given a specific American musical cast: *Flivver Ten Million*, *California*, and the *American Sketches*. Completed in 1926, *Flivver Ten Million* had a first performance with the Boston Symphony the next year. Converse stated that he was fascinated by the announcement of the building of the ten millionth Ford car, and decided to commemorate the event with a musical work: "The ancients had their Scylla and Charybdis; we have our semaphore [traffic signal] and 'traffic cop,' all equally perilous to pass; and I believe that the moon shines as tenderly on the roadside of Westwood [where Converse lived], as ever it did on the banks of the Euphrates. Hearing and admiring 'Pacific 231' [of Arthur Honegger], I said to myself, 'I too must try something of this kind for the 'Flivver.'" He created the score for his own amusement and with the notion that humor was a part of American life. The form was entirely free and made up of short episodes. Some chief motives underwent thematic development.[51]

Converse was not the first composer to deal programmatically with some aspect of the United States, but he, along with Carpenter, was one of the first of the mainstream composers to attempt a musical depiction of contemporary America. In order to do so, he modified his style to include a greater amount of modernisms than usual for him. (Possibly his admiration for Honegger's *Pacific 231*, a description of a railroad locomotive on the move described in astringent harmonies and machine rhythms, influenced him in this direction.) Escape chords, quartal harmonies, bitonality, and noise enter the score.

The first episode, "Dawn in Detroit," opens very softly. Producing an ethereally quivering effect, divided string basses and cellos murmur bitonally and bichordally.[52] A muted trumpet crows like a lackadaisical cock. Flute and oboe take up the cry. Volume builds as the listener is transferred to the second episode. "Sunrise" arrives on an assertive chord and flares out with a resplendent *fortissimo* sunburst. "The City Stirs" bestirs itself briefly. Next comes a "Call to Labor," complete with factory whistle. The "March of the Toilers" opens on a low pizzicato figuration in the strings. Muted trumpets sound. Chords with augmented intervals and a succession of consecutive fourths present a mettlesome motive.

The fugal fifth episode, "The Din of the Builders," is long and loud. It features pounding eighth and quarter notes that skip about in fifths and diminished fifths, with fierce accentuations, then proceed to hammered out repeated tones. This section puts an anvil to use. The resultant clamor is not confusing but uproarious. Snatches of "Yankee Doodle" are heard. The next episode announces the "Birth of the Hero," beginning with a long pause, then a trumpet and next a clarinet connoting the birth. "The Hero" emerges unexpectedly, marvelously, ludicrously to the honk of a Ford automobile horn. "He wanders forth . . . in search of adventure," in motor-rhythmic fashion. Episode eight, "May Night by the Roadside—America's Romance," bathes the ears with an expressive *adagio*, whose languorous melody is in long tones. A flute and French horn engage in a duet. Eventually a solo violin takes over. The considerable charm of this episode tellingly contrasts the surrounding music.

The mood abruptly changes with "The Joy Riders," fitted out with jazzlike sounds and rhythms, and hints of "Dixie." Then comes "The Collision." After the crash, basses play an inversion of the "Builders" motive, to indicate that the flivver is now unbuilt. The eleventh and last episode "Phoenix Americanus (The Hero righted and shaken)," turns the "Builders" motive right side up again. Tentatively at first, then faster, the flivver chugs along to an *allegro moderato e giocoso*. The horn honks again. Snippets of popular tunes add further perkiness to the section. The piece closes on an F-triad with an added-sixth tone.

In *Flivver*, Converse unveils the roguish side of his personality. Yet the musical result is both poetic and imaginative. This antidote to puffed up profundity won over the music public and immediately became his most celebrated work.

Flivver was swiftly followed by *California*, "Festival Scenes for Orchestra," completed in 1927 and first performed in April 1928 by the Boston Symphony. Again Converse wrote a descriptive work to please himself and, he hoped, to please his listeners. He had witnessed and thoroughly enjoyed the colorful celebration of the Fiesta in Santa Barbara, California, in 1927, and wished to give his musical impression of the historical procession of Indians, priests, explorers, conquistadores, Spanish women, and *gringos* that he had witnessed, followed by his dining at the café El Paseo, under the stars.

It begins with an vigorous "Victory Dance" (movement 1) of the first inhabitants, where Converse inserts a reminiscence of an Indian dance, to a tomtom beat, that he had heard in Arizona. "Spanish Padres and Explorers" (movement 2) follows. Here, one hears fragments of an old Latin hymn and sonorous counterpoint, and later the sparkling march of the conquistadores. "The March of Civilization" (movement 3) describes the foundation of the missions. A forceless reminiscence of the Indian theme from movement 1 suggests the vanquishment of Amerindian culture. "Land of Poco Tiempo" (movement 4) features a habanera-like dance to a soft Spanish tune, *"Chata Cara de Bale,"* which he found in a song collection of Charles Lummis. An English horn and, afterwards, a solo violin play the melody in rather lazy, sensuous fashion. The "Invasion of the Gringos" (movement 5) seems a rowdy, frolicsome, even boisterous event and musically exploits the traditional "Cape Cod Chanty." An Iowa traditional song, "The Unconstant Lover," furnishes a tender contrast. The final movement, "Midnight at 'El Paseo,' 1927," introduces Spanish melodies (*"El Capotin"* in waltz-time) and lighthearted tunes of the "Jazz Age."[53] Waltz and foxtrot sound together in a contrapuntal ending both sprightly and satisfying.[54]

Like *Flivver*, *California* is not weighty music. The orchestration strikes the listener as brilliant. Melody is fetching; rhythm, supple and nicely varied; overall conception, fresh; sound, full and rich. A little experimentation with non-major-minor scale and nontriadic chord construction occurs. The end result is a musical procession that lets the ordinary listener's imagination range widely by letting his senses perceive different peoples more completely than he could by merely reading about them. The cramped urbanite discovers redress in the experience of a past whose sweep is so much broader than what he has known. *California's* various borrowed melodies lure him into a former time. He cannot help but enjoy the grand, colorful spectacle the music surveys. The retrospective view of the passage of history in California can move him. It is no wonder that the work proved popular with the public.

American Sketches, a "Symphonic Suite for Orchestra," was completed in 1928, orchestrated in 1929, and first performed by the Boston Symphony in 1935. A few themes left over from *California* found their way into the score. "Manhattan," which starts off the composition, "expresses the activity and turmoil of a great city; the grandeur, as well as the sinister sordidness of its varied scenes. Through it runs a thread of loneliness which is often felt by sensitive souls in such overpowering surroundings," said Converse. Next comes "The Father of Waters," in which a broad tranquil tune represents the placid flow of the Mississippi. At intervals one hears an old African-American melody, "The Levee Moan," borrowed from Carl Sandburg's *The American Song Bag*. The third movement is "The Chicken Reel," a scherzo whose fiddler's tune also comes from the Sandburg book. The final movement, "Bright Angel Trail," investigates the mysterious depths, everchanging lighting, and grand vistas of the Grand Canyon, with particular attention paid to the legend that recalls the birth of the Hopi people in its abyss.[55]

The first movement never takes on the character of jazz, although portions of it contain skittish, syncopated rhythms. The dominant impression given by the seven contrasting divisions, the two fast and nervous sections notwithstanding, is that of solemn dignity. The second movement vacillates between a *molto largamente e tranquillo* river theme and an *adagio espressivo* spiritual-like song. A rambunctious "Chicken Reel" follows, which Converse interrupts in the middle with a touching *adagio espressivo*. The majestic last movement opens ponderously, as it tries to picture the "Depths of the Grand Canyon." Soon, a stream of descending parallel harmonies links up with a slightly faster moving passage. The music arrives at a section entitled "Birth of the Indian Race from the bowels of the Canyon," where an American Indian-inspired tune is built on a minor scale with the third and sixth tones missing and the seventh lowered.[56]

There is some, but not much, adventuring into the newer creative worlds of the twentieth century. The younger, bolder composers of New York, like Arthur Berger, found *American Sketches* derivative, and only superficially indigenous. Aaron Copland said the composition followed a familiar pattern, including the expected slow spiritual and fast fiddler's tune. The first and last were the more impressive movements to his ear.[57] This and all previous works of Converse were dismissed as too conservative and dated. Yet, Converse did have something to say through music, had undoubted ability to say it, possessed a fine ear to guide him, and exhibited a high level of craftsmanship in whatever he attempted.

That he was sincere and wrote music of integrity cannot be contested. That he was a capable artistic spokesman for his time and place is obvious. Assuredly, he was able to impress and delight the music public and the most astute music critics during the first thirty years of the century. To appreciate him, we must accept the fact that he preferred to work mainly within the commonly accepted musical idiom of his time, certain that its language was not exhausted and that he could find in it something fresh to say. With all his heart, he wanted to communicate with audiences, not merely to please them, but because he believed he had matters of importance to transmit. His music, at least the best of it, deserves reevaluation and rehearing.

NOTES

1. Waldo Selden Pratt, ed. *Grove's Dictionary of Music and Musicians, American Supplement* (Philadelphia: Presser, 1926), s.v. "Kelley, Edgar Stillman."

2. Maurice R. King, "Edgar Stillman Kelley: American Composer, Author, and Teacher" (Ph.D. diss., Florida State University, 1970), pp. 67–68.

3. Rupert Hughes, *Contemporary American Composers* (Boston: Page, 1900), pp. 72–73.

4. Arthur Shepherd, in *Cobbett's Cyclopedic Survey of Chamber Music*, vol. 2, 2nd ed., ed. Walter Willson Cobbett (London: Oxford University Press, 1963), s.v. "Stillman-Kelley, Edgar." An analysis of the quartet's structure is also given.

5. See A. Walter Kramer, "America's Most Notable Symphony," *Musical America* (18 December 1915), p. 35.

6. Edgar Stillman Kelley, *New England*, Second Symphony in B-flat Minor, op. 33 (New York: Schirmer, 1915).

7. Daniel Gregory Mason, *The Dilemma of American Music* (New York: Macmillan, 1928), pp. 4–5.

8. Robert Joseph Garofolo, "The Life and Works of Frederick Shepherd Converse (1871–1940)" (Ph.D. diss., Catholic University of America, 1969), p. 5.

9. Louis C. Elson, *The History of American Music*, revised to 1925 by Arthur Elson (New York: Macmillan, 1925), p. 204.

10. Garofalo, "The Life and Works of Converse," pp. 43–44.

11. Ruth Severance, "The Life and Work of Frederick Shepherd Converse" (M.A. thesis, Boston University, 1932), pp. 8–9. See, also, Garofalo, "The Life and Works of Frederick Converse," p. 138.

12. "Music of Frederick S. Converse," *Christian Science Monitor* (15 January 1910), p. 8.

13. John Tasker Howard, with the assistance of Arthur Mendel, *Our Contemporary Music* (New York: Crowell, 1941), p. 56.

14. "Music of Frederick S. Converse," *Christian Science Monitor* (15 January 1910), p. 8.

15. Frederick Shepherd Converse, Sonata for Violin and Piano in A Major, opus 1 (Boston: Boston Music (G. Schirmer, Jr.), 1900).

16. Arthur Shepherd, in *Cobbett's Cyclopedic Survey of Chamber Music*, vol. 2, 2nd ed., ed. Walter Willson Cobbett (London: Oxford University Press, 1963), s.v. "Converse, Frederick Shepherd."

17. George Chadwick, "American Composers," in *The History of American Music*, ed. W. L. Hubbard, The American History and Encyclopedia of Music, vol. 8 (Toledo, Ohio: Squire, 1908), p. 11.

18. Chadwick, op. cit., p. 11.

19. The score was published in 1903; see Frederick Shepherd Converse, *Festival of Pan*, opus 9 (Boston: G. Schirmer, Jr., The Boston Music Co., 1903).

20. William F. Apthorp, Program Book for the concert of the Boston Symphony Orchestra, on 21-22 December 1900, p. 294; Lawrence Gilman, *Stories of Symphonic Music* (New York: Harper & Brothers, 1908), p. 65.

21. Clipping from the *Boston Journal* (23 December 1900), in the Boston Public Library; see Microfilm No. ML 40.H3, roll 2; William F. Apthorp, "Music and Drama," *Boston Evening Transcript* (24 December 1900), p. 9. For other reviews, see *Musical America* (October 1908), p. 3, and the book of clippings in the Boston Public Library, Shelf No. **M.410.17. Shelf numbers are not always consistent; prefaced with one or two asterisks; the "M" sometimes followed by a period, or sometimes without a period.

22. Philip Hale, Program Book for the concert of the Boston Symphony Orchestra, on 11 April 1903, pp. 1162, 1164, 1165.

23. Frederick Shepherd Converse, *Endymion's Narrative*, opus 10 (New York: Gray, 1909).

24. See the clipping of the review by Philip Hale, in the *Boston Journal* (12 April 1903), in the Boston Public Library: Microfilm No. ML 40.H3, roll 2. Also see the review by William F. Apthorp, in the *Boston Evening Transcript* (13 April 1903), p. 7. Louis Elson waxes enthusiastic over the composition, in *The History of American Music*, p. 205.

25. Program Book for the concert of the Boston Symphony Orchestra, on 2–3 March 1906, p. 1241.

26. Frederick Shepherd Converse, *Night and Day*, Two Poems for Pianoforte and Orchestra, opus 11 (Boston: Boston Music, G. Schirmer Jr., 1906).

27. "Music of Frederick S. Converse," *Christian Science Monitor* (15 January 1910), p. 8.

28. Frederick J. Hoffman, *The Twenties* (New York: Free Press, 1962), pp. 149–51.

29. It was presented at London's Strand Theater as *Manola*, in 1882; M. Gustave Chouquet, with additions by Alexis Chitty and Gustave Ferrari, in *Grove's Dictionary of Music and Musicians*, ed. J. A. Fuller Maitland (London: Macmillan, 1906), s.v. "Lecocq, Alexandre Charles."

30. Frederick Shepherd Converse, *The Mystic Trumpeter*, opus 19 (New York: Schirmer, 1907).

31. Program Book for the concert of the Boston Symphony Orchestra, on 25–26 January 1907, p. 975.

32. "Edward Burlingame Hill, "A New American Composer: Frederick S. Converse and His Career," *Boston Evening Transcript* (29 January 1906); see the book of clippings in the Boston Public Library, Shelf No. *M 165.8, Vol. 7.

33. See Olin Downes, "New Work Played in Boston," *Musical America* (February 1912), p. 45; and also the report of "A.W.K.", *Musical America* (24 November 1914), p. 1.

34. The Converse quotation is from the Program Book for the concert of the Boston Symphony Orchestra, on 27–28 April 1917, p. 1461.

35. Garofalo, "The Life and Works of Converse," p. 114.

36. Frederick Shepherd Converse, Quartet in A Minor, opus 18 (New York: Schirmer, 1906).

37. Program Book for the concert of the Boston Symphony Orchestra, on 30–31 January 1920, pp. 892, 894.

38. H. T. Parker, "Symphonic Concert," *Boston Evening Transcript* (31 January 1920), section 3, p. 6. Parker mistakenly named it Converse's first symphony.

39. From an article printed in the *Boston Evening Transcript*, 29 January 1920, and reproduced in Garofalo, "The Life and Works of Converse," p. 85.

40. See, for example, the several reservations that Philip Hale had about the music, although he was quite approving of the work as a whole, in "Play Symphony Inspired by War;" clipping from the *Boston Herald* (31 January 1920), in the Boston Public Library; see Microfilm No. ML 40.H3, roll 5.

41. Program Book for the concert of the Boston Symphony Orchestra, on 21–22 April 1922, p. 1423.

42. The link to American Indian music is noted by Richard Aldrich; see "Music," *New York Times* (10 January 1923), p. 28.

43. Garofalo, "The Life and Works of Converse," p. 115.

44. See "New Converse Symphony at WPA Concert," *Boston Evening Transcript* (4 December 1936), p. 10.

45. Frederick Shepherd Converse, *The Pipe of Desire*: Romantic Grand Opera in One Act, opus 21 (New York: Gray, 1907).

46. "F. C. Converse, American Composer of Grand Opera in English," *New York Daily Tribune* (20 March 1910), p. 7.

47. Clipping from the *Boston Herald* (1 February 1906), in the Boston Public Library; see Microfilm No. ML 46.H3, roll 2.

48. Sidney Homer, *My Wife and I* (New York: Macmillan, 1939), pp. 202–203.

49. Program notes for the performance of *Job*, given by the Cecilia Society of Boston, on 11 February 1908, included in the book of clippings in the Boston Public Library, Shelf No. ** M 379.21.

50. Philip Hale wrote a lengthy criticism of the work, "Worcester Hears Converse's 'Job,'" in the *Boston Herald* of 3 October 1907 (see the clipping reproduced on Microfilm No. ML 40.H3, roll 3; in the Boston Public Library). See, also, H. T. Parker, "Music and Drama," *Boston Evening Transcript* (3 October 1907), part 2, p. 5.

51. Program Book for the concert of the Boston Symphony Orchestra, on 15–16 April 1927, pp. 1792, 1794, 1796.

52. Frederick Shepherd Converse, *Flivver Ten Million* (Boston: Birchard, 1927).

53. Philip Hale, in the Program Book for the concert of the Boston Symphony Orchestra, on 6–7 April 1928, pp. 1772, 1774, 1776, 1778.

54. Frederick Shepherd Converse, *California* (Boston: Birchard, 1929).

55. Converse provides this information in the Program Book for the concert of the Boston Symphony Orchestra, on 8–9 February 1935, pp. 662, 664.

56. Frederick Shepherd Converse, *American Sketches* (New York: Kalmus, 1937).

57. Arthur Berger, "Boston Hears American Works," *Modern Music* 12 (1935), 145; Aaron Copland, "Scores and Records," *Modern Music* 15 (1938), 111.

Chapter Three

Three New Englanders:
Mason, Hill, and Daniels

Willa Cather, in *Not Under Forty*, recounted a visit to the Boston home of Annie Fields, widow of James T. Fields, in 1908: "The unique charm of Mrs. Fields' house was not that it was a place where one could hear about the past, but that it was a place where the past lived on—where it was protected and cherished, had sanctuary from the noisy push of the present." Cather noted that: "The ugliness of the world, all possibility of wrenches and jars and wounding contacts, seemed securely shut out. It was indeed the peace of the past, where the tawdry and cheap have been eliminated and the enduring things have taken their proper, happy places." Yet, years later, when she wished to see the Fields house again, she found instead that it had been torn down and replaced by a garage.[1] This anecdote could stand as a metaphor for the New England music examined in this chapter.

Daniel Gregory Mason (1873-1953), Edward Burlingame Hill (1872-1960), and Mabel Wheeler Daniels (1878-1971), like Converse, were born and grew up in the Greater Boston area and shared in the heritage represented by Annie Fields and her home. Mason clung onto his inheritance more than the other two did, but all three of them felt its influence and never did repudiate it. They too wished to eliminate the tawdry and cheap from their writing and to include the enduring, although their understandings of what was tawdry and what was enduring were not precisely the same. Of the three, Mason remained the most conservative. All three persisted as eclectics, using methods of setting down music, themes, and other particulars selected from a multiplicity of sources, foreign usually, but domestic as well. Indeed, eclecticism would characterize most of the mainstream composers.

They began their careers during a period when New England composers had already brought a particular method of expression into existence on native soil, one German in derivation, romantic in spirit, and classical in structure. These older composers (John Knowles Paine, George Chadwick, Arthur Foote) hoped that they and younger generations of native composers would ultimately modify their styles in order to arrive at music that was uniquely American. This was to be accomplished not through a conscious and aggressive nationalism but through building on precedent, and by living in and absorbing the spirit of the New World so that one could not help but sound a part of it. Their attention, to be sure, was focused primarily on Yankee America and on a cultural tradition over 250 years old. Other expressions of the American spirit could be but incidental to their own. Revolt, primitive experimentation, tentative tries at the latest fashions in musical composition were just not in their nature.

Mason, Hill, and Daniels started their musical education with Paine and Chadwick, and at first absorbed the outlook of their mentors. For them, to be only original and creatively newborn was insufficient. They desired to preserve the best of the conceptualization, the idealism, and the life of the imagination that was a part of their Yankee past. They exerted their efforts toward a suitable cultural expression which seemed authentic and natural, at least to them. They tried to work out a system of principles that would enlarge their potential for discerning what techniques might be of value, and for giving a fresh tang to music. Their compositions show that first Germany, and next France, supplied the techniques; the United States added the fresh tang.[2] They were among the most thoroughly schooled branch of their calling living in America. Nor did many transatlantic musicians best them in craftsmanship and musical aptitude. However, by preserving the long-standing canons of musical excellence, they, and especially Mason, alienated a younger group of musicians residing elsewhere in the country, and particularly in New York. It is ironic that Mason spent his adult life in New York, teaching at Columbia University.

DANIEL GREGORY MASON

Mason was born in Brookline, Massachusetts, a town adjacent to Boston. His grandfather was Lowell Mason, of hymn writing and public music education fame; his uncle was William Mason, concert pianist and composer mainly of piano works; his father was Henry Mason, founder of the Mason & Hamlin piano and organ manufacturing firm. He credited his family with his turn to music: "As I consider the old problem of heredity and environment, then, in the light of my own experience, I feel sure that friendly environment in the form of my grandfather, father, uncles, brothers and companions did for my music what no heredity could have done alone. . . . It was because I heard music daily from piano, organ, glee club, or music box—it was because my family entertained musicians and discussed their problems . . . it was for all these environmental reasons that music became for me so early the most vivid thing in the world."[3]

After admission to Harvard, he studied music under Paine but gave up music study at the college after two years because he considered Paine's instruction arbitrary and not accommodating to students' viewpoints.[4] He then continued his education under George Chadwick and Percy Goetschius.

Mason composed his opus 1, *Birthday Waltzes* for piano, in 1894, and published his first book, *From Grieg to Brahms*, in 1902. He first appeared at Columbia University in 1905 and would remain there until 1942. He traveled to Paris, in 1913, in order to study under Vincent d'Indy. Throughout his life he would teach, compose, and write about music. In Mason's early works, Johannes Brahms, and in his post–1913 works, Brahms and d'Indy, were the main influences. He also valued the sort of romanticism that emanated from the music of Beethoven, Schumann, and Franck. Most program music bored him, except for a handful of works that he considered "of a high order," like Strauss's *Death and Transfiguration*, d'Indy's *Istar*, Dukas's *The Sorcerer's Apprentice*, and Rachmaninoff's *Isle of the Dead*.[5] He himself would compose very little program music.

Mason did not care for the music of Wagner, Bruckner, and Mahler. He liked a few works of Tchaikovsky, Strauss, and Debussy, that is, when he thought they did not sound exaggerated. The modernists, who rejected common-practice procedures, he found abominable. Mason and Hill befriended each other while students at Harvard, played music together, and certainly discussed their future artistic pursuits. Among the younger American composers, Mason favored John Powell, Samuel Barber, and Douglas Moore.[6] He disliked the ragtime-, jazz-, and blues-influenced songs and dance music of the popular composers, and the dissonant- and jazz-oriented works being written by the American avant-gardists, who were located principally in New York. Because so many of them were Jewish, a certain anti-semitic tone emerges from his earlier writings, especially in *Tune In, America* (1931). However, a letter sent to the *New York Times*, in 1933, which the newspaper did not publish, expressed Mason's appreciation for the Jewish influence in music.[7] Five years later, in *Music in My Time*, he admitted his error and said that the corrupting influences he opposed were not confined to one group but were widespread. It is quite possible that Mason's deplorable anti-Semitism and drift to the right was occasioned in part by the offensiveness of some modernists' demands for complete freedom from traditional practices. He saw them as advocating irresponsible license, whether in morality, social and personal relationships, or art.

He believed that music's appeal was not simply intellectual, but sensuous and emotional, conveyed principally through melody and its deployment in a movement. Rhythm was a second important conveyance. Good fortune alone was not responsible for a composer's happening on a fine melody and a stimulating rhythm. It was also a matter of self-discipline founded on a tradition going back at a minimum to Beethoven:

You can no more write a solid sonata without knowing Beethoven than you can work efficiently in biology in ignorance of Darwin. Yet on the other hand this assimilation of the past has to produce not an academic and sterile complacency with what is, but an equipped and curious advance upon what is to be: the artist, like the scientist, brings all his learning to the test in acts of creative imagination, leaps in the dark. . . . The great artist is bound to the past by love and docility, to the future by a faith that overleaps convention.[8]

Clearly, he wished to sustain music's spiritual ascendancy, and give it validity through the underpinning of tradition. By doing this, he was able to engage in an art that had a logically consistent array of precedents. It also provided cogent exemplars which supplied a method for appraising his own and other's work.

In addition, Mason said, an American composer achieves individuality not through abstracting the musical peculiarities associated with the New World, but through knowledge of the special beliefs or impulsive propensities in himself and his fellow Americans, "and taking his stand unflinchingly upon them." Among these beliefs are:

the reserve, the dislike of ostentation, the repressed but strong emotion masked by dry humor, that belong to our New England type. . . . In our literature the type is immortally enshrined in the work of Emerson and Thoreau and, in our own day, of Robinson and Frost. We hear it often in the music of Chadwick, sometimes in MacDowell and in Hill (a sort of tender reticence), in Kelley's *New England Symphony*, and in Powell's overture *In Old Virginia* (for it belongs to the old South as well as to New England). The essence of it is a kind of moderation— not negative . . . but strongly positive. . . .[9]

Works written during all phases of his creative life disclose an approach suitable to whatever the genre he was handling and the instruments he was using. A scholarly bent, an unambiguous design, a smooth rich flow of sound, and an ability to express himself easily, clearly, and engagingly are also evident. His was not a "go-as-you-please eclecticism," but one guided by rule and the imperative to seek out the best models, especially from the musical classics he loved.[10] He employed music characteristic of the United States rarely and cautiously. Singularly little that he composed betrays that he lived in the twentieth century. His boldest sallies were into the whole tone- or modal-scale flirtations, diffident display of open fourths and fifths, chromaticism, altered chords, and the dissonant piled-on dominant and non-dominant constructions of late romanticism. Because he was highly critical of himself, he often reworked and refined compositions after their first presentation to the public.

The Sonata for Violin and Piano, opus 5, dates from 1907-08, and is patently based on the style of Brahms. One hears expansive melodies, compact development of motives, malleable rhythms, amiable harmonies, and a nicely calculated dialogue between the two instruments. The strongest of its three movements is the middle one, an *andante tranquilo, non troppo lento* in ternary form. A melodically eloquent first and last section bracket a middle one that sounds more dissonant, syncopated, restless, and has as its goal a grand eruption of feeling. In 1909-11, Mason composed a Quartet for Piano and Strings, opus 7, whose derivation and virtues are similar to those of the sonata.[11]

Between 1912 and 1915, he worked on a *Pastorale* for clarinet, violin, and piano, opus 8. He said much of it came to him while vacationing in the Berkshire Hills of Massachusetts. His own description of what he was trying to express helps explain the limits he set on programmatic expression:

The first theme (violin, D Major), voiced the morning mood that filled one in that bright upland field, vocal with birds, steeped in sunshine and aromatic fragrance. Then with the change to minor and the entrance of the plaintive clarinet melody over the murmuring piano accompaniment I tried to suggest the change of mood that comes as a cloud passes over the sun. . . . There would come a sense of pause, of something both melancholy and ominous that is as characteristic of those Berkshire uplands as the gayer mood of full sunlight. I used the violin rather than the cello which more usually accompanies a clarinet in chamber music, because its brilliance gave just the contrast I wanted with the deeper liquid tones of the clarinet.[12]

Burnett Tuthill thought so highly of the *Pastorale* that he urged Mason to compose another clarinet piece. The result was the Sonata for Clarinet and Piano, opus 14, written between 1912 and 1915. Tuthill says he loved "its three graceful movements," which were "well contrasted with the central scherzo characterized by the augmented triad and the whole-tone scale."[13] The first movement captures a warm twilight mood deepened by a few impassioned climaxes and reminiscent of the late chamber works of Brahms. In the second movement, a wry liveliness invests the opening and its recapitulation; nostalgic tenderness, the middle. The Finale reverts to the moods of the first movement. At times, the music looks to the French, as in the augmented-fifth harmonies that enter shortly after the opening of the first movement.[14] Whatever its influences, the sonata is comfortable to play and gratifying to hear.

The most ambitious work of his early period was the Symphony No. 1 in C Minor, opus 11, composed 1913-14, and premiered in Philadelphia in 1916. Apparently, the public liked only the slow movement. It was then overhauled, with some complexities eliminated. This second thought was first done in New York, in 1922. Mason said that he spent a great deal of money, time, and worry on it, only to achieve discouragingly infrequent performances and modest success.[15] Twelve years would elapse before he would venture again into orchestral composition. Some time later, when he conducted a revival of the symphony, Howard Hanson stated, that he considered Mason "the last of the distinguished American romantic classicists carrying on in the Brahms tradition in this country," and "found [in] this early symphony . . . remarkably fresh and impelling music, which may well defy the ravages of time."[16]

The three movements are cyclical in nature and grow out of three germinal motives that appear in rudimentary shape in the opening *largo* introduction—a structural idea harking back to Chadwick, Franck, and d'Indy. The first, pensive and a bit sad, occurs in the flutes and clarinets. The second follows directly after, heard in the woodwinds, and prefigures the first theme of the *Allegro* to come; the third is a rising, questioning melody for solo violin and then oboe, which becomes the second theme of the *Allegro*. Most of the introduction concentrates on the materialization of the chief motive, the second one, as it changes into the principal theme of the *Allegro*. The moderately slow second movement begins with a new idea that graduates from the English horn to the full orchestra. The middle section retrieves the second germinal motive of the introduction, subjecting it to further development. The last movement has four horns sound a rowdy interpretation of the second germinal motive. The other two motives provide sharp and stimulating contrast. The movement concludes on a spacious hymnic restatement of the second motive. Personal and dramatic in spots, the symphony has no programmatic ambitions, inclines toward the austere, and devotes itself to the interaction of musical themes.[17]

The *Intermezzo* for string quartet, which Mason composed in 1916, has a great deal of charm and confident writing but the main interest is again in the interaction of musical ideas. It also shows some of the austerity noted in the symphony. When Elliott Carter heard it played almost 25 years later, he thought it one of Mason's best pieces, though lacking the personal quality of the *Lincoln* Symphony, his third.[18] Among his best pieces is *Russians*, a song cycle for low voice and piano, opus 18, written in 1916-17. It was later arranged for baritone and orchestra.[19] The Chicago Orchestra gave the premier of this latter version in 1918. Arresting settings of five singular and ungenteel poems by Mason's friend Witter

Bynner comprise the cycle. Ostensibly Russian characters speak out in the first-person singular. For example, in the first song, "A Drunkard," an intoxicated man is asked what he is singing about. Too far gone to know, he mumbles:

Vodka bakes me in my innards.
Drops of it are on my beard.

For a change, Mason loosens his inhibitions and produces a score vividly laid out for vocalist and orchestra, emotionally varied from song to song, dramatically telling when necessary, and running the gamut of feeling from warm poignancy to stony pessimism. Greater boldness of expression replaces the customary caution. The sound can be somewhat assertive, even vehement or grating. In short, it is a fine work.

Russians possibly helped relieve sundry restraints hitherto perceptible in his style. His next significant composition, the String Quartet on Negro Themes, opus 19, composed 1918-19, delves into African-American spirituals and sifts through impressionistic musical techniques. In the first movement, "You May Bury Me in the East" sounds; in the second, "Deep River;" in the third, "Shine, Shine," "Oh, Holy Lord," and "Oh, What Do You Say, Seekers." George Chadwick and Antonín Dvořák had already pointed the way to the use of African-American traditional music. Claude Debussy's impressionistic style, however much Mason had disapproved of it, proved too pregnant with fresh compositional possibilities for Mason to ignore it. Arthur Shepherd applauds Mason's handling of the spirituals. To transplant material like this into art music was a matter of controversy; success depended on skill and good taste, he states. To him, Mason has plenty of both qualities, for he realizes "the great potentialities of these tunes, particularly in the way of mood and rhythms." Shepherd especially enjoys the vitality and profound expressiveness in the handling of "Deep River." The composer effortlessly and tellingly counterpoises the spirituals, at the same time evoking "ample sonorities and piquant color-effects," which emerge "naturally and idiomatically" from the instruments.[20] Mason's friend Tuthill tells us that Mason's use of spirituals was not meant to be taken as a nationalist pose, but that he loved "beautiful simple tunes" of this sort.[21]

As for the impressionistic measures, Mason admitted to the attractiveness of Debussy's harmonies: "Debussy's harmonies, especially his sliding, clamped-together ninth chords reproducing a single melody at five levels simultaneously and thus virtually reducing harmony to zero, proved so seductive to the merely sensuous ear, that I used some of them with really startling inappropriateness, in the first version of my *Quartet on Negro Themes*, and only came to my senses [ten years later] in time to expunge them in a later edition. So slow was I to find my own musical ailment, and to perceive what, though food for others, was poison to me." He credits Hill with calling Mason's attention to the violation of the original character of the tunes.[22] Even in the revised version,[23] a Debussy-like sensuous quality, a freedom of voice-leading in the harmonies, and numerous coloristic touches persist in the music. In spots, as in the subsidiary theme of the first movement, the melodies also divulge a French influence not previously encountered in Mason's music.

The first movement opens in 2/4 time, with a strong main theme, syncopated and flexibly rhythmic, that emerges in short dancing phrases (a catching "You May Bury Me in the East"). For much of the movement, this earthy theme is effectively contrasted with diaphanous and atmospheric secondary ideas. The recapitulation of the main theme in the viola is particularly winning when we hear it accompanied by "banjo-strumming" violins. It is assuredly the most vernacular of the three movements. The eloquent second movement is a meditation on "Deep River" that surges up to trenchant peaks. Its joyous middle section has a blithe liveliness that freshens the return of the meditation. One detects hardly any link here to German romanticism. The brisk last movement makes its close on a reappearance of the "Deep River" melody, which provides a solid summation to the whole quartet. The music always maintains a high level of expressiveness, whether that of slow, deep contemplation or of vigorous, pulsing effervescence. Randall Thompson's allusion to the "sinister and foreboding pessimism," and the "dour and bitter irony in Mason's music"[24] seems somewhat off the mark here.

The year 1920 saw the completion of the Prelude and Fugue for Pianoforte and Orchestra, opus 20, a work dedicated to and premiered by John Powell with the Chicago Symphony, in 1921. No Americanisms appear in this thoroughly romantic score. One hears a great deal of sentiment, but no sentimentality. The prelude opens with the orchestra in unison playing an 11-note "motto-theme," tersely and portentously. The piano enters, its lyricism at times grave, at times poignant, always introspective—as if the personal voice of the composer himself. The two principal moods thusly introduced, make up the substance of the prelude, which builds to a first-rate climax, when the brass blares out the theme. The fugue, more truly a fantasy in a fugal vein, acts more as a continuation of the prelude's music, rather than as a separate movement. Announced by the piano, the melancholic subject turns out to be a variant of the theme of the prelude. The subject and the counter-ideas in the episodes are skillfully deployed and Mason supplies a monumental peroration. Thompson's "pessimism" and "bitter irony" would seem more appropriately applied to portions of this work, rather than to the quartet.

Mason was aware that the writing of an academic fugue could be deadly. However, he considered the fugue to be "one of the most moving and beautiful of all forms since it is in its very essence melody, all melody, and nothing but melody." Because he felt that the form lent itself to intense, subjective emotion and plastic beauty, he turned to it. Yet, he attempted to compose the prelude and fugue in "a modern idiom."[25] Mason's modernity, of course, stopped well short of that being practiced by Schoenberg and Stravinsky.

The composer had always admired Thoreau, who, along with other New England writers like Emerson and Whitman, furnished prime examples of the individualistic thinking that gave the United States stature in nineteenth-century literature. By age 25, Mason felt that Thoreau represented his own "purely literary side," and he hero-worshipped Thoreau as ardently as he did Brahms.[26] By July 1900, Mason was entertaining the thought of doing a biography of Thoreau: "I desire to make Thoreau vivid to the reader as a man among men, which means a great deal of description." A month later, he had written about 9,000 words and had a publisher, Beacon Biographies, awaiting the finished manuscript. Yet, he kept on putting off the completion of the biography; he then gave it up altogether in September 1908, when he suggested letting Edward H. Russell take on the assignment.[27]

Thoreau, nevertheless, was not forgotten. Mason finally paid his tribute to the philosopher of Walden Pond in the best way he knew how, the *Chanticleer* Overture of 1926, his opus 27. The composer made an important side of Thoreau "vivid to the" listener, through "a good deal of description." That the portrayal Mason attempts is not merely a literal one, he made clear in a comment on what he was endeavoring to capture:

"All health and success," says Thoreau in *Walden*, "does me good, however far off and withdrawn it may appear; all disease and failure helps to make me sad and does me evil, however much sympathy it may have with me or I with it. If, then, we would indeed restore mankind by truly Indian, botanic, magnetic, or natural means, let us first be as simple and well as Nature ourselves, dispel the clouds which hang over our own brows, and take up a little life into our pores." *Chanticleer*, an attempt to give musical expression to this same mood, bears as a motto the sentences Thoreau placed at the beginning of *Walden*: "I do not propose to write an ode to dejection but to brag as lustily as chanticleer in the morning, standing on his roost, if only to wake my neighbors up."[28]

The principal idea which opens this composition, in sonata form, centers on an artistic approximation of a cock's crow heard in the trumpet accompanied by brass, harp, and strings. Above the music of the score is a *Walden* quotation: "All climates agree with brave Chanticleer. He is more indigenous even than natives. His health is ever good, his lungs are sound, his spirits never flag."[29] The sound is open, diatonic, and in debt to traditional Anglo-American music. A second and third theme linked to the principal idea follow, played by the woodwinds and by four horns, respectively. The main theme makes a loud comeback in three trumpets against the full orchestra. This first part of the overture is intended to suggest the happiness in Nature and the joy it brings to mankind.

Dynamics grow softer and cackling bassoons chatter away on a contrasting "hen" theme. Thoreau's *Winter* is quoted: "Bless the Lord, O my soul, bless Him for wildness . . . and bless Him for hens, too, that croak and cackle." The tune is more chromatic and syncopated than the first one and hints at American popular song. The effect is charmingly capricious. A third idea, a unifying succession of five or six chords in parallel motion is heard throughout the work, often in a modal sequence. The development section that follows develops the main and subsidiary theme. Eventually, the recapitulation brings back the lusty crow of chanticleer and the answering chatter of the hens, then continues until an stirring conclusion is achieved.

No musical Americanisms are heard, yet the music encompasses the American vital force that Mason had hoped all native composers would eventually capture. One detects neither Brahms nor d'Indy peering over Mason's shoulder as he composed it. Instead he paints American figures into an American soundscape through a confidently employed musical language. The overture discloses dynamic, ebullient, and poetic attributes having no European parallels. As expected from Mason, the music is skillfully put together and conservative in style. Unexpected is the insistent, outspoken expression of joy and animal spirits. No pessimism or bitter irony here, just good-humored and genial music. Strong, evocative harmonic progressions and apt rhythms propel the sound along.

The overture quickly became a favorite with symphony audiences throughout the United States. Most amazingly to Mason, he made a net profit of $460.66 out of performance fees and royalties within a few years, instead of the usual net losses from his other works.[30] It is unquestionably one of the most appealing works he wrote. Its pages demonstrate that profundity is not synonymous only with tragedy. Reviewing a recording of the overture, in 1985, Paul Snook considers it one of several works that proved American music did not originate with the compositions of Ives or the teaching of Nadia Boulanger. *Chanticleer* is "delectably brash and bumptious." The music strikes him as harmonically free, open, and optimistic. The piece is "a kind of symphonic parallel to the self-assertive spirituality which animated Emerson, Whitman, and Thoreau . . . during America's cultural-democratic coming-of-age."[31]

After years of avoiding the genre, Mason composed another symphony, Symphony No. 2 in A major, opus 30, in 1928–29, and made some revisions to the score in 1941, 1942, and 1948. No program accompanied the music. The composer himself described the composition as romantic in tendency and style.[32] The piece strikes the ear as containing somber music, masculine in tone and weighty in texture. The unbuttoned exuberance of *Chanticleer* is abandoned. Conflict, sorrowful musing, and weary resignation are three of the symphony's dominant moods. Again, as in the first symphony, Mason deals with the four movements cyclically, with ideas traveling across movements. The most prominent idea of the entire symphony, a descending chromatic passage of three tones, *tutti*, launches the symphony on its way. Series of open fifths and fourths are heard. An aura of brooding dwells in the tones. Tuthill believes that Randall Thompson's comment on the "sinister and foreboding pessimism" and "dour and bitter irony in Mason's music" is appropriate to this work.[33] Themes heard in the first movement recur as variants in the third movement, *Scherzo*, and make up the principal material of the Finale. No conventional development and recapitulation take place in the first movement. Nor are they needed, since development occurs whenever the themes return, and the last movement can be taken as a free recapitulation of the first. The middle of the *Scherzo* displays a winsome folk like melody, treated laconically. The close of the composition is placid, but seems to imply exhaustion more than serenity. The austerity and the impression of holding back in one's feelings, noted in the previous symphony, are still apparent here. However, this second symphony is the surefooted work of a mature musician, worthy of high praise. Learnedness is everywhere apparent. One wishes, though, for less self-restraint.

A much less consequential piece, the *Serenade* for string quartet, opus 31, in three short movements, was completed in 1931. Fugato passages are tucked into all the movements—the first, a sonata structure sans a real development; the second, a rondo that thrives on two English folk songs; the third, variational.

Perhaps dealing with folk songs in the *Serenade* was a trial run before his next work, the *Suite After English Folk Songs*, opus 32, which Mason composed in 1933-34. It is a delightful change from the stiff *Serenade*. Fabien Sevitzky and the People's Symphony Orchestra premiered it in 1935, in Boston. One should keep in mind Mason's belief that the characteristic tunes and rhythms of a nation could serve as ingredients in a composer's music; but if allowed to dominate a composer's thinking, they could prove disastrous.[34] The first movement begins *moderato gioncoso* on "Oh, No, John!," shifts to a *sostenuto* with the lyrical "Young Sailor," then to a *vivace* with "The Two Magicians," and combines all three tunes for a climax at the end. The second movement, *andante tranquilo*, features freely rendered variations, each given an individual expression, on "Arise, Arise." It finishes on a canon. The last movement, a sprightly *allegro vivace*, turns to "The Rambling Sailor." Mason appears most comfortable with his material. The management of the agreeable tunes sounds just right. We discover the restraint and matter-of-fact repartee that stems directly from his New England upbringing. However, we also appreciate the rhythmic verve of folk dance, the artless and forthright expression of the folk singer, and the warmth of personal feeling with no hint of subjective pessimism. Nor do manifestations of scholarship bring on discomfort. The drawing power of the music stems not only from the attractive melodies, but also from the composition's homespun atmosphere and plain discourse.

The next, and grandest of Mason's compositions, the Symphony No. 3, *A Lincoln Symphony*, took shape in 1935-36 and had its premier in New York, in 1937. The musical depiction of Lincoln is tragic in the sense that it informs us of the contradictory and incongruous quality of humankind's striving against evil, and its sometimes fatal consequences. The tragedy embraces the events surrounding the Civil War, which brought Lincoln's age and its values into dispute. Mason possibly wanted to show that the aftermath of the battle against iniquity, in particular the battle against long-standing human enslavement, when pushed to the extreme, had ended in the reassertion of human worth and liberty. Regardless of the destructive power of evil, as seen in the suffering and dying of thousands of people and the assassination of Lincoln, this reassertion is a triumph (if only a nervous one, as history has proved). The music is not programmatic, in the sense of following a storyline. Its intent is to capture the moods of a discordant time and the fortitude of a leader seeking a common good.

When it was first heard, the symphony addressed the problem of American identity in the face of a debilitating economic depression that was pulling society apart during the 1930s. Its contribution to this struggle was an awareness of the convictions and standards of excellence, the travail and the sacrifice that have caused democracy to function. Lincoln is a figure from our heroic past, and the thought that this heroism showed itself in the men at Gettysburg and in the circumstances of Lincoln's life and death has always fascinated Americans.

The composer stated: "The only traditional theme is the *Quaboag Quickstep*, an actual popular tune of the 1860 period, used to suggest the thoughtless, restless, trivial people Lincoln had to inspire. The theme of the slow movement, *Massa Linkum*, it is true, is also conceived in the vein of the Negro spirituals, but is not based on any actual tune. Also my own are the themes of the serious Lincoln, of the humorous, gawky, yet tender Lincoln of the scherzo *Old Abe's Yarns*, and of the funeral march made from the *Quaboag Quickstep* in the finale, *1865*. I felt, and Douglas Moore, Chalmers Clifton, and other friends agreed, that this was a step in the right direction, away from the letter and toward the spirit."[35]

The first movement, "The Candidate from Springfield," begins *lento serioso* with the Lincoln motive, a downward skip of a fifth and an upward skip of a tenth, played by a trumpet, then a horn, then the strings.[36] Most of the particulars of the symphony come out of this motive. Gradually Mason portrays Lincoln's character, his outward cheer and inward struggles, and feelings from serious to comical. Then comes a *molto vivace* that features the brisk, nonchalant quickstep tune against a lightly skipping rhythm. After a cheery and highly syncopated clarinet solo, the quickstep returns *fortissimo* in the full orchestra, as if the composer was intent on hurling the sounds at the listener. Despite Mason's statements, could not this fast section also signify the common, human side of Lincoln? Soon a slower tempo arrives and the serious-Lincoln motive returns. It turns into a *fugato*, and after an acceleration of tempo, suddenly brakes to a somber funeral march. The ebullient, fast dancing tune returns. It again gives way to slow, reflective statements of the serious-Lincoln motive. This interchange between gaiety and heavyheartedness characterizes the movement.

The second movement, *Massa Linkum*, is an *andante dolente*, and slow and sad it is. It opens on an English horn solo playing a modal-minor tune, the seventh tone of the scale lowered. An oboe and a flute continue the tune's exposition. Shortly, a solo cello plays in the manner of a recitative and brings in the serious-Lincoln motive. The strings lyrically and expressively participate in a passage stemming from the recitative. Their tones burgeon into an eloquent *maestoso*, at which point the first theme returns in counterpoint with the Lincoln motive. Eventually, a variant of the opening is heard. The close is tranquil.

The very enjoyable third movement, "Old Abe's Yarn," fashions the motive into a theme of disjointed character. It is Lincoln taking on the character of a country bumpkin, a teller of cracker barrel tales. Gawky yet appealing, it starts and stops in jerky manner. Playfulness marks the motive's reincarnations in inversion, retrograde inversion, and augmentation.

The Finale, *1865*, starts with a tonally unfocused, chromatic rendition of the motive, *lento serioso*. A *tempo di marcia funebre* starts up. This theme is based on the first-movement quickstep, only now its expressive impact is totally opposite. This dramatic transformation is undoubtedly why the original, almost commonplace quickstep was used in the first place. The movement combines dignity with poignancy and continues to unfold until an emotional peak is achieved. The music grows quieter. Allusions to themes from the three previous movements are made. A final augmented version of the Lincoln motive sounds grandly. The symphony has ended.

After listening to the symphony, Lawrence Gilman writes in the *New York Herald Tribune*, 18 November 1937: "Mr. Mason . . . has demonstrated again and again throughout this work his depth of insight and of feeling, his power of salient and expressive utterance, his incorruptible honesty and dignity as an artist, his tact and sensibility as a poet and humanist in tones." Gilman praises the music's "lofty simplicity" and "noble austerity" that captured Lincoln's essence in concise fashion.[37]

Daniel Gregory Mason cannot be numbered among the very great composers of the United States, and we would be lacking in discrimination to give him that status. He missed out on the genius needed to create a large body of out-and-out masterworks. On the other hand, he nearly made up for it, if one takes into account the aesthetic pleasure one can obtain from his music, especially from its distinctiveness and impeccable technical construction. And a work like his last symphony deserves far more respect than critics have granted it.

Throughout his life, Mason tried to express his faith in the musical traditions and the Yankee vision of America he had inherited. That he worked sincerely within that tradition and labored to encompass the ideals of New England within viable musical forms cannot be doubted. However unresponsive to twentieth century innovation, he discoursed with some power and demonstrated not a little talent in those compositions that represent him at his best—the *String-Quartet on Negro Themes*, *Chanticleer*, the *Suite on English Folk-Songs*, and *A Lincoln Symphony*. Curiously, the compositions that have proved most rewarding to hear are outside his usual style in their references to African-American, Anglo-American, and popular American music—or, in the case of *Chanticleer*, to a beaming, optimistic, and typically American robustness unknown in his previous works. In them, his inhibitions are least in evidence and a spontaneity of utterance comes more to the fore. Moreover, in the late 1920s, he ceased looking so assiduously toward Brahms and d'Indy and revealed greater stylistic individuality. He was a master of his traditionalistic idiom and, within it, able to speak with a solid authority.

EDWARD BURLINGAME HILL

Around 1893-94, while students at Harvard, Hill and Mason engaged in an experimental activity similar to some engaged in by Charles Ives and his father. Charles Ives went on to incorporate the experiments in his music. For Hill and Mason, the experiment remained a matter of the moment, amusing but not artistically viable. Mason stated:

Hill and I would sometimes venture further afield, into Boston drawing rooms or studios, to regale our friends with music, two-hand or four—serious or frivolous. One of our favorite battle horses was *Between Two Bands*, a graphic representation of one march (E. B. H. in the treble) beginning very near and loud, and gradually disappearing into space and *pianissimo*, while a different march (D. G. M in the bass) would begin very far and soft and equally gradually approach into deafening *fortissimo*. There was a crucial moment when both bands were about equidistant, supremely relished by us if not always by our audience.[38]

Hill was born in Cambridge, Massachusetts. His grandfather, Thomas Hill, had been president of Harvard. His father was professor of chemistry at Harvard. Music was frequently heard at his home during his childhood and adolescence. W. F. Apthorp, the music critic, came there to play the German masterpieces, especially those by Bach; his father loved to sing the *Lieder* of Schubert and Franz. His father was also a friend of John Knowles Paine. During young Hill's stay at Harvard, Paine was his teacher in music composition and it was Paine's and Edward MacDowell's influence that he felt strongly. Some flirtation with the music of Russians and the musical vernacular of African-Americans also took place. He would later study with Chadwick at the New England Conservatory, with Arthur Whiting in New York, and Charles-Marie Widor in Paris. Perhaps it was during the course of his sojourn in Paris (1898) that Hill first felt the influence of Claude Debussy and Maurice Ravel.

Edward Ballantine, his colleague in the Harvard music department, stated in the *Boston Evening Transcript*, 25 May 1940, that Hill was one of the first Americans to make a thorough study of the more advanced contemporary French composers and to appreciate the teaching abilities of Nadia Boulanger. After he joined the Harvard music faculty, he encouraged his students to further their music studies with her in Paris, and thus initiated the parade of neophyte American composers to Paris beginning with Virgil Thomson. Hill himself once stated: "I was interested in French music when it was regarded as intensely radical, and trust that I have a liberal attitude towards Stravinsky, Schoenberg and Hindemith."[39] Such a standpoint set him apart from Converse and Mason. When he began teaching at Harvard, he gave courses on orchestration, about which he had become a master, and modern French music (d'Indy, Fauré, Debussy, and Ravel). Among his students were Virgil Thomson, Randall Thompson, Walter Piston, Elliott Carter, Ross Lee Finney, Irving Fine, Arthur Berger, and Leonard Bernstein.

As a teacher and composer, he contributed considerably to the dismantling of the barrier erected by German-oriented, nineteenth century musicians in the United States against the non-German, twentieth-century styles that departed sharply from the usual. He designed his own works lucidly and rationally, from the smallest detail to the all-embracing structure. At the same time, the fundamental emotional substance, which we recognize as infusing the design, is elegantly warm and fastidiously expressive. He was no lackey of French impressionism. What he learned from the French he eventually converted to American usages, especially after 1920. By the time he composed *Lilacs*, in 1927, whatever the impressionism that lingers seems American and personal. His music, with its astutely realized weave of sound and feeling, betrays a nature that is essentially contemplative.

The earliest compositions, written for the piano, derive mostly from MacDowell. In 1907 he completed his cantata *Nuns of the Perpetual Adoration*, for women's voices and orchestra, to a poem by Ernest Dowson. It proceeds from beginning to end almost entirely in lockstep homophony. After hearing an English performance in 1911, Ernest Newman praises its orchestration, "delicately poetical inspiration," and "half mystic, half passionate mood."[40] *Jack Frost in Mid-Summer*, a "pantomime" for orchestra, came out in 1908, and *Pan and the Star*, a "pantomime" for orchestra and women's voices, in 1914. Both works were praised for their orchestral scoring, rich sound, and imaginative conception.

Hill seemed to really break out on his own with the symphonic poem after Stephen Phillips, *The Parting of Lancelot and Guinevere*, opus 22, completed in 1915, and premiered in St. Louis on 31 December 1915. MacDowell's symphonic poem *Lancelot and Elaine*, composed in 1888, may have inclined Hill to write it. In its spare, focused, succinct, and trenchant language, it sounds not at all like the MacDowell work and reveals the ascendancy of French music and aesthetics. He has clearly moved away from his earlier influences. After a brief introduction, Guinevere's motive of tender longing is heard, played by the English horn. The motive is elaborated with increasing briskness up to the arrival of Lancelot's manly theme in the trumpets. An episode based on the Guinevere motive follows, serving as Lancelot's retrospection upon his love for the queen.[41] The dramatic conflict attendant on the parting of the lovers comes next and reaches a climax. The music subsides and changes into an epilogue with the melody given to the clarinets over triplet figures in the cellos and violas.

The normally abbreviated motives often abut each other and organize themselves into larger sections like bits of tile that are pieced together to form an overall design. These mosaic-like patterns struck critics as representing something ultramodern in musical style. Hill's procedures, derived from French impressionism, give the audience few lengthy tunes to chew over. H. T. Parker writes:

Short and impinging motives characterize Lancelot, Guinevere and, as it seems in the epilogue, their fate. These motives are not developed and interwoven in intricate polyphony, saturated with harmonic elaboration or drenched in instrumental color in the fashion of . . . the Straussian generation. In the newer and current mode, which flows out of Paris rather than Munich, they are wrought, bit by bit, into a fabric of tones that is more sensitive and incisive, that seeks harmonic subtlety rather than opulence; that prefers sharp or shaded instrumental tints to ornate vesture; that relies more upon adroit modulation and sharp-set juxtaposition than upon large and emphatic manipulation of the musical mass; that addresses itself to the comprehending mind and the sympathetic imagination of the hearer rather than to his nervous excitement.

Perhaps rightly, Parker concludes the work is mostly cerebral and makes only momentary illusions to scenes, moods, and the passion of the lovers.[42]

If *The Parting of Lancelot and Guinevere* showed Hill modifying his style to make room for French influences, the two *Stevensoniana* Suites show him definitely entering the new areas of tonal expressiveness pioneered by Debussy and Ravel. The suites pursue a parallel, not an imitative, course to that of Debussy and Ravel. They stand on their own as independent artistic entities. Poems from Robert Louis Stevenson's *A Child's Garden of Verses* supplied the inspiration. The listener is struck by the resplendently picturesque instrumental combinations, the textural clarity, the warmth of feeling, and the naïveté of manner. The first suite, opus 24, was written in 1916-17; the second, opus 29, in 1921-22.[43] Both of them became dear to the heart of the music public and gained Hill a name for urbane and shrewd wittiness, effortless ingenuity, and imaginative capriciousness. Scarcely any other contemporary American composer could write for orchestra with such appropriateness and esprit, or could set down harmonies of such spiciness and with such ear-catching expression of character. Only John Alden Carpenter's *Adventures in a Perambulator* and Deems Taylor's *Through the Looking Glass* come to mind as offering anything equivalent.

The first suite's movements are captioned "Marching Song," "The Land of Nod," "Where Go the Boats?," and "The Unseen Playmate." Of its premier at Boston's Jordan Hall, in 1918, an unnamed reviewer in the *Christian Science Monitor* writes: "The music made a favorable impression. The interest in the four pieces, march, lullaby—'The Land of Nod'—scherzo, and 'The Unseen Playmate,' is cumulative; and the last seems by far the best written of the four. The lullaby is frankly in the style of the modern French writers, particularly Debussy; and one suspects that Mr. Hill was especially interested in the last lines of the poem:

> Nor can remember plain and clear
> The curious music that I hear.[44]

Critics praised the suite's sophistication, gentle humor, and sympathetic interpretation of the verse. They liked the last movement the most. The march, though pleasant enough, was possibly too given to modulation and too highly refined in its use of instruments to project a childlike image.

The second suite received its premier in New York, in March 1923, and turned out even more popular than the first. In three movements—"Armies in the Night," "The Dumb Soldier," and "Pirate Story"—it possesses all the virtues and fine qualities of its predecessor. The outer movements have brilliance, stimulating rhythms, and a hint of the theatrical about them. The middle movement is a reverie enveloped in charm and whimsy. No expression is exaggerated, no movement too long. Every single portion of each movement is fittingly related to another and to the whole. Hill himself insisted that the music was not descriptive but an attempt to catch the moods of the poems.[45]

Between composing the two suites, Hill wrote *The Fall of the House of Usher*, Poem for Orchestra (after the story by Poe), opus 27. It goes to the opposite expressive extreme from the suites. Composed in the summer of 1919, and revised in the fall and winter of 1919-20, it depicted no story, according to Hill, but tried to capture the macabre atmosphere of the tale as a whole. Two themes, however, are associated with the morose Roderick and the dying Madeline Usher.[46] The structure is an abridged sonata form, without development and with a brief introduction and coda. The music does suggest quiet horror, frenzied unease, and imminent catastrophe with an economy of means and without luridness. At the end, the music alludes to the collapse of the house and tragic denouement of the Ushers. Yet Hill's fastidiousness prevents him from conjuring the totally oppressive atmosphere and feeling of unbearable terror conveyed by the original. He appeals to the mind rather than agitates the emotions. He would seem to have been more comfortable with the moods in *Stevensoniana*.

One suspects that for a few years Hill was fishing within his being to bring to the surface a future direction for his creativity. Nine Waltzes for Orchestra, opus 28, came out in 1921. The explicitly light music veers away from the delineatory wit of the suites and the dark emotions of the symphonic poem. It features a set of sublimated dances—rich in melody, tasty in harmony, and suave in orchestration. The next year he worked on the judiciously conceived *Jazz Studies* for two pianos (more jazz studies would come out in 1935).

In 1924, Koussevitzky and the Boston Symphony played his new *Scherzo* for Two Pianos and Orchestra. The audience enjoyed the syncopated rhythms and the proliferation of zesty non-dominant seventh chords. Critics dedicated to "Art" found it coarse; devotees of jazz complained that it did not go far enough. After Oswald Villard wrote about how much pleasure the *Scherzo* had given him, Hill replied: "I fear it shares the fate of all *mulattos*, in that it is too lowly for the purists, and not positive enough for the 'jazz fiends.' "[47] The next year, two abstract works swimming in the traditional mainstream saw the light, the Flute Sonata and the Clarinet Sonata. Both are beguiling works. For example, one of Hill's best tunes lives in the second movement in C-sharp Minor, *tranquillo, non troppo lento,* of the Clarinet Sonata.

His strivings met with unqualified success in *Lilacs,* Poem for Orchestra, opus 33 (after Amy Lowell), which the Boston Symphony performed in 1927. The composition was dedicated to the memory of the dead poet, once a dear friend. Hill stated that he had long admired Lowell's poetry and thought her "Lilacs" an "excellent subject for musical treatment by one of New England ancestry." He chose not to follow the poem in his musical depiction. Instead he gave his impressions of its images, especially those in the beginning and end.[48]

Almost 20 minutes long, the piece starts with a short introduction. The effect is impressionistic, with delicate sounds coming from a small number of muted violins and a celesta against abbreviated woodwind phrases.[49] Woodwinds, strings, and full orchestra follow each other in rendering the main melody, swelling in volume from very soft to very loud, then back to soft again. The music is deeply felt. The orchestra sings with a sincere simplicity that is convincingly communicated to the listener. A contrasting middle section follows; its theme's opening tones clash quietly with the harmony. But the conflict is temporary. Volume again increases. A broad *largamente* section ensues, where the music is spun out in the high strings and woodwinds. Then the main theme returns, now elaborated in different fashion. The music of the coda quiets down to a *tranquillo,* in order to make succinct references to all of the ideas that have gone before. The final measures return to the *tempo dell' Introduzione,* and the material of the opening is enunciated more extendedly. The tones in the last measure fade away to nothing.

In *Lilacs,* Hill accommodates readily to the position of poetic scenic painter, one who is unmistakably expressing an American ambience, a musical approach inaugurated by Chadwick and MacDowell. For all too brief a length of time, he sings achingly and affectionately about the loveliness of his native New England. It is a self-aware expression of the nobility in garden-variety things, a nobility that in the 1920s, when America's social and moral fiber seemed to be fraying, seemed more precious than ever to Hill. Amy Lowell's poem chronicles people, places, and activities with perceptive and exact diction. Eventually the reader is jogged into the comprehension of her overriding subject—that the lilacs from their roots to their flowers represent both her native soil and herself. George Boas writes about the poem: "When one stops to think, it appears to be of no importance whether Miss Lowell was of New England or not. . . . As an individual she will have disappeared completely in a generation or two. But her ecstatic cry of identity with New England seems important to you hearing it and I wonder whether any poem, whether any work of art, ever seems important (except historically) unless its pattern takes on significance."[50]

The subject fitted Hill's state of mind and he too took the lilacs as symbols of home and country. Impressionistic he may be but hazy he is not. He invents unambiguous, songful images that expand in fervor until they erupt with heightened feeling. The warm intensity of expression is unusual for Hill. Taken in its entirety, it is a music of loneliness, of someone estranged from much that surrounds him in the present. The composition comes across not as heroic and prolix, but circumscribed and highly concentrated. It is not youthful, but adult. Cheer and hope make way for the earnest and the self-searching; the declamatory makes way for the lyric. He has managed to write fresh music in an idiom that can in no way be mistaken as avant-garde.

In the year that he completed *Lilacs*, Hill seems to have opted to relinquish program music altogether, in favor of abstract composition. Three symphonies followed, dating from 1927, 1929, and 1937. A Violin Concerto was heard in 1938; the Music for English Horn and Orchestra, in 1945. In all of them, the composer wishes only to advance musical ideas. The style is more conservative than that of younger colleagues like Walter Piston and Aaron Copland, less so than that of Mason. The structures are traditional ones and look back to the Classical period. Every measure is impeccably crafted. Every passage is given a distinct and unfeigned expression, however disciplined the feeling may be. Indeed, "sensuous" and "romantic" are descriptions applicable to much of this music. There is no point in describing them verbally. They must be heard. The five compositions contain music well worth getting to know. The same holds true for his late chamber music, the Sextet for Piano and Winds of 1934, the Quartet for Strings of 1935, and the Quartet for Piano and Strings, also from around 1935.

On the lighter side, he wrote a one-movement Concertino for Piano and Orchestra in 1931, a Sinfonietta in One Movement in 1932, and a Concertino for String Orchestra in 1940. All three are fine, entertaining works.

Hill always maintained throughout his creative life that the music itself had to come first, before emotional or programmatic considerations. Personal emotional expression might, even speaking precisely, be the objective of music, but a composer like Hill did not devote himself primarily to it. He considered that a composer whose major desire was to get his feelings (or his temperament, or the features of his society) into his compositions was at the same time attempting to legitimize an artistic means about which Hill himself had a few doubts. In this regard, he completely agreed with Mason. He felt no uncertainty in what he proposed to accomplish. He avoided the presumptuousness that comes with an achievement of easy results and the belief that one can dispense with an intimate understanding of one's medium. For this reason, novel expression, facilely achieved by means of an advanced style that spurned tradition, was not for him. Hill evidently thought that the composer should preferably compose his music first, consider what he had written, and, after this was done, come to a conclusion about what he was expressing. The music might not capture all that he conceived in his mind; it would capture much of what he heard inwardly and what was thus heard would provide firm substance to his music. The careful listener must conclude that Hill's music does have substance, a dependable substratum that upholds his considerable artistry.

MABEL DANIELS

American women had long been active as writers and performers of popular song. In the latter part of the nineteenth century and the first part of the twentieth, a few women wrote art songs worthy of notice, among them Harriet Ware, Gertrude Norman Smith, and Eleanor Everest Freer. Celeste Heskscher, in addition to songs, tried her hand at some piano and orchestral music. Mary Carr Moore (1873-1957), who lived on the West Coast, not only composed several excellent songs, a piano concerto, and a little chamber music, but also several operas, of which *Narcissa* (1911) was perhaps the best received. Its subject concerned the journey to the Northwest and eventual massacre by Indians of a missionary couple. The music, obviously beholden to Italian opera composers, has many moments of great melodic appeal. Moore made an attempt at introducing Amerindian music, although she altered what she used for the sake of artistry.[51]

On the East Coast, in the generation antecedent to that of Daniels, there was Margaret Ruthven Lang (1867-1972), daughter of the noted Boston musician Benjamin J. Lang, who worked in several music genres and gained a modest success. There was also the extraordinary Amy Beach (1867-1944), who grew up in Boston, then sallied forth as a piano virtuoso to win the respect of audiences all over the Western world. She was also a remarkable composer, with her *Gaelic Symphony* (1896), Piano Concerto (1900), and Piano Quintet (1908) numbered among the finest musical works by Americans of her time.

Daniels was born in Swampscott, Massachusetts. She acquired her parents' and grandparents' love for music and decided to gain as thorough a musical education as she could. George Chadwick, in Boston, and Ludwig Thuille, in Munich, were her principal instructors in theory and composition. In addition, she earned her B. A. degree (magna cum laude) from Radcliffe College. The Radcliffe Glee Club was under her direction during 1911-13. A teaching stint at Simmons College extended from 1914 to 1918.

She first attracted more than local notice in 1911, when she won two prizes offered by the National Federation of Music Clubs, for her song

"Villa of Dreams," and for two three-part songs, "Voice of My Beloved" and "Eastern Song." It quickly became apparent that though she interpreted tonality liberally, freely laced her harmony with dissonance, and borrowed certain congenial practices from impressionism, she was essentially a musical moderate not far removed in style from the temperance of Converse and Hill.

Her interest lay mainly in writing for voice. Her first consequential work was *The Desolate Cry*, a cantata for baritone solo, chorus, and orchestra, on a poem by Wilfred S. Blunt. It was performed for the first time at a MacDowell Colony summer festival, in 1913. Praiseworthy was the effectiveness of the vocal writing and the dramatic qualities of the whole work.[52] Another celebrated composition, *Exultate Deo*, a motet for chorus and orchestra, was composed for the fiftieth anniversary of Radcliffe College, in 1929. Its first and last divisions resound with a glorification of God. Just before the last division is a brief but heartfelt avowal of religious faith. She commemorated the seventy-fifth anniversary of Radcliffe with *Psalm of Praise* for chorus, trumpets, percussion, and strings.

Daniels heard one of her most ambitious compositions, *The Song of Jael*, a large cantata for dramatic soprano, chorus, and orchestra (text from Edwin A. Robinson's poem "Sisera") premiered at the Worcester Music Festival in 1940. It tells of Jael, a Jewish woman, who slew the tyrant Sisera. It begins and ends with exulting religious song; the middle is a brief *andante pastorale*. In it, Daniels dares to go beyond her usual musical conservatism. Mighty and sinewy musical rhetoric, chromatic harmonic progressions, stabilizing structures, and moments of eloquent spiritual probing give it a great deal of consequence. David Ewen finds the melody and harmony close to that of Honegger. Warren Storey Smith is quoted as writing, in the *Boston Post*, that *The Song of Jael* is "a prolonged hymn of triumph that comes to a mighty climax. . . . The outstanding feature . . . is the striking and frequent highly original handling of the chorus. There are, nevertheless, many effective moments in the orchestral score, while the long soprano solo is dramatic and impressive."[53]

Among her few orchestral pieces, the competently written *Pirate's Island*, premiered in Harrisburg, Pennsylvania, in 1935, won approval for its approachability and good humor. Its interesting rhythmic qualities caused Ted Shawn to use the music as a vehicle for theatrical dance. The *Pastoral Ode* for flute and strings, of 1940, is in the updated style of *Jael*, but more clearcut and winsome in its expression. Her most undoubtedly appealing instrumental work, *Deep Forest*, a prelude for orchestra, was composed for a small ensemble in 1931, then rewritten for a large one in 1934. Daniels said of it: "This little piece makes no pretense at being other than a simple prelude, frankly impressionistic in style."[54] This musical mulling over the sights and sounds of nature is free from harshness and emotional intensity. It is the counterpart to Hill's *Lilacs*, in that it evokes the ever-present New England countryside so dear to her, although without the symbolism of Amy Lowell's poetry.

Like Beach, Mabel Daniels had to carve her own way through a male-dominated territory. However, she did not go about it as aggressively as Beach did. Possibly aware of this, she once complained that because their obligations were more time-consuming than men's and because they normally lacked the stamina to compose many lengthy and ambitious works, women tended to compose briefer, more modest pieces.[55] She had the qualifications and talent to act more than modestly. Her vocal compositions are especially attractive. Ignoring them is inexcusable.

NOTES

1. Willa Cather, *Not Under Forty* (New York: Knopf, 1936), pp. 61, 63.

2. This was also the attitude of Willa Cather, according to David Daiches, in *Willa Cather* (Ithaca, New York: Cornell University Press, 1951), p. 188.

3. Daniel Gregory Mason, *Music in My Time and Other Reminiscences* (New York: Macmillan, 1938), pp. 14–15.

4. Mason, *Music in My Time*, p. 39.

5. Daniel Gregory Mason, "Democracy and Music," *Musical Quarterly* 3 (1917), p. 644.

6. Sister Mary Justina Klein, *The Contributions of Daniel Gregory Mason to American Music* (Washington: Catholic University of America Press, 1957), p. 22.

7. Klein, *The Contributions of Daniel Gregory Mason*, pp. 19–20.

8. Daniel Gregory Mason, *Contemporary Composers* (New York: Macmillan, 1918), pp. 39–40.

9. Daniel Gregory Mason, *Tune In, America* (New York: Knopf, 1931), pp. 158–59.

10. Letter from Daniel Gregory Mason to Jay Chapman, dated 24 April 1903, now at Houghton Library of Harvard University, Shelf No. bMS Am 1854 (1103).

11. Both works were published by Schirmer, in 1913 and 1917 respectively.

12. Mason, *Music in My Time*, p. 173.

13. Burnett C. Tuthill, "Daniel Gregory Mason," *Musical Quarterly* 34 (1948), p. 52.

14. Daniel Gregory Mason, Sonata for Clarinet and Piano in C Minor, opus 14 (Boston: Ditson, published for the Society for the Publication of American Music, 1920).

15. Mason, *Music in My Time*, p. 262.

16. Howard Hanson, *Music in Contemporary American Civilization* (Lincoln, Nebraska: University of Nebraska Press, 1951), p. 15.

17. Daniel Gregory Mason, Symphony No. 1 in C Minor, opus 11 (New York: Universal-Edition, 1926). Mason provided his own analysis of the piece in the Program Book for the concert of the Boston Symphony Orchestra, on 16–17 March 1928, pp. 1508, 1510, 1512, 1514.

18. Elliott Carter, in *Modern Music* 16 (1939), 101.

19. On 28 February 1918, Mason wrote to Bynner that he was scoring the Bynner songs and that he hoped to finish them soon in order to show them to Leopold Stokowski; the letter is in Houghton Library, Harvard University, Shelf No. bMS Am 1891.28 (334).

20. Arthur Shepherd, in *Cobbett's Cyclopedic Survey of Chamber Music*, 2nd ed., ed. Walter Willson Cobbett (London: Oxford University Press, 1963), s.v. "Mason, Daniel Gregory."

21. Tuthill, "Daniel Gregory Mason," p. 50.

22. Mason, *Music in My Time*, pp. 167, 366.

23. Daniel Gregory Mason, String Quartet on Negro Themes, Opus 19 (New York: Schirmer, published by the Society for the Publication of American Music, 1930).

24. Randall Thompson, "The Contemporary Scene in American Music," *Musical Quarterly* 18 (1932), p. 13.

25. The composer is quoted in the Program Book for the concert of the Boston Symphony Orchestra, on 29–30 December 1922, pp. 630, 632.

26. Mason, *Music in My Time*, p. 98.

27. Letters of Daniel Gregory Mason to M. A. DeWolfe Howe, dated 26 July and 25 August 1900, and 18 March 1908, now at Houghton Library of Harvard University, Shelf Numbers bMS Am 11524 (1984) and bMS 1524.1 (68), respectively.

28. Program Notes for the concert of the Cincinnati Symphony Orchestra, on 23–24 November 1928, in the book of clippings in the Boston Public Library, Shelf No. **M 481.267

29. Daniel Gregory Mason, *Chanticleer*, Festival Overture for Orchestra, opus 27 (Boston: Birchard, for the Juilliard Musical Foundation, 1929).

30. Mason, *Music in My Time*, p. 386 fn.

31. Paul Snook, review of New World NW 321, *Fanfare* (March/April 1985), p. 361.

32. Olin Downes, "Music in Review," *New York Times* (19 February 1932), p. 15.

33. Tuthill, "Daniel Gregory Mason," p. 53.

34. Ralph B. Lewis, "The Life and Music of Daniel Gregory Mason" (Ph.D. diss., University of Rochester, 1957), p. 14.

35. Mason, *Music in My Time*, p. 387.

36. Daniel Gregory Mason, *A Lincoln Symphony* (New York: American Music Center, 1944).

37. Quoted in John Tasker Howard, *Our Contemporary Music* 4th ed. (New York: Crowell, 1985), p. 44.

38. Mason, *Music in My Time*, pp. 35–36.

39. David Ewen, *Composers of Today*, 2nd ed. (New York: Wilson, 1934), p. 116.

40. Quoted in George Henry Lovett Smith, "Edward Burlingame Hill," *Modern Music* 16 (1938), p. 12–13.

41. Philip Hale, Program Book for the concert of the Boston Symphony Orchestra, on 24–25 January 1916, p. 1114.

42. H. T. Parker, "The Symphony Concert," *Boston Evening Transcript* (25 March 1916), Part 2, p. 10.

43. I have seen the first suite in a manuscript dated "1916–1917," which is now at the Boston Public Library, Shelf No. **M 451.74; the score of the second suite that I have studied was published in New York, by Schirmer, in 1925.

44. "Hill Orchestral Piece," *Christian Science Monitor* (13 April 1918); see the book of clippings in the Boston Public Library, Shelf No. **M 451.74.

45. Program Book for the concert of the Boston Symphony Orchestra, on 21–22 March 1924, p. 1366.

46. Program Book for the concert of the Boston Symphony Orchestra, on 29–30 October 1920, p. 208.

47. Letter to Oswald G. Villard, dated 14 April 1925, in the Houghton Library of Harvard University, Shelf No. bMS Am 1323 (1678).

48. Program Book for the concert of the Boston Symphony Orchestra, on 26 April 1927, p. 10.

49. Edward Burlingame Hill, *Lilacs*, Poem for Orchestra, opus 33 (New York: Cos Cob, 1931).

50. George Boas, *Philosophy and Poetry* (Norton, Massachusetts: Wheaton College Press, 1932), pp. 14–15.

51. Edward Ellsworth Hipsher, *American Opera and Its Composers* (Philadelphia: Presser, 1927), pp. 289–290.

52. "New Music," *Musical America* (28 March 1914), p. 30.

53. David Ewen, *American Composers* (New York: Putnam's Sons, 1982), s.v. "Daniels, Mabel Wheeler."

54. Program Book for the concert of the Boston Symphony Orchestra, on 16–17 April 1937, pp. 1101–02.

55. Christine Ammer, *Unsung* (Westport, Connecticut: Greenwood, 1980), p. 91.

Chapter Four

Colorists, Theatricians, and Melodists: Hadley, Taylor, and Cadman

Of all the composers taken up in this study, these three—Henry Hadley (1871-1937), Deems Taylor (1885-1950), and Charles Wakefield Cadman (1881-1946)—have been the most criticized by later writers, when noticed at all. At least some vindication of their music and aesthetic values would seem in order. We should keep in mind that what is in vogue does enter into musical erudition and evaluation. The latest mode in criticism orbits around forward-looking composers like Charles Ives and Rodger Sessions and forsakes those content with the *status quo*, like these three musicians. Musical inquiry also leans toward extending current gauges of value into the past, turning the spotlight of contemporary censure on, for example, the operatic art of Taylor. Music experts on the whole become apathetic to the accomplishment of men like these three, because their hearing accords more with the sounds made, say, by Edgar Varèse, Carl Ruggles, and Wallingford Riegger. They make the mistake of assuming that Hadley was crass because Ruggles said so, Cadman callow because he believed strongly in entertaining the public, and Taylor lacking musical gifts because his style is unlike that of Aaron Copland. However much respectability it has gained in the twentieth century, American scholarship is still fettered by a narrow outlook circumscribed by time and space, still oblivious to the fact that every composition should be heard with awareness of the circumstances that produced it, and still discovering how to relish the extensive diversity of America's musical achievement and not just talk about it.

None of these composers is an anachronism. They had benchmarks of musical value, but they were *established*, not newfangled, benchmarks of value. Each resisted the radical changes taking place in music and

remained largely oriented toward the European music styles of the common-practice tradition. Each wished to present a picture of cultivation
and sophistication that the generality of concert- and opera-goers endorsed. They knew that the public was predominantly sentimental and
melody-prone in its taste and did not want music that faithfully reproduced the "machine age." Each of these composers was favorably inclined toward this view. Each illustrates the observation once made by
Willa Cather that if we note an artist's limitations, we also define his
talent. A creative person can do his best "only with what lies within the
range and character of his deepest sympathies."[1]

In fairy tale, the beast changes into a handsome prince. Children find
comfort in the ugly duckling that grows into a graceful swan. But a piece
of music with incomprehensible and repellent sound can never become
handsome or take on the grace of a swan—so these composers believed.
Their most important works proclaim a partiality for picturesque tonal
tints, theatrical gestures, and vocally-oriented lyricism, whether exotic
or expressive of direct personal emotion—hence the title of this chapter.
Indeed, catchy tunes, lush harmonies, nicely realized orchestral colors,
and soupçons of the strange and exciting were their stock in trade. In
the main, given their temperaments, their music could not help but
comprise programmatically descriptive instrumental compositions and
dramatic stage works.

The most exhausting of their creative efforts centered around the composing of operas. While doing so, the energy-draining puzzle for Hadley,
Taylor, and Cadman was one that John Knowles Paine, George Chadwick, and Horatio Parker had faced. No American operatic traditions
existed for guidance. Foreign-born operatic directors, singers, and instrumentalists confronted them and had to be placated. The audience
for opera took direction from the national practices of Italy, and, to a
lesser degree, Germany and France. The composers found it difficult to
surmount the problem of skeptical audiences and critics, of less-than-
friendly opera companies, and of vocalists unattuned to native musical
drama. To have written completely original yet highly significant and
enduringly successful operas under these adverse conditions would
have been miraculous. Finding suitable libretti, making the English language come alive musically, and regulating the flow of relaxation and
tension in dramatic scenes were the formidable tasks that confronted
them, in addition to the most formidable task of all—establishing the
means for determining what an American opera should be. Lack of
experience, lack of precedent, lack of encouragement, and lack of native
stylistic exemplars dogged their every operatic effort. Something
uniquely American was already emerging from the popular musical
stage: in the operettas of Sousa, the Broadway offerings of George M.
Cohan, and the musical skits modelled after those of Harrigan and Hart

or Weber and Fields. Regrettably, owing to the attitudes prevalent in the American operatic world, little of the ferment affecting the popular musical stage was transferrable to grand opera. If they dared to write an aria sounding like a popular ditty, spokespeople for the operatic world said it was obviously trash. If they unveiled an American scene and featured ordinary men and women whose speech centered on the American vernacular, critics claimed it nullified artistic standards. If they were rash enough to employ the syncopated rhythms of ragtime, jazz, and Broadway to underlay the stage action, the cognoscenti would decide that the utmost in vulgarity had been achieved. Since these three composers believed in cultural cohesiveness that was achieved through the acquiescence of performers and audiences, they did not exercise what force they could muster in order to proclaim a novel artistic vision. They stayed with what they thought would work on the operatic stage, and for their performers and audience.

HENRY HADLEY

Somerville, across the Charles River from Boston, was Hadley's birthplace. His father was a music teacher in the Somerville schools, and his mother was a singer and pianist. A great deal of chamber music was played at the Hadley home, with Hadley on first violin, Henry Gilbert (who was also born in Somerville) on second violin, Hadley's father on viola, and his brother Arthur on cello. Later, he would marry Inez Barbour, a professional vocalist. His father first, then Stephen Emery in theory and Chadwick in composition, gave him his instruction in music. (By now, it should be clear to the reader that Chadwick's instruction figures importantly in the early musical careers of a majority of the mainstream composers.) Although Hadley went on to complete his music studies with Eusebius Mandyczewski in Vienna and Ludwig Thuille in Munich, his friend and mentor for years continued to be Chadwick. The older man implanted in Hadley the necessity of giving heed to musical ideas that would sound telling, in a practical sense, and to laying out his melodic outline, harmonic movement, sectional contrasts, and overall scheme for maximum effect. While in Europe, he met Brahms and heard him play. He also listened to Tchaikovsky's *Symphonie Pathétique* and "left the auditorium in such a state of agitation that, in spite of a blind snowstorm, he did not realize that he had forgotten his hat."[2]

During most of his life, Hadley conducted symphony orchestras in the United States, Europe, and Japan. He would also help found the National Association for American Composers and Conductors. His main conducting posts were those of the city theater in Mainz, Germany, of the Seattle Symphony, and of the San Francisco Symphony. During the 1920s, he was associate conductor of the New York Philharmonic, and in 1929 he organized the Manhattan Symphony, which he directed until 1932. In the summers of 1934 and 1935, he led members of the New York Philharmonic in what was called the Berkshire Symphonic Festival, before Koussevitsky and the Boston Symphony superseded him and his players. As a conductor, Hadley devoted himself to advancing the cause of the American composer, championing the works of Chadwick, Frederick Shepherd Converse, Taylor, and Henry Gilbert, among others. The works of the more advanced American composers unsettled Hadley and were bypassed. He of course was diligent in putting his own compositions before the public.

Converse had nothing but praise for Hadley's "generous, unselfish encouragement to other composers, both young and old. He seems to have been utterly free from any taint of envy, and was just as ready to help his contemporaries by bringing about performances of their works as he was ready and anxious to help real talent, wherever he found it among his younger colleagues. . . . His achievements in this direction, especially as assistant conductor of the New York Philharmonic Orchestra and later with the Manhattan Orchestra . . . were notable."[3]

Hadley's was a cosmopolitan musical style distinguished by a knowledgeability and adroitness that in part emanated from residing in cities and travelling extensively. His cosmopolitanism drew on the styles of composers he admired (Wagner, Strauss, Tchaikovsky, Chadwick, MacDowell), the song and dance of various sections of the United States, and, to a lesser degree, the traditional music of some European countries, the Middle East, and the Far East. He would have agreed with a statement made in 1900 by John La Farge, after he returned from a painting expedition to the South Seas and Far East, who said that American artists differed from Europeans: "We are not as they are—fixed in some tradition; and we can go where we choose—to the greatest influences, if we wish, and still be free for our future."[4]

On the other hand, there was an ever-present danger that relishing and replicating the cultural styles and traits of others might be at the expense of one's own identity. Hadley's critics have judged that this did happen to him. Yet, we should heed Allen Tate's counsel about John Peale Bishop's poetry and apply it to Hadley's music: "It has been said that Bishop has imitated all the chief modern poets. . . . But the observation is double-edged. In our age of personal expression the poet gets credit for what is 'his own': the art is not the thing, but rather the information conveyed about a unique personality. Applauding a poet only for what is uniquely his own, we lose thereby much that is good. If a poem in Yeats's manner appears in Bishop's book, and is as good as Yeats's, it is as good there as it is anywhere else."[5]

Herbert Boardman, Hadley's biographer, feels the composer escaped the danger of being all things to all men. He claims Hadley's art was universal in scope, but distinctively American as well, not so much because he employed an identifiably national musical idiom, but because his music reflected the drive, youthful enthusiasm, optimism, and idealism of contemporary America.[6] We also have the estimation of James P. Dunn, program annotator for the Manhattan Symphony, who wrote in 1918: "Generally speaking, I have always looked upon him as the foremost American composer in point of actual achievement. To me it has always seemed that he painted his musical canvasses with such a colossal sweep, gave utterance to ideas of such deep significance and commanded such a gorgeous opulence of tonal expression as to dwarf into insignificance the efforts of most of his contemporaries."[7] Such was the opinion of many music lovers of this century's first two decades.

Hadley was a prolific composer and perhaps wrote too facilely. His music is not always a result of deep thought, nor does it suggest any sort of profound probing of the psyche. Yet, his melodic creations once sounded fresh; his expression, free, sincere, and forthright; and his technical attainments, impressive to contemporary listeners. He swayed them with his striking orchestral effects, astute musical narrations, and measures of poetic rhetoric which occasionally came off with sizable force. His works were often commended for their vigor, power, and immunity to morbidness and immoderate dissonance.

Hadley tried his hand at every genre, from songs and operettas to symphonies and operas. Moreover, he has left us enticing examples in each genre. Assuredly, several of his around 200 songs are among the best written in the United States during the early twentieth century. Amy Lowell felt honored when he set her poem "In a Taxi," reporting that others had told her that the music was "very beautiful."[8] William Treat Upton praises the technical adroitness, fitting harmonization, and solid workmanship of Hadley's settings, singling out "The Time of Parting" (1921), the poem by Tagore, and "Colloque Sentimentale" (1923), the poem by Verlaine, for special mention. The latter, he states, bears comparison with Debussy's setting: "While it lacks the eerie quality of the French song (particularly Debussy's organ point maintained with such uncanny effect throughout the entire ghostly conversation), [it] is in most respects . . . superior. Not so extreme in its characterization, it still obtains the appropriate atmosphere and is a fine, musicianly song. *The Time of Parting* is less involved, less dramatic in treatment, but no less effective."[9] Scheduling songs like these in recitals can continue to elicit a hearty public response.

Hadley's Instrumental Music

The first work to attract national attention to him as a composer was the Symphony No. 1 in D Minor, *Youth and Life* (1897), opus 25. Enhancing its attractiveness for Hadley's generation were frankly stated and plentiful tunes, sprightly rhythmic vigor, and imaginative orchestration. As was usual for Hadley, extra-musical perceptions, here idealistic, inspired the work. He stated, around 1925, that when he sat down to compose music, the emotional ideas came first, the musical themes after. The first movement concerns the mix of good and evil in human life; the second, the dark remorse felt over one's wrongdoing, "then a sound of bells, bringing solace with the thought of aspiration and redemption, then a return of the gloom;" the third movement, young comrades bring happiness; the last movement, the feeling of "achievement, of confidence, power, and hope—a strain that speaks of love. The thought of gloom and despair is recalled for a moment—but hope and joy return."[10]

Such a statement establishes without question Hadley's ready acceptance of the totality of suppositions about, and approaches to, creativity made by nineteenth-century romanticism, especially of the German-grown species. This affirmation both freed him to work proficiently in his medium and limited the eventual impact of his music on listeners with antipathetic twentieth-century sensibilities. As a result, his music won instant approval from the large number of Americans already attuned to his musical tendencies and to the symbolization explicated. What is more, the work retains its attractiveness even to today.

In the symphony's first movement, motives of good and evil struggle for ascendancy. These ideas, in musical formats sanctioned by usage, are communicated efficiently and swiftly to the audience. At the end the "evil" motive heard in the trombones in a major key signals good overcoming evil. The second movement's "fate" motive sounds in the strings; it rises to a passionate climactic cry of despair. A gong sounds a death knell. Then a tender Angelus gives hope, the three tones of the bells, on *B*, *A*, and *D*, constantly heard. Eventually the opening motive reasserts itself, but the movement ends on a prayer-like passage, signaling the possible return of hope. The third movement is the expected Scherzo, an *allegretto giocoso* with a parody of a fugue. The Finale's main theme sounds forceful and heroic; the subsidiary theme implies feelings of love. A return to and final vanquishing of the "evil" motive takes place before the symphony concludes.

The year 1901 saw the birth of the *Herod* Overture and the Second Symphony. The overture is in accord with the basic sentiments inspiring the first symphony. Written to preface a tragedy by Stephen Phillips, it dramatically contrasts a vehement main theme with a disarmingly soothing subsidiary theme. The awaited mighty climax signaling disaster arrives. The conclusion resolves the musical conflict with a return to the restful second theme. Yet, despite the plethora of orthodox gestures, the music seems to work and may still give pleasure.

The title page to the score of Symphony No. 2 in F Minor, opus 30, *The Four Seasons*, states that the music won the Paderewski and the New England Conservatory Prizes.[11] It is an immensely attractive work, completely within the bounds of common practice, apart from occasional modal effects achieved mainly through the lowered seventh tone and some gapped-scale melodies. As is usual with Hadley, extra-musical ideas are bound up with the music. He said the notion of writing the music first came during a hunting trip in the Adirondacks, in October 1898. He roughed out a few bars of music as he listened to the quiet fall of leaves and the guides' horn calls. At first intended for a symphonic poem, the initial thoughts were soon channeled into the "Autumn" movement of the symphony. He wrote the other movements during their respective seasons. For example, he was in an Indian canoe on Lake Saranac on a summer night when the nocturnal material for "Summer" occurred to him.[12] The premier of the entire work took place in New York, in December 1901.

The first movement, "Winter," deals with the moods, not the description, of the wintry term. A massive, passionate, Tchaikovsky-like first theme, *fff*, in full orchestra, *moderato maestoso*, evokes the dour stormy soul of winter. Afterwards, four horns introduce a melancholic subsidiary theme, along which are strung a number of poignant sounding appoggiaturas (a "longing for spring,"[13] perhaps?). Strings play a syncopated, pulsating accompaniment. After a codetta based on the main theme, a unfettered development follows. The mix of the two themes shows a wonderful sense for the dramatic, and Hadley achieves his principal climax at the point where he recapitulates the main theme. The secondary theme and codetta return as expected. A last climax, and the music ends on hushed dynamics.

The ternary-form second movement, "Spring," is an *allegretto con moto*. The opening flute melody generates a benign atmosphere ("nature's awakening"?) and suggests a British-American folk connection with its stress of the submediant tone and hint at a gapped scale. We hear more than a little intimation of Chadwick's style. In the midst of the first section, the music looks back briefly at the main theme of the first movement. The middle section's tune begins in the horns, the music given a suave, rocking conjunct motion. Later when the violins enter, the expression becomes graceful and elegant. The affecting "Summer," an *andante*, not unlike something that Chadwick of the Second Symphony and MacDowell of the *Indian Suite* might have jointly written, comes next. Mysterious harmonies of vague tonality introduce the movement, followed by a flute, then an oboe, on a syncopated melody featuring a Scotch-snap. The program notes call this opening a visualization of a midnight lake scene and the tune that is elaborated an "Indian Love Song."

"Autumn" completes the symphony. A sadly singing legato theme ("destiny"?), *andante con moto,* in the lower instruments sounds against a staccato sixteenth-note filigree from the violins (the "falling leaves"?). An *allegro molto* brings in a bit of cheer with hunting calls in the horns. The music expands on the new theme until three abrupt staccato chords halt the merriment and return the music to the grave opening *andante* (the "inevitability of the coming winter"?).

Hadley is like a masterful actor audaciously exploiting the entire scope of his acting ability. His virtuosity may be detected in the fine-edged opposition of different ideas and undiluted feelings encapsulated within neatly balanced formal structures. The musical results are unabashedly set forth with much naturalness and complete confidence. He produces atmosphere and expression mostly through rightly discerning what might be the fitting orchestral color and melody for every passage and then achieving a highly effective tone picture. A composition like this, satisfyingly realized through the standards adhered to by Hadley, demands courage, because lack of conviction or timidity immediately translates into hackneyed and boring music. Instead, what he has left us is music that continues to give much pleasure. Arthur Farwell thought highly of the work, finding in it "a delicate balance, within the classical form, of romanticism, impressionism, and symbolism. It is romanticism that predominates, however, although such distinct impressions as those of wintry blasts and falling autumn leaves are happy and noteworthy features of the work. The languor and sun-warmed luxuriance of mid-summer finds poignant and beautiful expression."[14]

A marvelously unstudied and blithe *In Bohemia* Overture dates from 1902; the *Oriental Suite,* from the following year. The last is tolerably evocative of the melodies and rhythms of the Eastern world, but of course is written in his own manner.

Hadley wrote *Salome,* opus 55, a tone poem for large orchestra after Oscar Wilde's tragedy, in 1905-06. The Boston Symphony premiered it in 1907. When *Salome* was first heard, critics considered it his best work up until that time. Orchestras in America and Europe took it up. Hadley apparently completed the score before Richard Strauss's drama of the same name was produced. A preface to the published music gives a detailed description of the program projected in the music: Salome hears and is moved by the voice of John the Baptist. She sees and loves him, and finds her love rejected. She dances the Dance of the Seven Veils for Herod, who grants her wish for the Baptist's head as a reward. Herod is repulsed by Salome's making love to the severed head and has her executed.[15]

The piece begins slowly and peacefully, with a languorous delineation of a moonlit site just outside Herod's palace. A theme indicative of Salome's desire for John the Baptist occurs here. Hadley endeavors to capture her sensuous, torrid personality. The more animated second section centers on loud trombones declaiming the Baptist theme. The third section, *con ardore*, dramatically contrasts the two themes. Then comes the section, labelled in the score as *Salome's Dance*, an *allegretto ben ritmato* in triple time. Next, we hear Herod's trumpet theme, a brief reference to the Baptist's trombone theme, and again Salome's love theme. A fiery fast passage indicates her psychotic passion for the head, soon followed by music marking her death. At the very end an English horn very softly and sadly sounds her motive.

His Symphony No. 3 in B Minor, opus 60, was written mostly in Italy in the summer of 1906 and premiered in Berlin, Germany, in 1907. He attached no program but admitted that the second movement was suggested to him while hearing distant church bells near Monza.[16] Nothing in it parallels the outsized fancies of the previous two symphonies. The first movement's sonata-allegro form shows the usual deployment of two themes, one intrepid, in strings and trumpets, the other quieter, in the strings. The moderately slow second movement depicts an engaging pastoral scene, with faraway bells chiming the announcement of a devotional hour. The third movement is a conventional Scherzo but difficult to play. Its capricious principal theme incorporates a bird song Hadley heard in the Adirondack woodlands.[17] The compact Finale sounds brilliant and affirmative in spirit.

Popular for several years after it was written, in 1908, *The Culprit Fay*, a Rhapsody for Orchestra, opus 62, stems directly out of incidents related in Joseph Rodman Drake's poem of identical name. It won the $1,000 prize of the National Federation of Music Clubs in 1909. Completed in Europe, it has, like Drake's poem, the accouterments of Central-European romanticism. Its incidents take place on a summer midnight. A fairy has dared love a mortal maiden, and the fairy king sits in judgment. Tasks are assigned the prisoner in order to win redemption. He successfully completes his assignments and is welcomed back into the company of his peers. General merriment breaks out until the cock crows to signalize the coming of dawn and the end of the festivities. Tonality is fluid throughout. Although closing in E major, broad stretches of G major are heard. In five sections, the nighttime opening, including the motive assigned to the culprit fay, shares a few similarities with that of *Salome*.[18] A mysterious *andante* gives way to a light *allegro*, where another motive, a chromatic half-step descending tonal stream, also shows kinship to ideas in *Salome*. The third section, in moderate tempo, begins in a droopy manner, the descending chromatic motive mixing with the fay's motive until a large climax is achieved. Next, we hear a cheerier variant on the fay's motive, followed by a waltz, also on the fay's motive. The fifth section starts *allegro scherzando* and changes into a frisky march, based on a horn motive first heard at the beginning of the piece. After a brief reference to the music of the second section, the cock crow sounds in two oboes. Reed instruments play a descending glissando-like passage and the music dies away.

In a review of the music, published in 1938, Elliott Carter praised both *The Culprit Fay* and *In Bohemia*, finding that "both achieve a real character and a deeply felt quality that in spite of their lack of strong individuality make them worth hearing more often in our orchestral concerts."[19]

Hadley's tone poem *Lucifer*, inspired by Joost van den Vondel's *Lucifer*, saw the light in 1910, but waited until June 1914 and the Norfolk (Connecticut) Festival for a first performance. Five themes supply its primary materials: one, Gabriel's trumpet announcement of God's message of love; two, Lucifer's theme of baleful cast; three, a hymn from angelic voices; four, music assuring peace and happiness; and five, a theme of joy and victory during and after the battle with the forces of Lucifer. The work revolves around Lucifer's revolt and the heavenly hosts that gather, oppose the evil legions, and eventually prove triumphant.[20] Skillfully and picturesquely written, the music at times glows with incandescent eloquence.

The Symphony No. 4 in D Minor, opus 64, *North, East, South and West,* of 1911, like *Lucifer*, received its premier performance at the Norfolk Festival, but three years earlier, in June 1911. It aims to capture the moods of the frozen North, the Far East, the Southern-black ragtime of the United States, and the American West and Pacific Coast. The profusion of well-known materials—polar-zone brass chords, picturesque exoticisms, syncopated rag, Amerindian tunes and rhythms—produce a carnival spirit designed to please listeners. Everything is expertly whipped together and served for the delectation of the audience. There is more of the pleasureful suite, less of the serious symphony, about the music. The efficacy of the music is never in question.

A competently written *Othello* Overture had its premier in 1919. Classical in structure, earnest in character, and slightly daring in harmonic usage, it is a lesser work than *Salome*. A tone poem, *The Ocean*, came out in 1921. Hadley's music follows portions of the poem "Ocean Ode," by Louis Anspacher. Listening to it, one is reminded a little of Wagner and Strauss. The first part has a brief introduction with imposing harmonies, including an ocean motive of three chords. The motive returns throughout, normally sounding energetic and threatening, aside from the conclusion where the brass play it softly. The *allegro* that comes next suggests the tempestuous sea. The poetically charming second part introduces a "sea-sprites" motive played by three flutes against an accompaniment connoting the flux of waves. The final part depicts the serene ocean enduring through all time. The double basses and harp convey the rise and fall of the waves with the higher strings sounding arpeggiated chords. A peaceful melody begins in the horn, is taken up by other instruments and grows, until finally the entire orchestra intones. After a decrescendo, the sea motto sounds amidst some bell effects, and the piece ends. It has more satisfying and enjoyable program music than either *Lucifer* or *Othello*.

The *Streets of Peking* Suite for orchestra, in seven short movements, was heard in 1930. Pleasant enough with its pseudo Oriental music, it at times calls Puccini's *Madama Butterfly* to mind. The *San Francisco* Suite for orchestra followed, in 1931. The three movements are labelled "The Harbor," "Chinese Quarters," and "Mardi Gras." Again we hear engaging music. An impression of a foggy harbor, complete with the sound of foghorns, opens the suite and eventually we hear a traditional American sea chanty. The Chinese scene is conveyed through trombone slides, pizzicato strings, open fifths, and an oboe d'amore playing a pentatonic tune. The last movement brims with joyfulness. Three years later came a bit of unabashed fluff, the *Scherzo Diabolique*, which entertains the listener with a depiction of a speeding automobile and the crash that follows.

Hadley's last major instrumental composition was completed in 1935, the Symphony No. 5 in C Minor, opus 140, *Connecticut Tercentenary*. Hadley conducted it at the Norfolk Festival in June of that year. The initial movement has the title *"1625,"* and makes reference to Amerindian music and to the Doxology. The idyllic slow movement, *"1735,"* features the chorale *Ein Feste Berg*. And the final *allegro brilliante, "1935,"* brings the audience up to date. Again, competently written and highly listenable music results.

Hadley had no compelling desire to compose chamber music. He did produce a violin sonata, two string quartets, and two piano trios, all of them decently written, but his most noteworthy effort was the Quintet in A Minor, for Piano and Strings, opus 50, of 1919. The listener detects no venturing into the realm of strong dissonance and elusive tonality. The structures of the four movements are traditional ones; the style leans toward that of a slightly updated Brahms or Franck in the outer movements. The first movement is fast; the second, moderately slow; the Scherzo, swift and jesting; and the Finale, brilliant.[21] The composition displays a high level of technical proficiency and exuberance of spirit. Especially attractive are the arcadian atmosphere of the slow movement, where the piano plays a decidedly subordinate role, and the zesty piano-led dash of the Scherzo, not unlike music by Chadwick.

Hadley's Large Vocal Compositions

With the one-act *Safie, the Persian*, based on a story by the Englishman Edward Oxenford, Hadley made a trial of operatic writing in 1909, while he was a music director in Mainz. When it was mounted in Mainz, a news item in the *New York Times* stated: "The piece is said to bristle with dramatic situations and Oriental color."[22]

He waited until 1914 to complete his first full-fledged, three-act opera, *Azora: The Daughter of Montezuma*, the libretto by David Stevens. The subject was on the advent of Christianity among the Aztec Indians. The Metropolitan Opera of New York refused to produce it. He tried other countries to no avail. Finally, Cleofante Campanini, artistic director of the Chicago Opera Company accepted it, and the opera was staged in December 1917. As was usual in American opera, an inexperienced writer supplied a weak libretto; the composer, excellent music considering the handicaps faced. The Chicago audience heartily endorsed the work, despite the limp scenes. The orchestra is allotted much of the important music. The voices are allowed few set pieces—many of these are duets and ensembles rather than solos. The lush harmonies and the discordant music at points of conflict indicate a Straussian influence. Otherwise the style leans toward contemporary Italian operatic styles. The music is not recognizably American. Yet, the setting is in ancient Mexico and an occasional Amerindian tune gains admittance. The singing of the static chorus has the least interest; the first-act instrumental and vocal music, excluding that of the chorus, the most interest. Especially effective are the preludes to the three acts (particularly the third), the contralto solo in the first act, sung by Papantzin, sister to Montezuma, beginning "I dreamed that Death had claimed this mortal frame." The love duet of Xalca and Azora, "Hope's radiant smile," and the dance and festival procession music, all in Act I, are also captivating.[23]

With the one-act *Bianca* of 1917, Hadley went from tragedy to comedy. Carlo Goldini's *La Locandiera* (The Mistress of the Inn) supplied the story, out of which Grant Stewart fashioned a libretto. Although the libretto could have been stronger, it does give greater opportunity for action than did that of *Azora*. The Society of American Singers sponsored the first production in New York, in October 1918. The setting is a Florence inn, the year, 1670. Bianca is a headstrong young woman courted by many suitors, who ultimately yields herself to her faithful servant Fabricio. The orchestra again has a dominant role. The motives allotted to people and situations are interesting, yet experience little development. The characters sing in recitative or brief melodic snatches, since so much of the text calls for back-and-forth musical dialogue. As a result, the few longer melodic sections do grab the attention, as when Bianca tells Fabricio of her father's admonition on how to treat guests at the inn, "You'll find it too," a 24-measure ABA aria with a graceful minuet-like sway to it. Bianca's tender reflection on Fabricio's apparent willingness to be swayed by her, "Why is Fabricio so easy to disarm?", goes on at greater length. Another big moment in the opera comes when Fabricio sings of his love for Bianca, "The scar is here," an aria given an ABA form. Still other high points are Bianca's "Now why did I not think of that?", when caught in a deception, and Fabricio's "Hail, Gentles! Give me joy!", after he wins Bianca's love. In many ways, *Bianca* is a rewarding opera for audiences to enjoy and take to heart.

Probably his best endeavor at operatic composition was the two-act *Cleopatra's Night*, libretto by Alice Pollock, based on the Theophile Gautier story *Une Nuit de Cléopâtre*. Lafcadio Hearn had published a translation of the Gautier tale in 1882. The Metropolitan Opera Company gave the opera a first performance in January 1920. Chadwick's symphonic poem *Cleopatra* (1904) may have spurred Hadley's musicodramatic treatment of the subject. In addition, the fashionable decadence of Strauss's opera *Salome* (1905) may have intrigued him. Hadley had visited Egypt and treasured the unusual ambience enveloping the Nile and its riverside cities and towns. Yet, he excluded references to Egyptian music from the opera, explaining to William Guard: "I visited all the cafés chantants and native theatres in Cairo, determined to take down some material, but found it all so crude and primitive and atrociously out of tune that I fled the country to seek inspiration from nature."[24] Without question Hadley reveals his lack of sympathy for and ignorance of Egyptian music in this statement. Whether twentieth-century Egyptian song and dance would have been suitable for an event that took place 2,000 years before is another matter.

In the opera, a love-besotted Meïamoun slips into Cleopatra's palace and confronts Cleopatra with the urgency of his passion. Intrigued, she conditionally accepts him: in exchange for one night of lovemaking, he must give up his life at dawn. For the first time in American opera, erotic desire supersedes sentimental love; sexual reality, idealized phantasy; a self-centered Freudian drive, selfless concern for a beloved. Although not blatantly so stated, this shift is obvious.

The libretto, though feeble, shows awareness of the requirements of the operatic stage. Its exceedingly sensuous narrative provides Hadley with opportunities for dramatic action realized through orchestral scene painting, dance, and heated musical discourse. Although exotic colorations are rare, all of the musical paraphernalia of late-romanticism are brought to bear: chromatically slithering tones, acrid dissonances, augmented-fifth and diminished-fourth intervals, and elastic melodies that shrink or stretch out as needed.[25] Highly effective are Cleopatra's monologue "My veins seem fill'd with flowing quicksilver," and her blazing song in ternary form, "I love you." The dramatic scene between Meïamoun and Cleopatra, commencing with "Who are you?", proves electrifying in several spots. Pleasant contrast is afforded by a good-sized Intermezzo and the dances: one for solo ballerina, another, a sinuous "Dance of the Greek Maidens" and after this, a Mideastern-flavored "Dance of the Desert Girls." At the end of the second act, Cleopatra holds the dead Meïamoun to her breast and sings of her regret at his death and her emptiness, "See, I keep my promise," the most melancholic song of the entire opera. Hadley would write other works for the musical stage, but none would come close to matching the excellence of *Cleopatra's Night*.

In 1922, an estimable oratorio for soloists, chorus, and orchestra, *Resurgam*, came from his pen. The heroic text is by Louise Ayres Garnett. The musical style owes something to Mendelssohn and Brahms, with an added dash of Elgar. The music is always convincing, sometimes theatrically telling, and one of his more conservative efforts.

At his best—the first four symphonies, *Salome*, *The Culprit Fay*, *The Ocean*, *Bianca*, *Cleopatra's Night*—Hadley created compositions that won the admiration of his contemporaries and that deserve respect in our time. When performed, his music is always effective. More of it should be heard.

DEEMS TAYLOR

Born in New York City, Taylor took keyboard lessons for a few months, then went on to study music theory for even fewer months. That ended all of the methodical musical education he would receive: "Obtaining a small subsidy from a reluctant father, I went to work with Oscar Coon, a retired bandsman and a superb musician. Time was short. Somehow, I managed to get through Richter's *Harmony* and Jadassohn's *Canon and Fugue* in three months. Aside from ten months' piano lessons, at the age of ten, that was the extent of my formal musical training. Otherwise I am self taught."[26] He did, however, earn a B.A. from New York University, in 1906. For a while he worked in variety shows and wrote for newspapers. Composing functional music for Broadway productions would continue to command his time. For much of his life, he also wrote music reviews and articles for various newspapers and periodicals, and books on music. He became well known for his radio commentaries as well, especially those delivered from 1936 to 1943, during the breaks in the live broadcasts of the New York Philharmonic.

Taylor truly launched his artistic career in 1912, when he wrote the symphonic poem *The Siren Song*, which was granted a prize by the National Federation of Music Clubs in 1913. This composition, inspired by a poem of Joseph Tiers, Junior, waited until 1922 and a revision of the original score for its premier. Taylor's link with the musical approach of Hadley is readily seen in its poetic, resourceful, and evocatively picturesque music—all drawing on an extra-musical source. Also in common with Hadley's music, it does not possess distinctly individual features—yet it is quite enjoyable. In three sections, the piece contains two main themes, that of the sea and of the siren.

He generated other competently written art works for orchestra and for voice, but it was not until the *Through the Looking Glass* Suite, opus 12, came out that he won widespread recognition as an art composer. He completed it in 1919 as a three-movement piece for chamber orchestra, then redid it in 1921-22 for full orchestra adding two more movements. The new version, performed in 1923, was an immediate hit. Fortunately, Lewis Carroll's fancies were not subjected to heavy Freudian analysis. The composition boasted incongruous musical imagery that, for contemporary audiences, captured Carroll's tone of raillery, caricature, and topsy-turvy reasoning. The music stuck these listeners as lighthearted, nicely imaginative, and neither portentous or pretentious. Many relished the absence of what they considered cacophony à la Schoenberg and of references to Greek legend or primordial tribal rituals à la Stravinsky. They felt relieved to hear music they could comprehend rather than an explication of a modernistic technique or an attempt at sounding provocatively original.[27]

The first movement, "Dedication," contains a guileless lyric melody, concisely exposed. In "The Garden of Live Flowers," a nimble musical playfulness mirrors the lively prattle of multihued flowers. "Jabberwocky" tells of the encounter with this strange creature; the entire orchestra describes the beast. A grumbling bassoon forecasts the Jabberwocky's arrival. A pocket-sized march announces the hero's advance; a pithy fugato, the battle. A xylophone glissando is the vorpal blade that snicker snacks the Jabberwocky; the Jabberwocky-bassoon expires on a cadenza; and the orchestra celebrates the hero's triumph. "Looking-Glass Insects" are granted sundry clever themes and unexpectedly droll sonorities. The amiable and hapless "White Knight" lurches along on his steed. A swaggering theme supplies his conceit about himself as a doughty adventurer. Another theme tells what he really is—innocuous, bathetic, and prone to falling out of his saddle.

In *Through the Looking Glass*, Taylor talks straightaway with his auditors. He made a considerable effort to freshen tonal melody and metrical rhythm in order to achieve his expressive objectives, rather than trusting in an individualized way of putting things. In all of these creative matters, his experience in the entertainment world was of practical help. Offhand, his suite may suggest no more than the unsophisticated representation of a fanciful caprice with the customary hodgepodge of freakish types. Taylor, however, utilized Carroll's fictional environment to gently spoof human foibles with winning musical banter. As for his programmatic intent, Taylor once wrote that "a program is a wonderful springboard for the imagination of a composer. . . . It gives him a ready-made framework for his music, and a prescribed set of emotions and impressions to convey. But a piece of music lives or dies, as a piece of music, and not as a sort of aural Baedeker."[28] This outstanding work deserves life.

At the request of Paul Whiteman, he composed *Circus Days*, Eight Pictures from Memory, for orchestra, in 1925: "Street Parade," "The Big Top," "Bareback Riders," "The Lion Cage, The Dog and Monkey Circus and The Waltzing Elephants," "Tight-Rope Walker," "Jugglers," "Clowns," "Finale." This version was orchestrated by Ferde Grofé. Nine years later, Taylor himself rescored it for full orchestra. The music is agreeable but of little weight.

In the same year, at the request of Walter Damrosch, he composed *Jurgen*, a symphonic poem for orchestra, opus 17, based on James Branch Cabell's novel. At first it was to be a suite, but this turned out infeasible. The several facets of Jurgen's personality needed depiction: amorous, bellicose, bosstful, and awareness of his illusory quest for the beautiful. Taylor said that he "tried to show Jurgen facing the unanswerable riddle of why things are as they are; Jurgen clad in the armor of his hurt; spinning giddily through life, strutting, posturing, fighting, loving, pretending; Jurgen proclaiming himself count, duke, king, emperor, god. Jurgen, beaten at last by the pathos and mystery of life. . . ."[29] Revisions of the score appeared in 1926 and 1929. Separate themes depict Jurgen, Koshchei the Deathless and maker of things as they are, Mother Sereda who renders life futile, and the vision of beauty—possibly one of Dorothy la Désirée or Helen of Troy. *Jurgen* received favorable reviews but never really caught the public's fancy. In later years, other orchestral works saw the light; none stayed very long in the repertoire.

Other than *Through the Looking Glass*, Taylor's claim to fame rests on two operas: *The King's Henchman* and *Peter Ibbetson*. Commissioned by the Metropolitan Opera Company to compose an opera, he completed *The King's Henchman* in 1926 and heard its New York premier in February 1927. Edna St. Vincent Millay, the noted poet, contributed the libretto, based on a story from tenth-century England, which she found in *The Anglo-Saxon Chronicle*, an early account, compiled over many years, of events in ancient England. Her poetic tragedy, whose subject resembles the Tristan and Isolde story, exhibits a lyricism descended from the poetry of Keats and Shelley. Regrettably, the language is sometimes too archaic. The text is often alert to an intricate web of feeling, with personal sorrow predominating. It hints at twentieth-century concerns—repression of human impulse, relinquishment of a sense of duty, and loss of hope. One even detects an element of sexual rebelliousness and bravery that shows the author's penetration into the lovers' situation, her romantic embellishments notwithstanding. Finally, she has a sensitivity for dramatic situations, though hardly any for character development.

Taken all in all, it was the best written and most workable libretto ever handed to an American composer up until that time.[30]

The introductory music to the three acts[31] sets the mood of the work and serves as an efficient curtain-raiser. In the hall of King Eadger, Maccus, a bass, sings the simple, modal "Song of the harper." Throughout the act, compelling music delineates the impetuous henchman, Aethelwold, who pledges himself to the king ("I'll ride to hell for thee!") and leaves to fetch the king's bride-to-be, Aelfrida. A highpoint is the finale of Act I, "Oh! Caesar, great wert thou!", a drinking song sung by everyone.[32]

In the second act, Aethelwold sleeps, concealed by mist. Aelfrida enters and chants two attention-grabbing numbers—an incantation so that she can see the person she is to love, "Red haws in the hedge," and a touching dance-song of narrow melodic range, "Thousand blossoms, white and red." The mist recedes and Aethelwold is revealed. She feels tenderness toward him, then kisses and awakens him. Their love grows, culminating in an ardent duet, "Ah, could we hide us here in a cleft of the night," one possibly encouraged by a similar duet in Wagner's *Tristan und Isolde*. The prelude to the last act has fetching music. The lovers have been married. At first they plan to flee together and sing a piteous good-bye to their country that is of disarming loveliness. On second thought, they agree that Aelfrida should make herself look hideous when the king sees her so that he will feel repelled by her. But shortly, Aethelwold suffers guilt at the betrayal of his king and dies. Curiously, Aelfrida apparently longs for the queenship. She dresses to look her comeliest and comes to greet the king. A rather similar ending had taken place in Hadley's *Cleopatra's Night*, when Cleopatra regrets the death of her lover Meïamoun, yet prepares to meet and win over Anthony.

Taylor had an incontestable feel for dramatic impact, composing music of succinctness that suited the action and struck the audience as sincere. Nevertheless, he never went beyond the conventions of late-nineteenth century romanticism and utterly disregarded the modernisms in use during the mid-twenties. He showed a flair for inventing, metamorphosing, and conjoining motives. At the same time, he devised melodies to delight the ear—some simple and folk-like, others sweeping and sensuous.

Such was the audience's enthusiasm that the Metropolitan kept *The King's Henchman* in its repertoire for three seasons. On the other hand, those writers on music who believed in one or another aspect of modernism raged against the opera, hating its success. They found it unadventurous, without a spark of originality, full of banalities derived from Wagner, Debussy, and Mussorgsky, and without contemporary significance. The audience, they said, was unthinking and liked the music because it went down like pablum, offering no challenge to the intellect.[33] A more objective assessment would come down on Taylor's side. It is no small thing to write a fine theater piece replete with music that catches the public's fancy.

The Metropolitan commissioned another opera. *Peter Ibbetson* was the result, with a libretto by Constance Collier, based on the George Du Maurier romance. It was performed in February 1931. Peter Ibbetson is portrayed as oppressed by his despotic uncle, from whom he craves to escape. He does so through dreaming of the Mary he loves and through the murder of his uncle. Imprisoned for the killing, he continues to dream of Mary over three decades, then learns of her death. His desire to live ebbs. As he dies, the walls of his cell dissolve, and he rises, a young man again, to meet his Mary. The music is excellent throughout, though none of it boasts great individuality. There are, however, an abundance of warmhearted melodies, some of them French folksongs, agreeable orchestrations, and a kaleidoscopic variety of harmonies. In short, its strengths are those of the earlier opera. These won him the just admiration and celebrity that goes with capturing the public's fancy. Finding its popularity greater than that of *The King's Henchman*, the Metropolitan Opera kept on performing *Peter Ibbetson* for four seasons. It was also hated more than the previous opera by several critics who thought Taylor's music was insufferably reactionary and reprehensible because nothing strikingly innovative took place. Lehman Engel gives a fascinating account of how he and other "unwashed young avant-garde 'composers'" attended the opera's premier. Taylor was called "Damn Stealer" by them; the opera was called "*Peter Rabbitson.*" They hated it before even hearing it, deciding it had to be overly conventional, "too 'vanilla,' " boring, and beneath contempt. Yet, when they came to the end of the performance, something happened: they found themselves "caught up in the *occasion.*" The applause was enormous. The cheering for the composer never let up, and at last he came to the front of the stage. The audience's demonstration grew deafening, "and by this time, we neophytes—undoubtedly seeing ourselves in Mr. Taylor's place—joined in the excitement." They wondered what the composer would say. Taylor stretched out his arms and after holding this position for a long while, he "spoke, simply and tastefully, and we with our snobbishness were annihilated because we were deeply moved." Taylor said: "When you go to your homes this evening, please remember that you have just seen one completely happy man."[34] Soon, like *The King's Henchman*, it became yesterday's American opera. The Metropolitan felt no compulsion to revive it.

He tried again with *Ramuntcho*, for which he himself wrote the libretto. It was done in Philadelphia in 1942 and met with the usual enthusiasm from the audience, and the usual denunciation from the reviewers for its lack of originality. No one questioned the craftsmanship, nor the musicalness of the score, nor the aptness for the stage. It, like his previous two operas that had been enthusiastically received, was undeservedly relegated to the dustbin. All three stage works merit better treatment. Taylor must have felt considerable annoyance with the writers on music, some of them influential, who wished his music to disappear from programs because it kept faith with a romantic age that was declared to be as extinct as the dodo. He complained that the contemporary American composer was valued only if he accepted revolt and dissonance as positives and was "busy Facing Life." Such a composer wrote music self-consciously, thinking he had to reflect "the spirit of his own age." Otherwise, he would be regarded as "just a swooning romanticist and *ipso facto* old hat." Furthermore, stated Taylor: "I can't help distrusting artists who are too conscious of being path-breakers. When I see composers issuing statements, and essays, and pamphlets explaining, not the aesthetic qualities of their work, but its technical virtues, I become uneasy. I begin to wonder whether they haven't spent too much time writing the words and not enough in writing the music."[35] Taylor deserves recognition as a major composer who knew how to write *music*.

CHARLES WAKEFIELD CADMAN

Cadman is taken up in the same chapter with Hadley and Taylor because he too put a sizable creative emphasis on writing operas and achieved a major success in this genre. Like them, he delineated atmosphere or expressed emotion forthrightly and paid no regard to being profound.[36] He also accepted the conventions of romanticism, including its stress on melody and color, whether harmonic or orchestral. Moreover, even more than the others, he courted the public's favor. We gather from statements he made, and made about him, that, at least during the beginning of his musical career, he thought of his pieces as commodities and the public as customers.[37] He found nothing despicable in fostering what he insisted was a necessary connection with the real world. Yet there was a danger. Popular esteem can corrupt the composer who zealously aims for it. It speaks well for Cadman that he was able to earn approval without letting the desire for esteem to dominate his thinking.

Although he gained widespread fame as an "idealizer" of Amerindian music, he was not considered a true nationalist by the dedicated Amerindianist Arthur Farwell.[38] Indeed, Cadman's turn to the musical traditions of the Amerindians seems at first more an adroit and possibly wily means for him to achieve popularity. He started off an admirer of Victor Herbert and Reginald DeKoven, wishing to follow in their footsteps as a composer of music so popular with the public it earned large royalties. When he seemed to get nowhere with what he was writing, he searched for some novelty to help him along. It was then, around 1906, that Nelle Richmond Eberhart turned him toward Amerindian music. Cadman had also read that Farwell's Wa-Wan Press was interested in publishing music using Amerindian or African-American material. He knew nothing about this music at the time. Going to a library, he found Alice Fletcher's *Indian Story and Song* (1900) and copied out tunes for his own use.[39] By the mid–1920s he was easing away from this phase even as the country tired of works centered on the Amerindian.

Cadman himself said, in 1934:

Though I was the first composer to utilize Indian themes successfully as the basis of song literature, I do not believe that the employment of any style of folk song indigenous to America leads to what is broadly called "American music." I acknowledge the fact that the occasional introduction and use of Negro, Indian, cowboy, and even Kentucky mountain music may add "color" and "locale" at times in the compositions of American composers, but I never believed or declared that the use of this 'native material' is at all necessary to significant music."[40]

He thought indigenous musical expressions were only the ingredients of music. None of them represented "the real idiom of American music."[41]

Cadman forsook the customary relationship between art-music's representatives and the public. For one, he made every effort to call the public's attention to his compositions. His goal was to vacate the fringes of the music world and hammer out a position for himself and his works solidly in the center. He asked himself what inexperienced listeners made out of the grave and enigmatic music of his time. He decided that they readily discarded it for sounds more instantly pleasing. They certainly were not absorbed by and converted to highly complex idioms. Compositions permeated by intricate puzzles and premeditated obscurities could in no way acquire the allure that went with art tailored to the popular taste. Still, trying for more compliance with the public's desires brought on the risks attendant on an obliteration of aesthetic distance and a capitulation to the lumpen proletariat. His difficulty was to communicate with a large segment of the public, without resorting to superficial creative solutions. If done right, his music might effect subtle penetrations into the realm of public imagination and feeling. For him, the attempt, however dangerous, was worthwhile.

Needless to say, of all the mainstream composers taken up in this study, he was the one most despised by twentieth-century composers professing high artistic ideals and writing in an advanced style. He was also one of the composers most loved by contemporary audiences. For example, Cadman's *Dark Dancers of the Mardi Gras* (1933) made quite a hit with American listeners during the 1930s. However, the young Elliott Carter, lately feeling self-assured and fairly self-important as a forward-looking composer, declared the music had no musical interest and was "bad enough to be funny." He dismissed it, along with Henry Gilbert's *Comedy Overture on Negro Themes* and *Dance in Place Congo* as containing meager material and representing what "American" meant before music "went modern." The "stupidity of the style amused me," Carter wrote. He did condescend to call Mason's *Abraham Lincoln* Symphony, dated but a bit more sophisticated, as not without charm but "small music about a great subject."[42] In this manner did he sweep aside Cadman and other mainstream composers with a few words.

Born in Johnstown, Pennsylvania, Cadman could point to a grand-father, Samuel Wakefield, who built the first pipe organ west of the Allegheny Mountains and composed sacred music.[43] His mother was an amateur singer. He studied music in Pittsburgh, under Lee Oehmler, Luigi von Kunitz, and Emil Pauer. He tried his hand at writing operettas after the example of Herbert and DeKoven, but with little success, and acted as music editor and reviewer for the *Pittsburgh Dispatch*. He met Nelle Eberhart for the first time around 1902 and began setting her poetry to music. The songs resulting from their collaboration, though shaped for acceptance, produced negligible results until John McCormack championed his song "At Dawning" (1906) and until Cadman himself became an Amerindianist after becoming acquainted with the ethnological investigations of Fletcher and Francis La Flesche. "At Dawning," lyric by Eberhart, had to wait about five or six years before McCormack's singing propelled it into best-sellerdom and won it admiration for its spontaneity, tunefulness, and direct expression.[44]

Meanwhile, Cadman busied himself composing the *Four American Indian Songs* to Eberhart's verses, which were published in 1909 as opus 45.[45] The first song, "From the land of the sky-blue water," makes use of Omaha tribal music collected by Fletcher. The prelude and postlude employ a "flageolet love call" and the body of the piece introduces a "Love Song." The fourth and seventh tones are missing from the melody, although the seventh tone is heard in the harmony. The Scotch-snap, stressed short note followed by a long note, is prominent in the tune, which is of limited range. The simple accompaniment utilizes a gently syncopated rhythmic pattern. It was this song, along with "At Dawning," that put Cadman in the American limelight. Both are enjoyable to sing and hear.

The second Indian song, "The white dawn is stealing," borrows an "Iroquois Tribal Melody" from the collection published by Theodore Baker. A purely supportive accompaniment is given to a melody lacking the second, sixth, and seventh tones. The third song, "Far off I hear a lover's flute," draws on Fletcher ("an Omaha flageolet love call").

Surprisingly, the tune and the way it is treated sounds quite Celtic-American. Unless told, one would not take it as Amerindian. Yet, when shown the four songs, Francis La Flesche, whose father was a chief of the Omahas, thought this was the most Amerindian-sounding. Number four, "The moon drops low," has an Omaha tribal melody taken from Fletcher. The tonality is elusive. Although Cadman asks that it be performed "Majestically, with great dignity," we hear an impassioned rush of sound, much of it invented by Cadman and not Amerindian at all. Instead of the tender words of love in the previous songs, this one declaims on the perishing of the "Red Man's race." La Flesche found this last song overly complex and not representative of the way an Amerindian sees himself.[46] It is a superb song, nevertheless. The Cadman version of Amerindian music is not satisfied with the original short-phrased chants set off by rests. Instead, he tries for longer melodic lines. Except in the last song, he keeps harmony plain and accompaniment discreet in order not to intrude on the vocal melody. The Eberhart verses have no relation to the original words.

In 1909 Cadman and La Flesche sojourned with the Omaha and Winnebago Indians on their reservations, recording their songs. Later, Cadman would do the same with the Pima and Isleta Indians. He also traveled for many years with the singer Tsianina Redfeather, of Cherokee and Creek Indian extraction, giving lecture-concerts throughout the United States and Europe. During the years up to 1925 Cadman would compose many vocal and piano pieces featuring Amerindian music. The *Thunderbird* Suite for Orchestra, opus 63, of 1914, constituted five items from the incidental music to the Norman Bel Geddes drama of the same title. All numbers suggest or employ Amerindian material and have abundant appeal, an air of mournfulness, and intimate a remote time and place. The Piano Sonata in A Major, opus 58, of 1915, is a instrumental interpretation of Joaquin Miller's poetry eulogizing the Southwest. No direct quotation of American Indian or other traditional music occurs in the three movements. The music is modal, rhapsodic, strong in melody, and loose in structure. Cadman said: "It is more or less programmatic. The spirit may be (according to one's point of view) more or less American, in that the first and third movements reflect the out-of-doors feeling of 'The Ship of the Desert' and 'Song of the South' by our good poet Joaquin Miller of the Pacific Coast. I am a great admirer of Miller and used excerpts of his wonderful poems to head my movements. I would not go so far as to say I have written 'American music,' for as yet there 'is no such animal,' though I feel that I have caught something of the Western American spirit, the Indian elements, the pioneer feeling, of these broad reaches."[47]

An outstanding success was Cadman's opera *The Robin Woman (Shanewis)*, composed in 1918, one of three Indian operas that he composed, the other two being *Daoma or The Land of Misty Water* (1912), later revised as *Ramala*, and *The Sunset Trail* (1918), which was denominated an operatic cantata. The Metropolitan Opera performed *Shanewis* (as it is now more widely known) in March 1918, alongside Henry Gilbert's *Dance in Place Congo* and continued to perform it over two seasons. In one act, *Shanewis* is divided into two parts.[48] Indicative of the enthusiasm of most reviews, in a report entitled " 'Shanewis' Indian Opera Captivates," an unnamed *New York Times* reporter, on 24 March 1918, enthuses: "Walt Whitman would have 'heard America singing' in such a day's music." There is much to be enthused about.

The libretto, ostensibly based on the life of Tsianina Redfeather, came from Nelle Eberhart. The story is unambiguous and moving when required. Eberhart invariably hits upon words felicitous for musical setting. In Part One, Shanewis is an educated twentieth-century American Indian girl with musical talent. Her sponsor has been a Mrs. Everton of California. During an evening song-recital, Shanewis gains the love of Lionel Rhodes, who had been engaged to Amy Everton. Shanewis refuses to approve his suit until he visits the reservation of her people. Shanewis sings two songs of Amerindian derivation: "The Spring Song of the Robin Woman," drawn from a Tsimshian myth, and an Ojibway canoe song, which resembles its source both in text and music. Part Two opens on the Oklahoma reservation. Mrs. Everton and Amy arrive and plead with Rhodes not to squander his future on a native Indian. Shanewis learns of his engagement to Amy, then dismisses Rhodes, feeling she is under obligation to Mrs. Eveton, who has befriended her. Enraged by what has taken place, Shanewis's fanatic brother Philip slays Rhodes with a poisoned arrow. The powwow music in this scene is, of course, borrowed. Rather incongruous is the "jazz band" entertainment rendered by the young men and women. We hear no Wagnerian development of motives, since Cadman felt it would be too pretentious to do so, given his simple story and the aboriginal music with which he was working. He knew that most opera-goers attended to hear the singers rather than to listen to a dominant orchestra or an unrelenting elaboration of a few ideas. His opera established itself as a string of songs, and these gave endless pleasure. No serious attempt was made to unify the larger musical sections. This did not bar him from conjuring up fitting atmospheric impressions with his orchestra. His own melodic invention is unerring (if sometimes sentimental), as is his feel for the dramatic musical gesture. Although around 20 American Indian themes enter the score, Cadman claimed that three-quarters of the score's melodies were original. Nor did he want *Shanewis* classified as an Indian opera.[49] If he derives from other composers, they are the Italians, certainly not Wagner or Strauss. *Shanewis* is an effective musical-stage work. Its forte is persuasive melody and a candid representation of his ideas.

Cadman wrote two more operas of some significance, neither of them based on Amerindian material, whether in the plot or the music. Both comprehend fluent and enticing melody, but neither achieved the eminence of *Shanewis*. The modest one-act *Garden of Mystery* was completed around 1915-16, but waited until March 1925 before it received a first performance in New York, as a benefit for the local Music School Settlements. The libretto by Eberhart stems from Hawthorne's *Rappacini's Daughter*, on the fatal attraction of a young man to a young woman who dwells in a lethal garden. The music is far more chromatic, dissonant, and harmonically varied than that of *Shanewis*. Two intermezzos are inserted into the work; the first sounding thoroughly charming; the second, "Death," lugubrious (based on an Italian folk song, which Cadman identified as "As rays of the setting sun").[50] The start of the opera, on the meeting of the lovers, contains the expected eloquent and gratifying melodies, a high point being the contralto solo "I was a rose." The unnamed *New York Times* reviewer of the first performance states: "In later scenes of the love nocturne and the poisoned death, Mr. Cadman was not loath to seek for his suggestion of harmonic terror among the discords of 'modernists' less lyrical in their impressionism. Plucked strings tinted bright flowers in a shimmer of poison sound, as melody again brought its antidote."[51]

The second opera was the three-act *A Witch of Salem*, composed in 1925 and premiered in Chicago in December 1926. The libretto, another by Eberhart, finds overwhelming ardor, vengeance, and, at the last, true devotion activating the Puritans of the seventeenth century. Sheila loves Arnold, who loves Claris. Finding herself rebuffed, Sheila successfully denounces Claris for practicing black magic. However, Sheila offers to save her rival from hanging for one kiss from Arnold. Given the kiss, she dies instead of Claris. The music, all by Cadman, features lyrical song from beginning to end and pleased the audience.

Chamber music was not his strong suit. Almost everything he attempted in this genre strikes the ear as rhapsodic and underdeveloped. One of his best efforts is the Trio for Violin, Cello, and Piano in D Major, opus 56, of 1913, which he dedicated to Chadwick. In it, he strove to eliminate his identification with song alone by composing an idiomatic and well thought out instrumental composition. However, no cogent interrelation of its diverse musical elements distinguishes it. An idea, usually lyrical, after an initial appearance, experiences little elaboration other than sequential treatment. Yet, there are notable moments—the engrossing forward-striding start of the first movement, which owes much to Chadwick; the Amerindian-tinged lyricism of the pensive second movement; the ragged tunes and nervous vigor of the last movement. The work is cyclical in that first the *affetuoso* tune from the slow movement, then the principal one of the first movement, return in the last movement.

Interestingly, the Sonata for Violin and Piano in G Major, of 1930, is also beholden to Chadwick, although lacking Chadwick's strong grip on structure. Forthright and sincere expression harnessed to songfulness is its strength. The movements are decidedly rhapsodic. The music is Cadman's own, except for a few measures in the last movement that remind us of the "Flageolet love call of the Omahas," which opens the song "From the land of the sky-blue water."

He wrote several pleasantly picturesque compositions for orchestra, mostly of the non-Amerindian "suite" variety, among them *Oriental Rhapsody* (1921), *Hollywood* Suite (1932), and *Suite on American Folktunes* (1937). Even his *Pennsylvania* Symphony, written in 1939-40, is more a suite-like depiction in three movements of the forest primeval, the pioneer spirit, and the glorification of industry and labor. The two most interesting of the late compositions are *Dark Dancers of the Mardi Gras* for piano and orchestra (1933) and *American Suite* for string orchestra (1936).

The once popular and still fascinating *Dark Dancers of the Mardi Gras* is more progressive in style than previous works and has taken lessons from the jazzy syncopated music prevalent on the popular circuit. Sometimes it harks back to the march-rag style of the century's beginning, sometimes it recalls the jauntiness or tenderness associated with Gershwin's songs. However, because it is Cadman's, one also hears luxurious melody, apt orchestration, and, for the most part, opulent triadic harmonies. The composition depicts the bizarre, fanciful, and unrestrained vitality of the Mardi Gras celebration. Although the music is Cadman's, the opening motive, which will percolate through the piece, is meant to impart an African-American élan vital. Repetition, key transposition, and sequential treatment characterize its recurrences. Expression varies from episode to episode: now exalted, now savage, now gently yielding. All in all, it offers a marvelous concert experience.

American Suite is in three movements. The first movement, "Indian," is "based on an authentic Omaha Indian tune from 'The Omaha Tribe' by Alice C. Fletcher and Francis La Flesche."[52] We hear some tomtom rhythms at moderate tempo and some discordant major seconds; otherwise, the pentatonic tune is discreetly harmonized. The second movement, "Negro," is very expressive and slower. The composer warns the performers: "Don't drag." He states at the bottom of the first page of the score: "This number makes use of two South Carolina Negro Melodies recorded by Rosa Warren Wilson." The music is not sweetly sentimental; it has dignity and eloquence of a fine order. The third movement, "Old Fiddler," bright and fast, uses "two old American

fiddler tunes, 'Dere's sugar in de Gourd' and 'Hoop-de-doo-den-doo.' "
Diatonic dance tunes scurry along in the violins until the middle section,
where the music slows and smooths out. Then it's back to the scurrying.
The entire composition is attractive and shows some boldness in its
variety of dissonant harmonies and in the occasionally elaborate accompaniment of the tunes.

Cadman, Hadley, and Taylor knew exactly what they wanted to
achieve in the music they wrote and how to go about achieving it. What
is more, all three of them had an expertise more than adequate to their
purposes. These musicians were basically pragmatic in the way they
thought about and worked with their musical materials. Nonetheless
they did attain renown as eminently creative composers. While they did
not wish to dig deeply into the innermost recesses of the human soul,
they did mirror precisely those moods and feelings valued by contemporary American audiences. As is doubtlessly true, they did not always
concoct their sounds newborn in their heads. When necessary, they
appropriated what they needed from existing styles, doing so with exceptional discernment. This is true of the vivid musical atmospheres in
Hadley's Symphony *The Four Seasons,* of the flitting, whimsical imagery
in Taylor's *Through the Looking Glass,* and of the affective redeployment
of Amerindian music in Cadman's *Shanewis.* In addition, they valued
the employment of technique in the cause of ready comprehension,
whether for the amusing music invented to depict the gossipy flowers
in Carroll's Wonderland or the ominous shimmer of sound illustrating
the poisonous growths in Hawthorne's garden.

They did concentrate on musically descriptive or vocal pieces, rather
than abstract and complexly integrated instrumental works. This, for
some reason, magnifies the sensation of déjà vu when coupled with the
frequent restating of thematic figures and design patterns that play such
a large part in their artistry. In light or heavy musical discourse, their
ideas, though carefully shaped, would seem to slip from one procedure
and section to another, each time acquiring new breath, if the work is
a fine one. At the same time that the ideas expose each composer's
accomplishments, they lay bare the way he works out problems and the
manner of his growth from work to work. If a work is of inferior quality,
then they underscore its tediousness and betray the composer's
limitations.

Nevertheless, hearing their best pieces can be a stimulating experience. If we were able to hear several such compositions by any one
composer performed, we could realize the variety of delights he offers
us, and the scope of his multifaceted evocations of mood and feeling.
Otherwise, we must passively accept the critical evaluation of others,
unable to form our own judgments because the music, however worthy,
is no longer played.

NOTES

1. Willa Cather, *Not Under Forty* (New York: Knopf, 1936), p. 81.

2. John Clair Canfield, Jr., "Henry Kimball Hadley: His Life and Works (1871–1937)" (Ed.D. diss., Florida State University, 1960), p. 45.

3. Frederick Shepherd Converse, "Henry Hadley," included as Appendix E, in Robert Joseph Garofalo, "The Life and Works of Frederick Shepherd Converse" (Ph.D. diss., Catholic University of America, 1969), see p. 236.

4. Richard Guy Wilson, "The Great Civilization," in *The American Renaissance, 1876-1917* (New York: Brooklyn Museum, 1979), p. 37.

5. Allen Tate, *Essays of Four Decades* (Chicago: Swallow, 1968), pp. 351–52.

6. Herbert R. Boardman, *Henry Hadley* (Atlanta: Banner Press, 1932), p. 88.

7. Ibid., p. 78.

8. Letter of Amy Lowell to Henry Hadley, dated 9 June 1919, in Houghton Library of Harvard University, Shelf No. bMS Lowell 19.1 (579).

9. William Treat Upton, *Art-Song in America* (Boston: Ditson, 1930), p. 159.

10. Canfield, "Henry Kimball Hadley," pp. 56–57.

11. Henry K. Hadley, *The Four Seasons*, Symphony in F Minor, No. 2, opus 30 (Boston: Schmidt, 1902).

12. Canfield, "Henry Kimball Hadley," pp. 61–62.

13. In this and the other quotations within parentheses, I follow the notes of Henry F. Krehbiel, prepared for the New York premier; they reappeared in the Program Book for the concert of the Boston Symphony Orchestra, on 14–15 April 1905, pp. 1425, 1427, 1428, 1430. It is interesting to note that the *Boston Evening Transcript*'s "P.R.G.," who reviewed the Boston concert on 17 April 1905, said that the elaborate program furnished for the music was more Krehbiel's than Hadley's; see the book of clippings in the Boston Public Library, Shelf No. **M 412.6.

14. Arthur Farwell, in *Music in America*, eds. Arthur Farwell and W. Dermot Darby, The Art of Music 4 (New York: National Society of Music, 1915), p. 376.

15. Henry Hadley, *Salome*, Tone Poem for large orchestra after Oscar Wilde's Tragedy, opus 55 (Berlin: Reis & Erler, 1906).

16. Program Book for the concert of the Boston Symphony Orchestra, on 10–11 April 1908, p. 1604.

17. Boardman, *Henry Hadley*, p. 105.

18. Henry Hadley, *The Culprit Fay*, A Rhapsody for Orchestra, opus 62 (New York: Schirmer, 1910).

19. Elliott Carter, "Season's End, New York, Spring, 1938," *Modern Music* 15 (1938), 233.

20. Hadley gives these explanations in his score: Henry Hadley, *Lucifer*, Tone Poem for Orchestra, opus 66, After the poem by Vondel (Boston: Birchard, 1927).

21. Henry Hadley, *Quintet in A Minor*, for Piano and Strings, opus 50 (New York: Schirmer, 1919).

22. *New York Times* (14 March 1909), part 3, p. 2.

23. Henry Hadley, *Azora: The Daughter of Montezuma*, an Opera in 3 Acts, opus 80, text by David Stevens (New York: Schirmer, 1917).

24. Quoted by Henry T. Finck, in the *New York Post* (2 February 1920); see the book of clippings in the Boston Public Library, Shelf No. **M 422.45.

25. Henry Hadley, *Cleopatra's Night*, An Opera in Two Acts, opus 90, Text by Alice L. Pollock (Boston: Ditson, 1920).

26. Madeleine Goss, *Modern Music-Makers* (New York: Dutton, 1952), p. 104.

27. See Philip Hale, *Philip Hale's Boston Symphony Programme Notes*, ed. John N. Burk (Garden City, New York: Doubleday, Doran, 1935), pp. 339–340. Hale's full review of the Boston Symphony's performance of Taylor's work appeared in the *Boston Herald* (16 February 1924) and may be found in the book of clippings in the Boston Public Library, Shelf No. **M 462.89.

28. Deems Taylor, *Of Men and Music* (New York: Simon & Schuster, 1937), pp. 47–48.

29. John Tasker Howard, *Deems Taylor*, Studies of Contemporary Composers, 5 (New York: Fischer, 1927), p. 30.

30. For further discussion of the libretto, see Edmund Wilson, *The Shores of Light: A Literary Chronicle of the Twenties and Thirties* (New York: Farrar, Strauss & Young, 1952), pp. 198–200.

31. Deems Taylor, *The King's Henchman*, opus 19, Lyric Drama in Three Acts, Book by Edna St. Vincent Millay (New York: J. Fischer, 1926).

32. Howard calls it a rousing choral arrangement of the only folk song used in the opera; see Howard, *Deems Taylor*, p. 35.

33. See, for example, Paul Rosenfeld, *An Hour with American Music* (Philadelphia: Lippincott, 1929), pp. 114–15; Herbert Peyser, "Now it can be told," *Modern Music* 4 (May/June, 1927), pp. 33–34—the pagination is by issue, not by volume.

34. (A.) Lehman Engel, *This Bright Day* (New York: Macmillan, 1974), p. 45.

35. Taylor, *Of Men and Music*, pp. 45–46, 168.

36. See John Tasker Howard, *Our Contemporary Music* (New York: Crowell, 1941), p. 47.

37. Arlouine G. Wu, *Constance Eberhart: A Musical Career in the Age of Cadman*, ed. Leland Fox (n.p.: University of Mississippi Press, 1983), p. 6.

38. See what Farwell says about Cadman, in *Music in America*, p. 425.

39. Wu, *Constance Eberhart*, p. 15; Anon,, "Charles Wakefield Cadman," *The Musician* 20 (1915), p. 688.

40. David Ewen, *American Composers* (New York: Putnam's Sons, 1982), s.v. "Cadman, Charles Wakefield."

41. "Seeking the 'Real' American Music," *Musical Courier* (2 June 1934), p. 20.

42. Elliott Carter, "Vacation Novelties, New York," *Modern Music* 15 (1938), p. 97.

43. See the "Preface" to Charles Wakefield Cadman, *American Suite* for Orchestra (New York: Composers Press, 1944).

44. "Charles Wakefield Cadman," *The Musician*, p. 688.

45. Charles Wakefield Cadman, *Four American Indian Songs* (Boston: White-Smith, 1909).

46. Wu, *Constance Eberhart*, p. 20.

47. John F. Porte, "Charles Wakefield Cadman, An American Nationalist," *The Chesterian* New Series, No. 39 (1924), 225; the pagination is by series.

48. See Charles Wakefield Cadman, *The Robin Woman (Shanewis)*, An American Opera (Boston: White-Smith, 1918).

49. Harry D. Perison, "Charles Wakefield Cadman: His Life and Works"

(Ph.D. diss., University of Rochester, 1978), p. 182; see also, Edward Ellsworth Hipsher, *American Opera and Its Composers* (Philadelphia: Presser, 1927), pp. 98–101.

50. Perison, "Charles Wakefield Cadman," p. 159.

51. *New York Times* (21 March 1925), p. 16.

52. Printed on the bottom of the first page of music, Charles Wakefield Cadman, *American Suite* (New York: Composers Press, 1944).

Chapter Five

The Pursuit
of National Music

A society's dominant attitudes, and the principles behind them, help define what styles and compositions will comprise the normal musical language of a culture. At the turn of the century, American attitudes and principles concerning art music were usually those shaped by Central Europe and the music of its composers, from Beethoven to Strauss. Nevertheless, the traditional and popular music indigenous to a nation, or characteristic of a distinctive portion of a nation, can figure importantly in a musical language. Indeed, more than a few of the finest musical works of the Western world have drawn on the songs and dances peculiar to a single nation. We easily call to mind, for example, Mussorgsky and Russia, Grieg and Norway, Dvořák and Bohemia, Falla and Spain, and Vaughan Williams and England. Since time immemorial, composers have drawn on popular and traditional music for use in their own compositions. However, nationalism itself, in all its aspects including the musical, emerged out of the American and French Revolutions, at the end of the eighteenth century, and gathered strength throughout the nineteenth century. It involved a consciousness of nation: a stress on the culture, concerns, and even idiosyncrasies of one's own country. By the twentieth century, musical nationalism was an established trend, especially in those countries trying to break away from Germanic cultural domination, among them the United States.

The surge of interest in America's indigenous music, which came in the closing decades of the nineteenth century and the first two decades of the twentieth, is an important milepost in our musical history. Music historians have yet to acknowledge its complete significance. Among those involved were composers, performers, ethnic historians, and writers on musical matters. *Slave Songs of the United States*, for which William Francis Allen, Charles Pickard Ware, and Lucy McKim Garrison were responsible, came out in 1867. The Jubilee Singers of Fisk University, from 1872 on, were electrifying the country with the performance of African-American spirituals. Black American musicians, real and would-be, were advancing the novel sounds of minstrelsy and ragtime, and later, blues and jazz. Theodore Baker pioneered the study of Amerindian music with his *Über die Musik der nordamerikanischen Wilden* (1882). Alice Fletcher's *The Hako: A Pawnee Ceremony* (1904) and Frances Densmore's *Chippewa Music* in two volumes (1910-13) and *Teton Sioux Music* (1918) signaled a concerted effort to collect this music. Charles Wakefield Cadman has already been cited as a popularizer of Indian music. N. H. Thorp's *Songs of the Cowboy* came out in 1908, and J. A. Lomax's *Cowboy Songs and Other Frontier Ballads* in 1910. Collectors searched for the folk songs of Appalachia, other areas of the South, and New England.

By the 1850s, Louis Moreau Gottschalk had composed piano music that drew on African-American, Creole-American, Latin American, and popular American song and dance. George Chadwick was already incorporating American vernacular idioms, African-American and British-American, into his orchestral and chamber works in the 1880s. The Bohemian composer Antonín Dvořák had done the same while sojourning in the United States during the 1890s. Edward MacDowell had written an *Indian Suite* in 1895. Harry Burleigh, an African-American who had studied with Dvořák, made arrangements of spirituals and composed songs and other vocal pieces based on an African-American idiom in the earliest years of the twentieth century. Previous chapters have mentioned Frederick Shepherd Converse and Daniel Gregory Mason as incorporating diverse American tongues into their art music.

In addition, novelists, short story writers, painters, sculptors, and entertainers were mining the same vein. William Sidney Mount commenced his striking paintings of black musicians in the 1850s. Joel Chandler Harris began to issue his *Uncle Remus* stories in 1881. Bret Harte's and Mark Twain's tales highlighted unique aspects of America in vernacular language. Ned Buntline induced Buffalo Bill Cody to perform in his play, *The Scouts of the Plains* (1872), which quickly became popular and won fame for Buffalo Bill. Then, Buffalo Bill's Wild West Show, organized in 1883, promoted the exploits of the plainsmen, Amerindians, and Annie Oakley. Starting in the 1830s, George Catlin, Karl Bodmer, and Alfred Jacob Miller were making portraits of Amerindian men and women and graphic portrayals of their life, thus bringing an unknown world to Americans of the eastern seaboard and to Europeans. Next, Frederic Remington's sculptures and paintings of cowboys, cavalrymen, and Amerindians, in the 1890s, called attention to the American West as never before. Shortly thereafter, Zane Grey's Western novels, especially *The Last of the Plainsmen* (1908) and *Riders of the Purple Sage* (1912), were avidly read.

The composers taken up in this chapter—Henry Gilbert (1868-1928), Arthur Farwell (1872-1952), John Powell (1882-1951), and Arthur Shepherd (1880-1958)—were acutely aware of this nativist movement. They joined a large minority of musicians and music lovers who aspired to a distinctive American music, identifiable not only by the spirit of the music but also by the unmistakably native elements that invested melody and rhythm primarily, and harmony secondarily. They believed that a usable cultural past and present existed beyond the borders of New England, in the lives and music of African-Americans, American Indians, the inhabitants of Appalachia, and the cowboys of the West. All of these people, after their own fashion, seemed to have an imposing core and to emit a life force approaching that of stalwart Americans' past. Moreover, their cultural expressions seemed to unite spiritual things closely with earthly interests and values—unveiling a humanism quite different from the ideology conveyed by the sometimes foggy incorporeal yearnings or subconscious conflicts of German expressionism.

They welcomed the refreshingly honest naïveté that was inseparably wedded to native music, in contrast to the precious sophistication shown in some of the newer European compositions. In an attempt to explain composers like Gilbert and Powell, Mason commented on how they "shared, I think, the intuitive conviction that American music must be more active, restless, humorous and sentimental than European; that to this end it must, or at least might, draw upon naïve elements of folksong capable of answering and guiding its own naïveté; and that somehow the native style into which its elements were built must be simpler than European styles, more childlike in feeling, yet contented in its childlikeness—in short more naked and unashamed."[1] Nor, it should be added, did they disdain popular music—for example, the music of sentimental ballads, jaunty minstrel ditties, and syncopated ragtime pieces. These were in their own way unique, American-people related, and amenable to utilization.

The preoccupations of these composers also imposed certain limits on what they created, those limits determined by the native idioms they chose to employ. To be sure, their eclecticism did on occasion concentrate narrowly on sequestered areas of Americana. Yet, if properly handled, this approach to art could enable them to display humanity in a more sharply defined rather than a more expansive sort of musical expression. Furthermore, it did not necessarily indicate bantamweight thinking. Through means of the vernacular, a sensitive composer could capture in his music a pungency and an actuality not found in big transcendental works. Moreover, in the case of Gilbert and Powell, it allowed room for a subtle comicality that was at the same time compassionate. All four composers insisted on creative autonomy and displayed signally dissimilar temperaments. Each obstinately traveled his own divergent road and sought his own manner of speaking. However disparate their sympathies, musical education, and modes of expression, they were alike in two particulars, none of them ever freed himself completely from Germanic influences, and each of them succeeded in composing works nourished by an American rootstock that their contemporaries considered clearly American in mood and tone.

One other composer must be added to the four already named, Scott Joplin (1868-1917). It is appropriate to discuss, at the chapter's end, his major authentic contribution to indigenous expression in American art music, the opera *Treemonisha*.

HENRY GILBERT

Gilbert's mother sang, his father played keyboard instruments, and his birthplace was Hadley's: Somerville, Massachusetts. Ole Bull's violin playing spurred his own study of that instrument. Independent, unwilling to undergo the discipline necessary for thorough musical training, he nevertheless did study theory and composition with George Elbridge Whiting, George H. Howard, and MacDowell. According to Katherine Longyear, it was Gilbert who responded to MacDowell's request for American Indian melodies for use in the *Indian Suite* by offering him a few from Baker's study of American-Indian music, *Über die Musik der nordamerikanischen Wilden*.[2]

Gilbert only partially digested his learning and displayed an awkwardness in most of his compositions that remained evident throughout his creative career. Katherine Longyear reports that Shepherd once told her "that Gilbert realized that his lack of training was a handicap, but that Gilbert preferred to acquire the needed craftsmanship in his own way rather than to risk contamination of his own style."[3] Clifton Furness, who thought Gilbert the first American composer whose work was individual and indigenous, quotes him as saying that his aim from the first was to write American and un-European music, that would "smack of our home-soil, even though it may be crude."[4]

Possibly, as H. G. Sear claims, the heart disease with which Gilbert was born syphoned off his strength. It did set bounds for the field studies that might have resulted from his interest in the music of African-Americans and American Indians.[5] Yet, he managed to visit the Chicago World's Columbian Exposition in 1893, keeping himself solvent with some menial work, and thus became acquainted with the music of Asia. Here he learned also about Russian music from a friend of Nicolai Rimsky-Korsakov, Prince Galitzin. Joseph D. Whitney, of the Harvard faculty, sent him to Europe in 1894 to obtain music scores. In 1901, his celebrated cattle-boat trip to Paris took place, where he went to hear Charpentier's *Louise*. All of the above was a great deal of activity for a man with a serious congenital heart condition.

During adulthood, Gilbert was fortunate in his marriage to Helen Kalischer, for she made his domestic life peaceful and agreeable. Unfortunately, he was less than successful in earning a living. For a while he was a vioilinist in pit orchestras, at dances, and for resort-hotel entertainments. Labor in a factory was tried and rejected. He worked briefly for a printer, a real-estate agency, and a music publisher. Eventually, though poor in health and financial means, he withdrew to Quincy, Massachusetts, where he worked part time tending farm animals.[6] The withdrawal, of course, was not a retreat from music. In addition to his composing, Gilbert helped Farwell with the running of the Wa-Wan Press, dedicated to issuing American music with a leaning toward the vernacular. The Press would publish a half-dozen of his piano pieces and over a dozen of his songs. Gilbert also transcribed American Indian music that Edward S. Curtis had collected for volume six of *The North American Indian* (1911), acted as associate editor for *The Art of Music* (1916), and sent numerous articles to journals, including the *Musical Quarterly* and the *New Music Review*. Finally, Harvard called on him now and again for lectures on music.

Throughout his life, he framed his own opinions independent of any authority and informed himself through the writings of diverse authors: Ralph Waldo Emerson, Henry Thoreau, Walt Whitman, Edgar Allen Poe, Herman Melville, Mark Twain, John Millington Synge, and Thomas Huxley.[7] In music, he wished no other composer's or country's style to take him over, although he admitted to having studied the music, and particularly the folk music, of many nationalities and races from around the world.

In 1915, Gilbert wrote that though American composers still had to learn their art from Europe, their failing was to accept European ideals of beauty. Moreover, most musicians in the United States, from soloists to orchestra conductors, were Europeans, not Americans. They were biased against American and toward European compositions, and actively educated the American public in European ideas of beauty, which produced a preference for European music. This discouraged or made impossible any hint of an American spirit in native compositions. Undoubtedly having in mind the reception of his own music, Gilbert said: "One always feels that music by an American is not wanted, especially if it happens to be *American music*. It is merely tolerated with a sort of good-natured contempt. It is true that American music as such is still very much in its infancy. But an unwelcome child always has a very hard time and sometimes fails to grow up."[8]

He defined himself as a nationalist composer, that is to say not an imitator of Europeans but an artist of an independent turn of mind, a seeker of "new rhythms, and piquant and unusual melodic turns, to express something which shall at least be different. . . ."[9] However, he warned against bizarre rhythms, freakish melodies, gratuitous dissonances, and cultivation of originality for its own sake, which he considered debilitating factors in most of the music by modernists. The works of Debussy and Ravel aside, "the musical world of today," he wrote in 1921, "is as prolific of tricksters, conjurors, and tone-jugglers as it ever was. . . . The majority of these lesser composers . . . [try to] astonish rather than delight . . . substitute pretense for worth, and . . . attain an attention-provoking eccentricity rather than to express a genuinely felt emotion."[10]

Lastly, he came out foursquare in favor of humor in music: "Personally I like to laugh, and my sense of humor I conceive to be one of my most precious possessions. . . . The sense of humor is not to be decried or by any means belittled, for, in its highest manifestation, it is at least a first cousin to philosophy. It is a great resource against the continuous ills of life, a shield against the too serious effect of the tragic, and a sovereign remedy and preventive of petty annoyance."[11]

Furness, who furnished the article on Gilbert in the *Dictionary of American Biography*, divides his music into three periods.[12] The first period, Furness asserts, saw open exploration of available musical means within the bounds of the European styles that affected him, mainly Germanic, then French. This is exemplified by works like the songs on poems of Irish authorship (from the mid-1890s), *Salammbô's Invocation to Tänith* (1902), and the Symphonic Prologue to Synge's *Riders to the Sea* (1904). Furness states that the second composition gave Gilbert celebrity in Russia, where he became an admired American composer. It is necessary to add to Furness's information that Gilbert was also actively studying the music of Russian and Bohemian composers, as well as the folk music of all regions of the world.

That Furness's three-period division requires modification is made clear when we come to his second stage. He states that Dvořák moved Gilbert to utilize native American matter, leaving out the probable influence of the Americanist compositions that Chadwick commenced writing before Dvořák's Symphony No. 9, *From the New World*, of 1892-93, and of Chadwick himself, who lived in the same area of Boston as Gilbert. Moreover, there is an overlap of time between Furness's first two period designations. The *Two Episodes* (Legend" and "Negro Episode") for Orchestra date back to 1895-97. According to Furness, this work was praised by Jules Massenet, and hailed in France as the first appearance of "autochthonous American orchestral writing." Subsequently, Gilbert composed the *Comedy Overture on Negro Themes* (ca. 1905-10), *The Dance in Place Congo* (ca. 1906-08), *Americanesque* (ca. 1903-08) (later given the title of *Humoresque*), the *Negro Rhapsody* (ca. 1912) (also known as *Shout*), and several ragtime- and jazz-influenced dances. Also on the list are two songs that were popular, "The Pirate Song" (1902) and "Fish Wharf Rhapsody" (1909), and some desultory experimentation with Amerindian material.

The last period, Furness claims, constitutes works in a mature, original style that show an assimilation of various indigenous idioms. These pieces Gilbert "attempted to make expressive of American optimism, youthfulness, and buoyancy." Four compositions are cited: the opera *The Fantasy in Delft* (ca. 1915), *Symphonic Piece* (1925), *Strife* (1910-25), and *Nocturne, after Walt Whitman* (ca. 1925).

What distinguishes Gilbert's music after 1904 is the goal he set for himself of speaking definitely and honestly as he tried to delineate human experience through the vocabulary and rhythms of workaday sound. His compositions, which acknowledge his immersion in both African-American and popular idioms, are dynamically envisioned, meant to come keenly alive, and carried to a flavorful conclusion. The music tends to be spare, abrupt, rugged in countenance, and out at elbows—advancing like a song-and-dance vaudevillian who is simultaneously sad and comical. Gilbert may not have had an exceptionally individual style, originality not being one of his high priorities, but inarguably he did have a new and forceful point of view and he did pioneer the use of the American vernacular in music. His friend Farwell points out that his technique, though resourceful and showing a rich imagination, was often lacking in finish—a defect perhaps, but also the source of his appeal. Possibly, the unevenness was a direct outcome of what Farwell tells us was Gilbert's disenchainment from tradition and fashion, "whether in art, dress, or speech," and his fight for freedom.[13]

An examination of Gilbert's scores reveals melodies, lyric or angular, that are always tonal and mostly diatonic, which normally suggest a connection with traditional song. Harmony is triadic and only occasionally piles on tones of the ninth to the eleventh, or resorts to chromatically altered chords. Rhythms are clear-cut. Duple time predominates; triple time is much less frequent. Modulations can be precipitous; sections within a movement are usually kept quite distinct. Orchestral pieces offer fine displays of instrumental color. The writing of descriptive rather than abstract compositions is favored.[14]

Salammbô's Invocation to Tänith, for voice and orchestra, opus 6, was composed in 1902 and draws from Flaubert's novel *Salammbô* (1863). With this piece, the composer tries to come to terms with contemporary French music—in the evocation of the novel's atmosphere, in the rich and varied orchestration, and in the employment of coloristic harmony. Gilbert's composition is impressive enough but the work of a follower, not a master. Nor does the music particularly capture the ambience of the ancient Carthage that Flaubert had in mind. In an important sense, the piece represents a serious attempt to discover alternatives to the dominant Germanic style from which Gilbert was trying to break away. For similar reasons, piano pieces like the *Mazurka*, published by the Wa-Wan Press in the same year, look back to Chopin but introduce some sonorities, occasionally evasive secondary modulations, and suspicions of modal practices that again look to the French.

Celticisms offered him another avenue of escape from the Germanic impasse. In this regard, he had the examples of MacDowell's Piano Sonata No. 4, *Keltic*, of 1901, and several characteristic Celtic piano pieces, like "An Old Love Story,"[15] number one of *Fireside Tales* (1902), to encourage him. Songs like the pathetic "Lament of Deidre" show him allied to the moods and music of the Celtic-speaking peoples. The Symphonic Prologue to *Riders to the Sea*, a one-act play by Synge, was an ambitious effort in this direction. Composed in 1904, it was revised in 1913. At first, he had written a 94-measure prelude, requiring only a chamber ensemble, for a Twentieth-Century Club performance in 1905. He then reworked the melodic material into the 164-measure Prologue of 1913, scored for full orchestra and performed at the MacDowell Festival at Peterborough, New Hampshire, in 1914. Gilbert stated that the music encompasses two dominant moods from the play: one, elemental and impersonal like the unchanging sea; the other, the sound of human lamentation. The music climaxes on the lament, then subsides into quietness.[16]

Gilbert draws on an old Irish melody, which pervades most measures of the score,[17] thus making the work almost monothematic. The slow opening in the low strings is in a modal minor scale with the seventh missing. The tempo then vacillates between slow and fast, but finally picks up as the music intensifies for a grand tragic statement. This passage, developmental in nature, is also modal. The slow tempo returns with the melody in the first violins, while muted instruments supply an accompaniment. The last 14 measures are in a major key and indicate Maurya's resignation at the loss of husband and sons to the implacable sea. The folk-related sounds are nicely done; the work is likeable. The mood of darkness, anguish, and surrender is ever present. The absence of musical and emotional contrast is a detriment. The continual melodic expansion is not very smooth. Yet, on balance, it is a stronger work than *Salammbôs Invocation*. After hearing the Prologue, Philip Hale wrote in the *Boston Herald*, on 21 February 1919: "This Prologue is impressive music. It owes nothing to Munich or Paris. . . . He thinks for himself; he belongs to no school. . . . Even his crudities, showing a certain ruggedness that is not wholly displeasing, are those of a virile thinker."[18]

A third possible alternative to the Germanic style lay in the exploitation of the American vernacular. Gilbert during the 1890s grew firm in the belief that folk music was beneficial to artistic composition. After the turn of the century, he would consider a folk tune to be a valuable musical kernel from which to develop a significant work. If the composer learned to do this well, Gilbert believed, he could present "in an intensified, enlarged, and extended manner the *spirit* of the original folk-tune."[19] He saw the futility in treating traditional music with the scholarly respect of a cultural anthropologist. To create an artistically viable composition, the artist inevitably had to juggle with his material. Gilbert tried a tentative rapprochement with Celtic folk song, but attained a more intoxicating relationship with indigenous American song. In January 1896, the Boston Ladies' Symphony Orchestra performed "Legend;" in December 1896, the Manuscript Society of New York performed "Legend" and "Negro Episode;" in 1897, Gilbert himself was the publisher of both pieces as *Two Episodes* for orchestra.[20] "Legend," moderately slow, in 6/8 time and D Minor, is lovely, lyrical, and indebted to the music of his teacher, MacDowell. (The first movement of Mac-Dowell's *Indian Suite*, which he worked on from 1891 to 1895, is also entitled "Legend.") Introducing the music to the "Negro Episode" is a note from the composer that states two Negro musical ideas are used, taken from W. F. Allen's collection, *Slave Songs of the United States*. The second, "Nobody knows the trouble I see, Lord!," makes its initial appearance in measure 15. There seems to be a relationship between the music in the beginning of "Legend" and that of the middle part of "Negro Episode," labelled "Melancolia." Both episodes are miniatures, satisfying in their own right, and the modest offerings of a still diffident composer. The *Two Episodes* come off because Gilbert did not drive himself to achieve something of significant size. Thinking small, in this early stage of his career, helped to insure success. He was not then ready to accomplish anything on a larger scale.

In its initial appearance in 1903, it was called *Americanesque*; when published in 1913, *Humoresque on Negro Minstrel Tunes*, opus 5.[21] This piece represents a pioneering attempt at a national music and is constructed around three minstrel tunes: "Zip Coon," "Dearest May," and "Don't Be Foolish, Joe." The music puts Gilbert's comic faculty on display. The choice of melodies suggests, but only suggests, an appreciation of the contradictory temper of man's impulses, those of self-centered nonchalance and other-centered solicitude. In the "Note" that prefaces the score, Gilbert wrote of "the vigor and heart-touching qualities" of minstrel song, claiming it approaches "true folksong." He added that he was trying for the comedy, pathos, and mirth inherent in the minstrel show of old.

The music from beginning to end can also be interpreted as an agency for displaying the folly lurking in the decorum of priggish, high-cultural compositions. It revels in the vulgarities that overly refined Americans disclaimed as part of their nature. The satirical mode, after all, had been a telling function of nineteenth-century minstrelsy, which had relished the drollness, the foolishness, and the piteousness of human behavior. Lest I be thought too fanciful, one should keep in mind Gilbert's belief in rendering "in an intensified, enlarged, and extended manner the *spirit* of the original" melodies he used.

It is curious that at the time he was composing the *Humoresque*, the French and Russian figurative painters known as *les fauves*, the wild beasts, were active in Europe. Like a *fauvist* painting, *Humoresque* sounds sturdy, clothes itself in starkly simple musical colors, and contains more than a modicum of energy. The painterly two-dimensional designs are, here, the sharp-edged sectional divisions and the two dimensions of melody and accompaniment, in mostly homophonic textures, occasionally alleviated by contrapuntal activity. The robust dances of the outer sections are contrasted to a slow middle section, where horns, later woodwinds, and still later violins intone a melody sounding like a sentimental plantation ballad of the 1850s. The listener hears no classical elegance, no romantic expansiveness. *Humoresque* is not an important work. It resembles a garment so roughly stitched together that all of its seams continue to show. Yet, it stood out in bold relief against many of the works then being heard in the concert hall.

A clash with the conservative, German-oriented tastes of the time was inevitable. Gilbert's presumption seemed not far removed from brazenness when he demanded that his common-dirt materials be considered worthy components of serious artistic discourse. Nowhere did the music seem to preserve even a smidgen of propriety. Vulgar and simplistic were verdicts often delivered by cautious contemporary critics. Olin Downes, on the other hand, liked the music's vigor, freshness, and individuality. He writes that the piece "smells to heaven of the crowd. A sort of rowdy, drunken dance rhythm precedes the rustling of 'Zip Coon' in the double basses," which next is rendered brilliantly by the full orchestra. "The most interesting pages are those in which all three themes, after the statement of the second theme by the brass, rush along to the conclusion, cheek by jowl, with ingenious counterpoint and spicy instrumentation."[22] On the other hand, Mason states: "In his [Gilbert's] actual work, I must confess, even in [compositions] . . . lauded by Downes, I always found the originality of the intent largely defeated by the crudity of the workmanship. But his aims one could not help admiring."[23]

As early as 1905, Gilbert was toiling on an opera based on the *Uncle Remus* tales of Joel Chandler Harris (1848-1908). The libretto had come from Charles Johnston, who had been a member of the Bengal Civil Service, but was now retired.[24] Undoubtedly his creativity was spurred by two piano pieces: "From Uncle Remus," number seven of Mac-Dowell's *Woodland Sketches* (1896) and "Of Bre'r Rabbit," number two of MacDowell's *Fireside Tales* (1902).

The Georgia-born Harris had worked on a plantation where he encountered a great deal of African-American folklore. His first story had appeared in 1879. He was attracted by the animal legends through which Southern blacks reconciled themselves to their circumstances. Interpreted by a sympathetic white man, these tales tried to maintain the viewpoints, speech patterns, and traditional knowledge of African-Americans. Unfortunately, Gilbert failed to get the musical rights for the opera because they were already assigned to another composer. Therefore he had to be satisfied with recasting the prelude to the opera into the *Comedy Overture on Negro Themes*, which was finally completed in 1909. It was heard at an Open-Air Mall Concert in New York, in August 1910, and then performed by the Boston Symphony in 1911.

The overture,[25] in five sections, is built on three motives of four measures each, and one theme of eight measures taken from traditional African-American song and dance. The first section, which is featherweight, jocose, and full of vitality, has a tune fashioned from two four-measure phrases found in Charles L. Edward's *Bahama Songs and Stories*. The leisurely and spacious second section contains the only complete melody, from a former worksong of Mississippi roustabouts and stevedores, "I'se gwine to Alabammy, Oh," found in Allen's *Slave Songs of the United States*. The third section is a sparkling fugue, whose subject is the start of the spiritual "Old Ship of Zion," from Jeanette Robinson Murphy's *Southern Thoughts for Northern Thinkers*. It closes on this theme played in augmentation by the brass and interwoven with "I'se gwine to Alabammy, Oh." Next comes a brief passage which returns to the mood of the beginning, followed by the return of the first theme. The work closes on increased merriment and with allusions to ragtime. The ending sounds a raspberry at self-mortification and itches with tomfoolery.

The syncopated rhythms and overmastering vivaciousness of the opening, the entertaining fugue that describes Bre'r Fox's chasing after Bre'r Rabbit, the majestic restatement of the spiritual "Old Ship of Zion," the laughing inflections of Americana, and the spontaneous feeling of the whole did cause music circles to talk about Gilbert. A few people considered the piece undignified; most responded "to the youthful vigor, the racy humor and the romantic nature of this new music," states Downes. Hale writes: "The overture stirred the blood of the audience. All rejoiced in hearing a new voice with something to say and an original way of saying it. The fugue did not dampen the interest of the hearers, for the old form was used with dramatic spirit. No wonder that the audience, surprised and delighted, was for once in no hurry to leave the hall. . . . The overture is distinctively, but not bumptiously, not apologetically, American."[26]

Several American orchestras took up the *Comedy Overture*. Moreover, the Russian composer Alexander Glazunov found the work "simple, original and powerful, well orchestrated and melodious"[27] and recommended it to Reinhold Glière for Russian performance. Ivan Narodny states that when performed it "struck a note absolutely new to Russian audiences. One Russian critic writes: 'Gilbert is a composer who does not seek after artificial effects and forced phrases. . . . His music is spontaneous, natural and beautiful. One can feel the powerful individuality of the American composer in his direct and classic message. Though the work is based on negro music . . . it does not belong to the class of popular compositions.' " Later, Glière is quoted as saying: "It is melodic, pleasing, and well orchestrated. America should be proud of a genius like Gilbert."[28]

The references to ragtime in the *Comedy Overture* are not isolated ones. Surely, he was aware of Scott Joplin's and other African-American composers' piano rags, those effervescent compositions in syncopated march rhythm that he and the public first got to know at the Chicago fair of 1893. Around 1906, he started writing a number of keyboard dances in ragtime rhythm, several of them originally intended for the *Uncle Remus* opera. Among the dances are the three *American Dances* of 1906, the five *Negro Dances* of 1914, and the six in *A Rag Bag* of 1927. They are close to the style of Joplin. Thirty years after they were written, the *American Dances* and *Negro Dances* were reexamined by Eliot Carter. He found them "delightful," rich "in homey American humor," and "without pretence."[29]

Gilbert possibly achieved his greatest success with *The Dance in Place Congo*, begun in 1906, which New York's Metropolitan Opera premiered as a pantomime-ballet, alongside Cadman's opera *Shanewis*, on 23 March 1918. After the first performance, it was usually presented as a an orchestral tone poem at symphony concerts. Gilbert had been attracted by the intriguing pre-Civil War life in New Orleans. In addition, he had avidly read George Washington Cable's article, "The Dance in the Place Congo," published in the *Century Magazine*, February 1986. The Place Congo was where the black slaves gathered once a week to enjoy themselves. The musical illustrations, especially of the "Bamboula" dance, that went with the article excited him. He turned to writing a piece that would capture "certain dominant moods" he had gleaned from his reading.[30] One cannot help also wondering if Gilbert was familiar with Louis Moreau Gottschalk's piano work, *Bamboula, danse de nègres*, published in 1849.

The first section is somber and full of emotional suffering. It features a musical phrase from Cable's article that is made to cry out in tragic protest against slavery. Little by little the rhythms of a dance invade the music until "the theme of the Bamboula is ripped out in its triumphant vulgarity by the full orchestra."[31] A climax results, followed by a quieter lyrical music which depicts the more tender activities, including love-making, of the slaves. This section, too, mounts to a climax. A barbaric free fantasy on the Bamboula tune comes next with the dance finally combining with the other motives. A bell sounds, calling the slaves to their quarters. The dance disintegrates; the cry of protest returns and with it, despair. Fragments of musical remembrances are heard until a pause interrupts the music. At the end the tragic cry returns in the full orchestra.

The roughness and seeming naïveté associated with Gilbert's music continues in this piece. Yet, rhythm, which is often complex, produces a marked effect. The harmony can sting. Orchestration is brilliant, and expression, powerful. Because Gilbert preserves a distinct space between himself and his topic, the consequence is a precisely managed emotional approach that permits the composer to impart the notion of passionate release and grievance minus any triteness and maudlinism.

Gilbert made a final use of African-American music in a major work when he wrote the *Negro Rhapsody (Shout)* for performance at the Litch-field County Festival in Norfolk, Connecticut, in June 1913. The "shout" was a powerfully felt religious dance of African-American slaves, as-sociated with hand-clapping, foot-stamping, and a shuffling gait exe-cuted to the music of exuberant spirituals. The *Rhapsody* starts off with wild, untamed explicitness, on a savage dance based on the spiritual "Where do you think I found my soul?" The second section is rather unsettled but melodious and utilizes the poignant melody "I'll hear the trumpet sound."[32] The "shout" recurs, treated differently, and achieves a delirious climax. Harmonies scrape rudely against each other. An ag-itated drum roll sounds. At the last, wind instruments intone "I'll hear the trumpet sound." The savagery subsides; dignity increases as the music depicts a yearning for spiritual enlightenment.

The closing off of Gilbert's indigenous-American period came not with an African-American but an Amerindian piece, *Indian Sketches*, an or-chestral suite in six movements: Prelude, Invocation, Song of the Wolf, Camp Dance, Nocturne, and Snake Dance. The work was started in 1911; but the premier did not take place until 1921, when the Boston Symphony undertook to give it a hearing. As mentioned earlier in the chapter, Gilbert had transcribed Amerindian music from the phono-graphic cylinders that Curtis had collected for volume six of *The North American Indian*. He then examined other collections of Amerindian mu-sic. Although he considered most of it to be monotonous, he found some of it "striking and piquant." This work was intended to suggest the untamed primitivism of Amerindian life, in a series of mood pictures grounded on fragments of this music.[33] The best of the suite is in the first three movements: the half-civilized emotion of the first, followed by the utterly simple religiosity of the second, followed in turn by the sad call of the Kutenai. The last three movements are more conventional: a pleasant and predictable group dance, an amorphous waterside song of night, and a Hopi prayer-dance.

Like Cadman, Gilbert realized that the interest in works completely given over to traditional African-American and Amerindian music was fading after 1915 and especially after 1920. Most such music that he had written, he had begun before 1915. He himself was also looking for other avenues to explore. His new works now took a different orientation. Never believing he had committed himself to only one creative direction, he began a one act opera in 1915 that had nothing to do with Amerindians or African-Americans, *The Fantasy in Delft*. Although he may have completed its musical setting within a few months, he kept on putting the music into working order over the next four years.

The libretto came from Thomas P. Robinson, an architect and writer-member of George Pierce Baker's *47 Workshop* at Harvard University, which was actively encouraging and producing plays by students.[34] The locale was Holland in the seventeenth century. The story involved two adroit young women, who were trying to get around their aunt in order to continue their liaisons with the young men they fancied. The finished composition was "delicate, poetic, and humorous," according to the several knowledgeable people who carefully read through the score.[35] Gilbert offered it to the Metropolitan Opera House. The Metropolitan rejected it, advancing no convincing reasons for its refusal. Giuseppe Marinuzzi, the orchestra conductor of the Chicago Opera in 1920, considered it the finest opera by an American that he had seen and wanted to produce it. He returned to Italy in 1921, and with his departure from Chicago died any interest in mounting the opera. Otto Luening said that, when associated with the Opera in Our Language Foundation, he had studied the score of *The Fantasy in Delft*, found the music highly praiseworthy, but unfortunately, the Foundation "lacked the resources for production."[36] Gilbert never saw his opera produced on the stage.

In 1920, George Pierce Baker, who had originally urged Robinson to write the libretto for *The Fantasy in Delft*, was put in charge of the Pilgrim Tercentenary Pageant commemoration of the founding of Plymouth, Massachusetts. Along with Gilbert, other composers were asked to write music for the celebration, among them Chadwick, Foote, Kelley, Converse, and Hill. Gilbert was responsible for the first of the pageant's four episodes. After fulfilling his commission, Gilbert reshaped his contribution into a concert piece for orchestra, Suite from *The Pilgrim Tercentenary Pageant*. The Boston Symphony performed it in 1922. In two parts, the first comprises a "Prelude and Norse Scene;" the second starts with a "French and Indian Pantomime," goes on to an "Indian Dance," and concludes with "Pestilence." The music sounds neither shallow, nor sweetly nostalgic, nor merely pleasing. The "Prelude," despite its brevity, manages to impart both potency and range. The "Norse Scene" does show awareness of Grieg's music and MacDowell's Piano Sonata No. 3, *Norse*. At the same time, something distinctly Gilbert's own is evident. Its one weakness is a motive that recurs too many times. Quite different, the "Pantomime" music gladdens the listener, owing to its generous, forthright, and sincere expression. The "Dance" conveys a grand wildness of spirit.

Hale reviewed the Boston Symphony concert in the *Boston Herald*, 1 April 1922. Gilbert is "singularly fortunate" in the "Pestilence" section, writes Hale, where he portrays "desolation without falling into the abomination of desolation." Hale finds the Suite to be "more than picturesque." It "conveys the feeling without the aid of any program; there is the hopeless, despairing, tragic note. . . . in these episodes Mr. Gilbert gains his effects concisely, with a few strokes. Only in the Norse episode does he grow somewhat diffuse."

During 1925, Gilbert was hard at work on the *Symphonic Piece*, which he finished in November. Its Boston premier came in February 1926. The composer said it was non-programmatic and originally intended as the first movement of a symphony. Echoing the sentiments of Whitman, he wrote:

My constant aim . . . has been to write some *American* music—i.e., some music which would not naturally have been written in any other country, and which should reflect, or express, certain aspects of the American character, or spirit, as felt by myself. That spirit, as I see it, is energetic—optimistic—nervous-impatient of restraint—and in its highest aspect, a mighty protest against the benumbing traditions of the past. This new birth—renaissance—of the human spirit, which is America, is a joyous, wildly shouting demonstration. Plenty of jingoism, vulgarity, and "Hurrah boys!" attaches to it, but the spirit of the new-birth underlies all, for him who can see it.

He said the first theme had a "Hurrah boys!" character; the second theme resembled, but only resembled, Foster's "Old folks at Home," with suggestions of "The Arkansas Traveler" inserted at intervals.[37]

The composition has nothing of a formal academic makeup about it. The opening sounds defiant, the continuation abounds with bracing rhythmic idiosyncrasies, the quasi-Fosterisms summon up a winsome mood, the development of ideas is convincing. The alternations among heated discourse, beamish shrieks, and gentler interludes do have a singular American savor to them, both in themselves and in their juxtapositions. The Boston audience responded enthusiastically to the music. The work represents Gilbert at his best. In all probability it was the Whitmanesque *Symphonic Piece* that the Boston Symphony performed, in 1926, at New York's Carnegie Hall, where Mason said he encountered Gilbert: "He rose on my approach, and standing there in full sight and hearing of many neighbors began to tell me, in no measured terms, how inadequately his piece had been rehearsed. I tried to put on a little soft pedal, to make extenuations or qualifications, but in vain. It was an American piece, and he was telling the world it hadn't been rehearsed enough."[38] One cannot but help wondering if this work of Gilbert's encouraged Mason to work on his *Chanticleer* Overture in 1926.

Gilbert was more explicit in acknowledging his regard for Whitman in his *Nocturne, after Walt Whitman*, which he composed in 1926. Pierre Monteux conducted its premier in Philadelphia, in March 1928. The Whitman passage he had in mind was:

> I am he that walks with the tender and growing night;
> I call to the earth and sea half-held by the night.
> Press close, bare-bosom'd night! Press close, magnetic,
>   nourishing night!
> Night of south winds! Night of the large few stars!
> Still, nodding night! Mad, naked summer night![39]

Gilbert wrote a letter to Lawrence Gilman, saying:

My composition was written in 1926. I've always wanted to write something on that beautiful passage from Whitman. . . . That piece is filled with melody; in fact, it is one long melody from beginning to end. Melody is, I believe, about nine-tenths of music, anyway. . . . I have heard so many of the devilishly clever, uncannily ingenious, but dry and soulless musical concoctions which are all the style nowadays that I desired to give myself the satisfaction of making an individual protest against all this super-intellectual, modernistic tendency. So I wrote the *Nocturne*.[40]

The music has the effect of an idyll, a pastoral musical poem charming in its simplicity. The listener hears a long hymn-like melody clothed in an impressionism whose equivalent occurs in the writing of the contemporary English school of composers. Now and again countermelodic activity takes place. However, no marked rhythmic underpinnings appear alongside the ever-expanding lyricism. When the composition arrives at the recapitulation of the music heard at the beginning, the ear relates the passage to the early "Legend," of *Two Episodes*. Both have a similar gentle beauty and innocent tranquillity about them. Yet, the "Legend" was a handiwork of youth, and here the composer is mature, sure of his technique, and individual in his discourse. Altogether, *Nocturne* is a rewarding piece to hear.

A final work was completed just before his death, the Suite for Chamber Orchestra, commissioned by the Elizabeth Sprague Coolidge Foundation. After Gilbert finished composing the music in 1927, Nicolas Slonimsky and the Chamber Orchestra of Boston played it for the first time in April 1928. The first movement, "Prelude," has next to no complexity and resembles a study for violins. The second movement, "Spiritual," has a manifest American intent and draws on the style of an African-American spiritual, without actually quoting one. The tentative opening, with its indeterminate tonality and fragmentary melodic phrases, struggles toward greater definition. Eventually this definition arrives, embodied in a pentatonic melody. The last movement, "Fantasy," seems mostly a dance laced with popular tunes set to ragtime rhythms. Gilbert died 13 months after the premier.

Gilbert exemplified a craggy individualism in his compositions. His music does frequently sound rough. He knew it did but would not change it. What naïveté it had, he considered a virtue. Standing out in everything he said through music was the sincerity with which he said it. He led the way in the use of traditional African-American music, ragtime, and even jazz in artistic compositions. He experimented with Amerindian material. With all his strength, he strove to bestow an American character on a great majority of his works. Here, too, he led the way. Beginning with *The Fantasy in Delft*, a mature and distinctive style emerged, American to the hilt, but not dependent on any one indigenous wellhead. Even though a European underlay to his music was evident to the end, the spirit was American and the predominant characteristics were American.

ARTHUR FARWELL

Farwell, born in St. Paul, Minnesota, had every intention of becoming an electrical engineer when he enrolled at the Massachusetts Institute of Technology, in Cambridge. Yet, after he attended his first symphonic concert in Boston, he discarded engineering in favor of music. His music education came in Boston, from Homer Norris (a Francophile), Chadwick, and MacDowell. (Later, in turn, Farwell would instruct Bernard Rogers and Roy Harris.) Unlike Gilbert, whose formal music education was confined to American teachers, Farwell left for Germany in September 1887 in order to continue his studies with Engelbert Humperdinck and Hans Pfitzner. He would also work with Alexandre Guilmant in Paris. Farwell returned to Boston in May 1899. He grew interested in an American music different from Europe's, and especially in Amerindian music's possibilities for artistic usage. In this regard he was possibly influenced by Gilbert, Chadwick, and MacDowell; he certainly was influenced by the pronouncements on the subject made by Dvořák during his visit to America in the 1890s, and by Alice Fletcher's *Indian Story and Song from North America*, which he studied during the summer of 1899. This led to his immersion in Amerindian mythology and music.[41] Others were cultivating this field alongside Farwell: Cadman, Carlos Troyer, Arthur Nevin, Harvey Worthington Loomis, Thurlow Lieurance, and Charles Sanford Skilton.

Farwell also swiftly learned that music publishers hesitated to print the music of American composers, particularly those younger composers who actively sought an American musical identity. Immediately, he took up the cause of American music: demanding that music education not be dominated by German views and tastes, that art music become available to the common people and cease its existence as an indulgence for the leisured class, and that native composers be given an honest hearing by the music world. Following through on his convictions, Farwell started the Wa-Wan Press in Newton Centre, just outside of Boston, and kept it going from 1901 to 1912, with negligible financial backing and scarcely any profits to support the venture. (Schirmer would take over the Wa-Wan Press in 1912.) "Wa-Wan" is the name of the Omaha tribe's ceremony of peace, fellowship, and song.[42]

The Press did publish music of American composers, among them Kelley, Cadman, Gilbert, Hill, Shepherd, and of course Farwell. Most of its issues were brief piano pieces and songs. Music with a distinctive American ambiance received preferential consideration. Farwell himself set about earning money to keep his Press going. Concert-lecture tours began in 1903, during which he played his Amerindian-directed piano pieces and proselytized for American music. The Southwest Society of the Archeological Institute of America had him collect and record Amerindian music of the Southwest during 1904-5. To strengthen the cause of American music, he established the American Music Society in Boston, in 1905, and the National Wa-Wan Society, in 1907. Twenty centers in scattered cities advanced the study of American music, as also did publication of the *Wa-Wan Press Monthly*, in 1907-8.

He moved to New York, and from 1909 to 1913 was a music critic for *Musical America*. For a while he was also supervisor of New York's park concerts and director of a music school settlement. Later he was a teacher and choral director in California for nine years, then taught at Michigan State College for 12 years, and finally returned to New York in 1939 in order to devote himself to musical composition.[43] When old age enveloped him, Farwell wrote a letter, dated 26 May 1948, to Noble Kreider. He considered himself an unfairly discounted artist: "None of the current generation of artists ever heard of me, especially as the leading orchestra conductors will no longer play anything of my generation. And now Schirmer is going to destroy the bulk of the plates of my songs which they publish."[44]

His beliefs about life and art diverged from those of influential musicians of the next generation. He spoke of two tendencies in his nature, one toward a "spiritual life of ascetic discipline;" the other "toward the ends of artistic accomplishment, in my case musical composition... where beauty and emotion seemed to exclude the rigors of ascetic life." He felt an obligation to both.[45] Every composer's "personal subjective mind," he insisted, had to become attuned to "the universal creative spirit,"[46] a visionary point of view close to that of the New England transcendentalists of the nineteenth century. The sincere artist struggled to reach "the Ideal," to search "beneath the eternal flux and shifting shadow-play of visible phenomena" for "the one Law of all phenomena."[47] At the same time, he fervently advanced the seemingly contradictory notion that "Art which does not give happiness is no art, and the artist who gives the greatest happiness to men will have the greatest success and win the highest reward. The public knows whether it is receiving beauty and happiness from an artist."[48]

He refused to trample on the less-cultivated sensibilities of the general public, an aesthetic blood sport that took strong hold among young composers during the Menckenian 1920s and later.[49] He was a cultural neo-Jacksonian, optimistic about the spiritual future of the American people. By 1915, he had formed strong opinions about music in America that ran contrary to those who found nothing but philistinism and sham in America's cultural life. "Too many persons," Farwell said, "are ready to suppose that the issues of music in America lie wholly within the scope of purely musical considerations, and that they do not depend, as is actually the case in certain important respects, upon the nature of the national ideals and tendencies. The national need will condition the supply, and the more truly and deeply a national need is fulfilled, the more vital will be the result." He inveighed against the powerful coalition of foreign musicians and narrow circles of wealth and culture that were "skinning the cream from as many communities as possible," without regard "for the broader interests of the people." He warned of "the spectacle of an American 'musical world' . . . no longer true to American conditions and which does not serve the people. In short, we have finally come face to face with the problem of the reaction of musical art and democracy."[50]

When he surveyed Amerindian life and its cultural manifestations, he romanticized both. He found exemplifications of spiritual lives guided by austere willpower in their society. The Amerindian's mind struck him as being reconciled to a universal creative spirit and sensitive to an unchanging Ideal. The simplicity, spontaneity, and sincerity of Amerindian song and dance was an antidote to the hypersophistication, excessive emphasis on monetary profit, and peacockish individualism he thought was taking over America. The music often captured a sense of religious rapture and mystery. It reanimated a faith in the integrity of one's inmost self, a desire for things eternal, and a susceptibility to the deeper meanings of the cosmos. Songs might pass on tribal lore and history, enjoin affection, grieve for the deceased, inspire warriors for battle, or aggrandize one's heroism. They always implied something more profound than the transient. They never merely entertained. This attitude of Farwell was analogous to that of Cyrus Edwin Dallin when he sculpted *The Appeal of the Great Spirit*, in 1908, which is now at the Boston Museum of Fine Arts. Personified in the sculpture is the sense of "the inherent dignity of the Indian, combined with a romantic nostalgia and melancholy. . . ."[51]

Yet, as his musical compositions show, Farwell's Amerindian influenced music represents only part of his total output. In a letter sent to Quaintance Eaton, 12 June 1935, Farwell mentioned the public misconceptions about himself. He argued that he had never claimed Amerindian music was or should be the basis of American music. Nor was he a follower of Cadman, since he was involved with Amerindian culture before he met him. On the contrary, around 1902-4, states Farwell, he himself advised Cadman "to tackle the Indian music or other American folk music."[52]

There can be no doubt that Gilbert reinforced Farwell's inclination to study the American musical vernacular. Gilbert would certainly have also encouraged the attention that the relatively inexperienced young Farwell was giving to Wagner, Strauss, Grieg, Dvořák, and various French and Russian composers. Farwell showed no interest in the post-triadic experimentation of Schoenberg and Stravinsky. Indeed, he disliked it. He would subtly lampoon the modernisms of these two composers in a late opera, *Cartoon* (1948). Except for certain Amerindian pieces and some late polytonal studies, his compositions are basically orthodox in style. They adhere to classical structures, display tonally oriented melodies, and state unambiguous rhythms that are not extraordinarily removed from late-nineteenth century European practices. Farwell's non-Amerindian melodies once in a while show kinship to popular-song tunes, and one wonders whether this is due to his democratic impulses. His music relies on triadic harmonies that are more chromatic than those of Gilbert and that show a fondness for intervals higher than the fifth. He is happiest in his songs and short piano pieces; uncomfortable in long works, especially those for orchestra.

In the Amerindian works, Farwell did endeavor to invent harmonies that would abet the indigenous melodic lines, although on occasion he would slip in an inappropriately rich harmony that sounds like a non sequitur. He tried sincerely to study the original stimulus for the material he used in order to remain true to its spirit. Interestingly, taken by itself, the music in the finished composition may sound at one and the same time gently poetic and steadfastly forbidding, like a caress from an iron glove. Some of Farwell's Amerindian pieces generate cryptic auras that withstand lucid interpretation.

Song was a comfortable ground for Farwell to cultivate, and usually represents this composer at his best. As Edgar Lee Kirk states: "The compositions of songs was ideally suited to the compositional technique of Farwell. His training and background were not of the sort that would give him any compelling motive to write in the larger forms."[53] He began to put out his versions of American traditional vocal music with compositions like *Folk Songs of the West and South* (1905), opus 19, which contains African-American spirituals and Amerindian music. Farwell said his harmonies resulted from dramatic and poetic considerations, not from the rules prescribed by theorists. The "Bird Song Dance," from this set, evokes an Amerindian atmosphere in part through nonfunctional harmonic dissonance whose discordant resonances enhance the effect of sound suspended in time.

In 1908, he issued *Three Indian Songs* (1908), opus 32, with Omaha melodies that Alice Fletcher had collected[54] and that had previously been included in a clutch of *American Indian Melodies* for piano (1900). The first, "Song of the Deathless Voice," calls forth the night-spirit of a warrior that occupies the space where he met death. Farwell speaks of the piece's strikingly subjective feeling. The first call of the spirit is fairly objective, but what follows is to sound legato and dreamy, the utterance of a spirit watching for a living warrior to absorb the courage of the dead one. Farwell comments: "It belongs to a dream-world which he must enter, who would truly voice the mystery of its haunting and echoing cadences." The second song, "Inketunga's Thunder Song," requests a novel voice production from the singer in order to interpret the disembodied experience of a man conferring with the Great Spirit, who controls rain, thunder, and lightening. The third song, "The Old Man's Love Song," is a serene *aubade* celebrating the life principle in love and beauty.[55] All three songs are brief and have an unusual dignity and solemnity about them. None of the chant-like melodies is of any length. The plain accompaniment with its unexpected harmonic progressions sounds impressionistic, but absent is any French delicacy and softness.

This description can serve as a guide to the contents of the many Amerindian songs he put out. His other songs, several of them fine ones, do not elicit any sense of a primeval way of life. The earliest of these songs, beginning with "A Ruined Garden" (1902), are romantic in feeling and indebted to various European composers (Wagner, Dvořák, Tchaikovsky) and American composers (MacDowell, Chadwick). The songs written after 1918 are, on the whole, free from complexity, although at times clothed in full, occasionally luscious, harmonies, and at other times, in idiosyncratic tonal combinations. Simple melody and rich harmony are found in "The Wild Flower's Song" of 1920; unusual harmonic effects occur in "On a Faded Violet" of 1927. The latter is to be sung with warmth and a sense of motion. In it, we hear dominant ninths, double appoggiaturas, the clash of a Neapolitan-sixth chord above a dominant-ninth chord, many non-dominant seventh chords, and much half-step chromatic motion in the bass. Yet, Farwell always gives a clear sense of harmonic direction within a definite tonality. Quite fine are the several settings of poems by Emily Dickinson, which distill into tone the message of introversive wonder contained in the words. Finally, the puissant "The Ravens Are Singing" (1929) is highly praised by William Treat Upton in his study of American song.[56] Upton is impressed by the bleak melody that Farwell inserts above the relentless pulsations of a death march in the accompaniment.

A great many of Farwell's piano pieces are Amerindian centered, and were subject to the same aesthetic and musical considerations as his Amerindian songs. Several of them were also arranged for orchestra. Already mentioned was *American Indian Melodies*. This was followed by *Dawn*, a fantasy on two Indian themes (1901), *The Domain of Hurakan* (1902), *From Mesa and Plain* (1905), and other pieces. The gritty "Navajo War Dance" and "Pawnee Horses," both included in the 1905 set, are usually numbered among his finest and most individual works. Of the first, Farwell said he has employed many open fourths because he heard the Navajos sing this war dance in fourths. He wanted the rhythms played precisely and with vehement accentuation. The meter is mostly 6/8 time; the melody, pentatonic. The second piece employs an Omaha melody as sung by Francis La Flesche, the title derived from the text: "There go the Pawnee horses. I do not want them,—I have taken enough."[57] Meter alternates between 9/8 and 6/8. Again, the melody is built on a gapped scale. The impression is decidedly one of wild fierceness. The ceaseless pounding and reiteration of a minimal number of phrase-fragments, however extraordinary the treatment, induces monotony. Of the non-Amerindian piano compositions, of interest are the *Polytonal Studies*, written between 1940 and 1952, and the one-movement Piano Sonata of 1949. The writing is bolder than usual; the music commands spotty interest, although two writers have praised the uniqueness of "the sonata's emotional intensity and dramatic impact."[58]

In the works he described as Symbolistic Studies, which he began composing around 1901 and continued to write to the end of the 1930s, a world beyond the scope of reason breaks into what might otherwise have been conventionally laid-out music. These Symbolistic Studies unbosom an approach to artistic creation distinguished by its trust in insight as a method for grasping what the composer should create. Farwell seems to have been apprehensive about the hardheaded realism invading the literature and painting of his time, and in rebellion against what he saw as the chill detachment from human concerns of the avant-garde music coming from Europe. He searched the center of his being in order to probe and interpret the changeless states which he thought were buried within the life-giving animus common to all humans. Music as symbol, he believed, allowed him to connote enigmatic and otherwise incommunicable emotion-laden ideas, and generate an aliveness to the puzzle at the hub of all life. Farwell's symbolistic music may seem to occupy a psychic region of phantasmagory than of ordinary existence, yet one he would give a vaguely programmatic environment.[59]

One regrets to say that his attempt to transmit in his music a metaphysical apprehension of life does not always succeed. The very vagueness of the musical medium, its inability to convey philosophical states with any concreteness, militates against Farwell's endeavors. The actual compositions are occasionally hampered by passages hazily arranged in structure or difficult to pursue in sound, though not without instances of exceptional expressiveness. The musical style is more conservative than that of the Amerindian pieces, satisfied to remain within the confines of the tonal-triadic conventions. One of the more interesting of these studies is *Symbolistic Study No. 3*: "Once I passed through a populous city (after the poem by Walt Whitman)," composed in 1905, considerably rewritten in 1921, and performed by Monteux and the Philadelphia Orchestra in 1928. Farwell said the poem offers two pictures: "The imposing city" on a material plane and as a memory of emotional experience on a psychic plane. His own bipartite composition observes the dual meanings of the original.[60] Also of interest is *Symbolistic Study No. 5*: "Vision of the Great City," (1905) also for orchestra.

The most fascinating of the studies is *Symbolistic Study No. 6*: "Mountain Vision." It began life in 1912 as a piano solo; in 1917, it became a one-movement piano concerto; and in 1938, it was given final shape as a piece for solo piano and string orchestra, with a second piano added, possibly to deputize for the absent wind instruments. Farwell stated that it represented a sequence of ideas about the reconquering of joy through and after unhappy experience, tragedy, and despair.[61]

Of Farwell's remaining major efforts, his suite, *The Gods of the Mountain* (1928) is considered his finest orchestral composition; the mammoth *Rudolph Gott Symphony*, one of his more boring. The former work came from the incidental music for chamber ensemble that Farwell composed for Lord Dunsany's play in 1917. There is some evidence of novel scale constructions and of musical exoticisms, especially when he tries to depict "the awful stone tread of the approaching gods," in movement four. The program of the initial movement, "Beggars' Dreams," mentions beggars impersonating the stone gods of the mountains in order to gain power. An attenuated opening idea refers to the hungry beggars. Next comes a motive indicating the realization of their goal. This section expands in splendor, but ends abruptly when the music foreshadows the heavy tramp of the gods. A motive on the terror felt by the beggars enters, then gives way to the opening idea, now sounding fairly toned down.

The second portion of the work, "Maya the Moon," shows the sharp dealings intended to bring about the delusion of godhood. Somewhat unsettling sounds introduce a sustained melody in the cellos, which later recurs in the violins and woodwinds. In the third part, "Pinnacle of Pleasure," the beggars are revered and honored with a feast. An exotic dance in the Phrygian mode is featured that implies ecstatic and frenzied celebration.

The last movement, "The Stone Gods Come," describes the arrival of the gods and the punishment of the beggars, who are turned into stone. At first the music, sounding faraway, portends calamity. The motive of terror mingles with the heavy tramp of the gods. Agitation and volume grow. A musical gesture announces the changing of the beggars into stone. At the last, the motive of the gods and that of terror subside to show that the gods have left the scene. Farwell wanted the last movement played very slowly in order to produce suspense.[62]

Farwell demonstrated his democratic leanings by writing several works meant to actively involve a community chorus or an audience in the music-making. Among these are the *Symphonic Hymn on 'March! March!'* (1921) for orchestra with (or, if needbe, without) chorus; and the *Symphonic Song on 'Old Black Joe'* (1923), for orchestra and audience. He also put together pageants and masques designed to attract the general populace (for example, the *Pageant Scene* of 1913, and the Christmas masque, *The Evergreen Tree*, of 1917).

By no means one of the most outstanding composers of his period, Farwell nevertheless did write a few worthwhile compositions and contributed importantly to the awareness of the possibilities in national music. He spoke against the stifling effect of too close adherence to the more conservative Germanic styles, and for the allowance of some place in the sun for American composers. Like Gilbert, he had a Whitmanesque vision of American democracy, with none of the cynicism expressed by so many writers of the 1920s and 1930s. He tried to educate the public to music of worth and to encourage the community music-making that seemed to be at the point of burgeoning in the first years of the twentieth century. Farwell deserves respect for his selfless efforts on the behalf of America's music.

JOHN POWELL

A Virginian, Powell began his music studies at home with Frederick Charles Hahr. He traveled, in 1902, to Vienna to study piano with Theodor Leschetizky and music composition with Karel Navrátil. He started his music career as a virtuosic pianist, in 1907, and toured in Europe until the onset of World War I, at which time he returned to America. Regarded as one of the leading pianists of his generation, he would continue to give solo recitals and performances with symphony orchestras.

Powell considered himself a gentleman and honored the history and traditions of his state. Moral principles were uppermost in his thoughts when he rejected operas like *Cavalleria Rusticana* and *Tristan und Isolde* that dwelt on marital infidelity. He found nothing beautiful in the frenetic harmonies and dissonances of Strauss's *Salome*. While still a student in Vienna, Powell claimed that Brahms bored him, although this did not deter him from later sounding Brahms-like at times; Beethoven, Tchaikovsky, Wagner, and the Dvořák of the *New World* Symphony held his interest.[63] Foreshadowing Powell's use of rag in some compositions, he is said to have played the piano rags of Scott Joplin in 1902, at the Viennese home of Theodor Leschetizky.[64]

The least interesting of the music he composed are those works written between 1907 and 1913 in a late-romantic German style: the *Sonata Noble* (1907), *Sonata Psychologique* (1909), and *Sonata Teutonica* (1913), all for piano, and the Violin Concerto (1910). The first is the easiest of the sonatas to take; the third, which has won the most attention of the three, is the most difficult. It took Powell eight years to finish the *Sonata Teutonica*. The motto on the title-page reads: "The Ocean is in the Drop as the Drop is in the Ocean." The philosophical program meant to go with the score connects the music to a contemplation of "Oneness" and "Universal Unity." These concepts, Powell said, are in sympathy with Lao Tse, Spinoza, Goethe, Darwin, and Beethoven. Nevertheless, one wishes he had elided the excesses of ecstasy and heroism that tend to come off as bombast in the music. The three movements rumble or thunder on, sometimes tediously, for around an hour and a quarter, and in a style sounding like a combination of Liszt, Reger, and Strauss. The textures tend toward turgidity; the earnest worrying of motives into every sort of shape oftentimes defeats clarity of expression. Rhythms strike the ear as indecisive; tonalities, obscured by incessant chromaticism. As a result, coherence threatens to become casualty.[65] Powell's good friend Daniel Gregory Mason called the sonata an important composition, but added that it was a manifestation of megalomania. Reviewing a 1977 recording of an abridged version of the piece, Irving Lowens describes Powell as a "strange person," but likes the work's "grandeur . . . reminiscent of Liszt in his more effective moments," and found the music to be powerful, vigorous, and most concise in the last of its three movements.[66] Mr. Lowens was being more kind than accurate in his praise.[67]

In contrast to the ripely romantic *Sonata Teutonica*, Powell's American-centered works are more direct in expression, precise in structure, and appealing in sheer sound. Such works demonstrate an acute awareness of the older pastoral South in general, and of Virginia in particular. Beneath the surface picturesqueness the listener may detect the moods arising from Southern myth, belief, and practices, and from aspects of nature. The link between music and mood is the traditional song and dance of Virginia. In the late 1890s, and before he left for Vienna, he had worked on a *Sonata Virginianesque* for violin and piano. In 1906, Powell completed its final version, as opus 7. The subject with which the music is involved, antebellum plantation life, contains a high coefficient of nostalgia. The music itself is free of unnecessary complications, makes immediate contact with the listener, and draws on tunes that Powell had heard as he grew up. The three movements: "In the Quarters," "In the Woods," and "In the Big House-Virginia Reel" employ white and black traditional songs and the Virginia reel. Not least of the composition's virtues are the absence of inflated speech and the presence of vivacity, comedy, and ingratiating melody. Of the four movements in his piano suite, *In the South* (1906), the second, a "Love Poem," at one point hints at rag; the third, a "Negro Elegy," has a melody Powell first heard on the lips of a black streetsinger in Richmond; and the fourth, a "Pioneer Dance," is based on the fiddle tune "The Arkansas Traveler."[68]

The first major work that won him national and international attention as a composer was the *Rhapsodie Nègre* for piano and orchestra, of 1918. The premier came that same year in New York, with Powell at the piano, backed by the Russian Symphony Orchestra. Joseph Conrad's *The Heart of Darkness*, which Powell read in 1910, was the original spur for its composition. The composer had wanted to convert the story into an opera, but Conrad convinced him that the symphonic poem was a preferable genre. In the program notes for the piece, Powell mentioned his fascination with the music of various oppressed peoples—music of despair, pathos, and mad gaiety. African-American music had all of this plus an additional characteristic of something "genuinely primitive": of the jungle, of superstitious terror, of protest against fate, and of religious emotionality. The *Rhapsodie*, he said, tries to synthesize all of these feelings. A lengthy description of the music's structure as related to its program came after these statements.[69]

The Introduction opens in a slow tempo and with a doleful wail, apparently taken from a watermelon vendor's cry. After this material is worked up a bit, one hears the zesty first section of the work, a moderately fast dance resembling a rag, which seems related to the theme of the introduction. A drumbeat forms part of the accompaniment. This attractive material in turn is developed until a climax is achieved. An allusion to the introduction is made, then an emotional second section begins: a sad melody heard against a syncopated background. Then a new tune sounds, which turns out to be a version of the spiritual "Swing Low, Sweet Chariot." Brief reference is made to the earlier dance theme before the next section begins, built on the spiritual "I Want to be Ready." The music gets wilder and wilder until the dance theme returns to represent the "frenzy of the Voodoo orgy." The piece ends "with a shriek from the brass, accompanied by a tempestuous *crescendo* streaming up the full range of the pianoforte."[70]

The work has flaws in its thematic elaboration, overall framework, and reconciliation of African-American musical ideas with rhetoric out of Liszt and Strauss. But it also has an abundance of energy, naturalness, and imagination. Powell makes a sincere attempt at realizing an American sound. The listener cannot help but like it. Most writers on music consider it his most successful piece.

In the years that followed the completion of *Rhapsodie Nègre*, Powell's views on America and the music appropriate for its national representation narrowed. He decided that materialism, unrestricted immigration, and racially mixed marriages were eroding the "white," "Anglo-Saxon" traditions that he insisted epitomized the United States at its best. He rejected the "Red Indian School" and "Negro School" of composition as not really typical of the nation. The "Stephen Foster School" overly resembled German traditional music. The "Popular Music School" of rag, jazz, and song-ballad was vulgar and too entangled with cheap entertainment. Although he voiced a little admiration for Charles Griffes's *White Peacock* and Marion Bauer's *White Birches*, he opposed what he considered to be the "Ultra-Modern School." He advocated the elevation of the "Anglo-Saxon Folk Music School."[71] Powell was especially concerned about preserving his Virginia heritage, which meant, musically, its Anglo-Celtic derived traditional song. In this regard he shared some of the views voiced by the Southern "Agrarian" writers: Allan Tate, John Crow Ransom, Donald Davidson, and John Peale Bishop. They deemed contemporary American life and culture to be a failure, and to have been imposed on all of America by the urban North, and New York in particular. In order for them to flourish, the arts needed a stable society, an agrarian orientation, and a scale of values removed from industrial materialism.[72] His fellow Virginian, John Peale Bishop, upheld his state's past, not for romantic reasons, he claimed, but because it was right for him in every sort of way. The simpler past, he said, could instruct the present, this current civilization that everyone was so intent in making over, where "all will be ordered for the best in the best of dehumanized worlds."[73]

Powell set about collecting Southern folk song in earnest and supported its study by others. He also was cofounder of the Virginia State

Choral Festival and energetically advanced the White Top Mountain Folk Music Festival. In 1921, he composed the overture *In Old Virginia* in order to commemorate the centennial of the establishment of the University of Virginia. One hears "Dixie" and two country dances: "Old Virginny Never Tires" and "I Love Somebody, Yes I Do." The traditional music is fine; Powell's development of it lackluster.

Two estimable compositions exemplify Powell's folk direction at its best: *Natchez-on-the-Hill*, three Virginian Country-Dances for Orchestra (1932), opus 30; and *A Set of Three* (1935), opus 33, also for orchestra. The first piece is divided into five sections, played nonstop. The tune "Natchez" goes on to "Hog-eyed Man," which in turn goes on to the jumpy "War-Whoop," then back to "Hog-eyed Man" and a close on "Natchez." He states the captivating melodies without adornment or elaboration, in textures that allow them to stand out utterly.[74] Much of the piece sounds modal and of British-American derivation. The music is polite; none of it as rough or adventurous as that of Gilbert.

A Set of Three has three movements, each identified by its main traditional tune: "Snowbird on the Ashbank," "Green Willow," and "Haste to the Wedding." Again, the music is modal and of British-American derivation, though all the folk themes originated in Virginia. The quick, chipper outer movements frame an intensely melancholic middle movement with a tune that weighs on the memory long after it ends. Later, he composed a Symphony in A, which was first performed in 1947 and afterward revised. Despite the attractiveness of the traditional music, inserted into all four movements, Powell's mistake was in attempting to achieve a lofty dignity of expression. The material cannot stand the treatment. The composition is too long, lasting more than an hour. Counterpoint destroys the drawing power of the simple melodies, crowded textures get in the way of understanding, and rambling structures make the listener lose patience.

His notions about Anglo-Saxon superiority and prejudices against people of other races and cultures were reprehensible. On the other hand, he did set the example for others to collect and use the American folk music that threatened to rapidly disappear in the twentieth century. In this regard, he made a considerable contribution. He was not one of the more significant figures in the mainstream group of composers. Yet, four works were laudable contributions to our musical literature: the *Sonata Virginianesque*, *Rhapsodie Nègre*, *Natchez-on-the-Hill*, and *A Set of Three*.

ARTHUR SHEPHERD

Although born in Paris, Idaho, to parents who had emigrated from England and, in 1877, had converted to Mormonism, Shepherd imbibed a great deal of the New England musical manner, especially as represented by Chadwick. A large reason for this was a musical education begun at the impressionable age of 12 that took place in Boston, at the New England Conservatory. His instructors were Percy Goetschius in theory, and Chadwick in composition. From 1898 to 1909, Shepherd taught and conducted in Salt Lake City, where he established a branch of the American Music Society after meeting Farwell. Farwell also instilled in him an abiding interest in America's traditional music. He then joined the New England Conservatory's faculty, retaining his teaching position until he joined the United States Army during World War I (1917-1920). After his discharge, he went to Cleveland, where he became an assistant conductor of (and furnisher of program notes for) the Cleveland Orchestra, a teacher at Western Reserve University, and, for a time, music critic for the *Cleveland Press*. In Cleveland, Shepherd made influential and helpful friends: Frank Ginn, Grover Higgins, and Mr. and Mrs. Dudley Blossom.[75]

Among the composers of the past that Shepherd admired were Bach, Haydn, Mozart, Beethoven, and Schubert. In addition, he had come to know and feel the influence of Fauré, d'Indy, and Vaughan Williams. He disassociated himself from the modernist fashions of the day, which he thought were destructive to the art of music, and rejected what he considered mere "laboratory techniques" and "hair-splitting aesthetics." He felt that when his music included large servings of dissonance, it required balancing with consonance, tonality, and recognizable melody. As for tradition, one had to respect it, learn from it, build upon it, and change it gradually and for good reason. The rejective and destructive tendencies in the modernism of his day were anathema to him.[76] On the other hand, he always kept himself informed about what the advanced composers were writing.

Shepherd worked slowly, circumspectly, and thought a great deal about what he was putting down. Indeed, at times he thought too much about it. He polished and revised constantly.[77] Not surprising, when one considers his background and his studies with Chadwick, a modal bent and an British-American (that is to say, Anglo-Celtic American) tinge colors much of his music from the beginning. Some melodies may reflect the popular ballad; others may draw on the dance of backwoodsmen and riverboatmen; still others owe their existence to the cowboys of the West. Paradoxically, musical passages can also appear that are quite contrapuntal and sound knotty to the ear. Shepherd is not content to leave his initial ideas alone. He goes about disciplining them and complicating them. Classical rigorousness in the construction of logical structures is joined to rather labyrinthine intellectualization. Thus, the music may at times suffer from an absence of the driving inspiration that otherwise would fire up every detail and bring to satisfying completion what was nicely started. On occasion, the music grows dynamic, or jocose, or displays a flash of rich fancy, as when an otherwise prosy sound glows briefly with a heightened illumination. But only briefly, in many of his works. In numerous instances, when Shepherd has punch, he lacks a sustained punch. Consummate compositions do exist. Yet an equal number of compositions exist that seem on the verge of succumbing to that awkward disorder of the artist given to frequent polishing and revision unguided by strong imagination: the defeat of meaningful expression before the end is reached.

The early *Overture Joyeuse* (1901), which won the Paderewski Prize, is enjoyable, if only in part. The Sonata No. 1 for Piano (1907) gives greatest pleasure when traditionally-based melody occurs from which the composer has not polished away the original freshness, as in the exuberantly syncopated opening tune of the Finale, to be played *giocoso, all burla*. It sounds like a minstrel show walk-around or a backwoodsman's dance.[78] The *Fantasie Humoresque* for Piano and Orchestra (1918) starts well, says Philip Hale, "but the treatment [of the thematic material] . . . is often confused."[79] The Sonata for Violin and Piano (1918) is one of his most successful early works—grave, decisive, stirring, and cyclical after the example of Chadwick and d'Indy. Richard Loucks praises the *Overture to a Drama* (1919) for the energetic mood and virile effect of the first subject and quiet expressiveness of the second. He says that the music is cast in a sonata form of "considerable scope, drama, and conviction."[80]

Shepherd's most successful works, however, came after he departed Boston for Cleveland. Modal constructions and British American melodies now appear with increased frequency. Triadic harmony continues, but with heightened dissonance via added seventh to eleventh tones and nonharmonic thickenings of texture. Up-to date chords involving seconds, fourths, and sevenths make their appearance. Tonality becomes more ambiguous owing to chromatic activity and not a few secondary-key references.

The *Triptych* for high voice and string quartet, completed in 1925, was published in 1927 by the Society for the Publication of American Music. Its three sections employ texts taken from Rabindranath Tagore's *Gitanjali*: the moderately paced "He it is," the slower "The Day is no more," and the faster "Light, my light." Regarded by critics as one of his notable works, it makes scarcely a bow toward national idioms. Instead, Gabriel Fauré and Charles Martin Loeffler seem to have been in the back of the composer's mind. Certainly, the words are sympathetically interpreted in a subdued sort of fashion. The work is decently formed and gratifying to sing and hear. Delicate, expressively reserved countermelodies provide a quiet backdrop for the vocalist. Rhythms flow gently. Lowered second and seventh tones and intimations of gapped scales add an archaic folklike dimension to the music. However, *Triptych* requires dedicated musicians to perform it effectively. Otherwise, its passages sound overly controlled, the composer unwilling to give uninhibited expression to the emotions in the poems. The ceaseless legato flow and unobtrusive rhythmic motion can add up to monotony. For example, the music for the joyous last poem does not capture any strong delight. The dancing in "The light dances" is fitful; why the restrained passage that describes "the wind" running "wild, laughter" passing "over the earth"?

Unquestionably, Shepherd's most successful and extensively played composition is his Symphony No. 1, *Horizons: Four Western Pieces for Symphony Orchestra*, premiered in Cleveland in December 1927. The four movements bear the titles "Westward," "The Lone Prairie," "The Old Chisholm Trail," and "Canyons." More than any of his other works, it makes considerable use of traditional American musical matter and allows this matter to mold the score. No obtrusive quirks or obfuscations get in the way of the music. From the first to the last note, the measures teem with the excitement of tunes generated by the earthy and generous life-styles of the American West.[81] In "Westward," the opening theme in the low strings, accompanied by woodwinds and high strings, does convey a pioneering feeling. The oboe playing the bucolic second theme suggests the loneliness and openness of the plains. The first melody returns to close the movement. "The Lone Prairie" movement incorporates the cowboy song "The Dying Cowboy," introduced by a tenor saxophone. Motives from the tune are elaborated to catch the different moods connected with the prairie, sometimes hushed stillness, sometimes fierceness, always a hovering melancholy. The livelier "Old Chisholm Trail" employs the cowboy tune of the same title and contrasts it with the spicy "Dogie Song." Tough-minded pleasantry prevails throughout. The last movement, "Canyons," is the weightiest one. The music has gravity and nobility. Its chief traditional material is a hymn of the Western pioneers, which Shepherd had known since childhood. An indirect reference to the main theme of the first movement enters before the close.

Reviewing a 1933 performance of *Horizons*, Olin Downes praises its "individual idiom " and "considerable degree of genuine atmosphere." He observes: "This music may not be of sustained strength throughout. It may have its bare places and its inept moments—its uncouthness. But there is the ring of sincerity and imagination in it. . . . it has mood and physiognomy. It is romantic in conception, but not sensuous." The last movement provides an admirable culmination to a composition "emphatically worth hearing."[82]

In 1946, the *Fantasia on Down East Spirituals*, commissioned by the Indianapolis Symphony, received a first performance. Its four modal melodies came from George Pullen Jackson's *Down East Spirituals*. The polyphonic treatment convinces the ear of its rightness. William Newman praises the "healthy fiddling" and designates the *Fantasia* as a surefire piece.[83]

Between *Horizons* and the *Fantasia*, other compositions were completed that were not overtly American but nevertheless incorporated certain Americanisms, usually of British-American derivation. One of these, the Sonata No. 2 for Piano (1930), is sturdily put together, tersely stated, and strikingly emotional. The *Exotic Dance* (1930) for orchestra has allure but sounds not at all like Shepherd. The *Song of the Pilgrims* (1932), a cantata for tenor solo, chorus, and orchestra, is based on a poem by Rupert Brooke. Aaron Copland found it well written, solidly constructed, and one of the finest things Shepherd had written.[84] Without question, Shepherd inserts an unusual amount of feeling into the music, and achieves a monumental peak on the words "Thine altar. Wonderfully white."

The Quartet for Strings in E Minor (1935) has a strong British-American alignment. It sounds at its best when melodies remain fairly open and diatonic, rhythmic patterns remain inelaborate, and textures remain lean and limpid. It sounds less attractive in the last movement, when the rhetoric tends toward the overblown, and the emotional expression toward prolixity. The Symphony No. 2 (1938) has similar virtues and liabilities. The Quintet for Piano and Strings (1940) in F-sharp Minor makes a stronger appeal than the quartet or symphony. Melodies are more inviting. The rhythms in the outer movements pile up strength upon strength. Unchained from meter, the variably stressed chant in the slow movement affords a welcome contrast. In 1946, Shepherd would complete his last major instrumental work, the Violin Concerto, followed by *Variations on an Original Theme* for orchestra (1952) and *A Psalm of Mountains* (1956) for chorus and orchestra. He died two years after the last work was finished.

Shepherd's music is late-romantic without the sensuousness associated with the term. His finest music rests on an American foundation, British-American and cowboy, without the conspicuous nationalism of Gilbert, Farwell, and Powell. Because he was so busy teaching and conducting, a few of his works may seem hastily finished and not thoroughly thought out. Others may seem so thoroughly thought out no spontaneity remains. Still and all, at his best, as in *Horizons*, his music is choice indeed.

SCOTT JOPLIN'S *TREEMONISHA*

Joplin was an African-American pianist and noted composer of piano rags. Born and brought up in Texarkana, Texas, he later lived in Sedalia, Missouri. He may have had some early instruction in music theory.

During a playing stint at the Chicago Columbian Exposition, in 1893, he encountered a great deal of rag music. In 1896, when he located in Sedalia, he did attend music classes at a local college. His remarkable musical talent was manifested in his many ragtime compositions, most of which were popular in his day and several of which have since become classics in their genre. They are splendidly crafted, with cogent melodies, canny harmonies, and expression that gives the listener a pleasure fused with sadness.

His abiding ambition was to compose for the music stage. To this end, in 1903, he composed an opera whose music centered on a rag style, *A Guest of Honor*, and assembled an opera company to perform it. It was not the first opera by an African-American, since Henry Lawrence Freeman (1869-1954) had heard the first of his several operas, *The Martyr*, done in Denver in 1893. The audience failed to respond with any enthusiasm to *A Guest of Honor*. Today, the score cannot be located.

He roamed from town to town until 1907, when he decided to live in New York City. Here, he was soon composing another opera to his own libretto, *Treemonisha*. He himself published it in 1911. Nobody assisted in financing its publication; nobody would mount it on the stage. Joplin's own money went into having it performed once, in Harlem, in 1915, to piano accompaniment. He could not afford an orchestra, scenery, and costumes. Yet again, he failed to win over the audience. The opera survives in piano score; the composer's orchestration now lost. He died in 1917, convinced of the prime quality of his music but without the recognition that he craved of his artistic merit.

That recognition finally came in the 1940s.[85] *Treemonisha* received its first complete performance in Atlanta in January 1972, with an orchestration by Thomas Jefferson Anderson. It was heard at the Wolftrap festival in 1973. The Houston Grand Opera gave a thoroughly professional performance of it in 1975, with an orchestration by Gunther Schuller. Ironically, about 60 years after his death, Joplin won the Pulitzer Prize for his music.

We now acknowledge the expertise, resourcefulness, and attention Joplin lavished on *Treemonisha*. We listen with admiration to the infectious melodies, piquant rhythms, comfortable harmonies with their subtle chromatic modifications, and the firm, logical progressions of the bass line. At the same time, we hear music that exceeds the merely entertaining and demands serious attention. Joplin had wanted to express through this three-act opera the spiritual values and goals of African-Americans, and to advance the idea of freeing the mind from ignorance and superstition through education. He tried to incorporate these concerns into the plot of *Treemonisha*, whose libretto is otherwise of inferior quality. Dialogue sounds artificial; and the didactic aspects of the tale are often hard to take. The confrontation of good and evil and the ultimate triumph of the former is at the core of the drama. The opera is best apprehended as an African-American fable set to music.

He also wanted to write music not based solely on rag but also on the practices and styles of the operas mounted at the Metropolitan Opera House. As a result, while *Treemonisha* contains a great deal of both ragtime and music designed after African-American traditional secular and religious song and dance, it also contains arias that sometimes sound Italianate or Schubertian and sometimes like the American popular ballad. The three acts comprise a succession of self-contained pieces—from solo songs to vocal ensembles and choruses, from dances and straightforward orchestral interludes to concerted finales.

The setting is morning, midday, and evening of the same day, on an Arkansas plantation near the Red River. Ned and Monisha had found a baby under a tree, adopted her, and gotten her an education through the good offices of a white family. On the one day that the action takes place, Treemonisha is 18 years of age and the only black person in her community who is literate. "Conjurors"—Zodzetrick, Luddud and Simon—dominate the people because of the latter's ignorance and superstition. Treemonisha wants to liberate her people by educating them. The culmination of the story comes as her life is imperiled after she challenges the conjurors. However, she is delivered from them, pardons her foes, and finds herself hailed as the leader of her people.

At first, the opera ambles along without great excitement, until "Aunt Dinah Has Blowed de Horn" gets fieldhands going in a veritable delirium of joyous dance activity when their day's labor ends. Effective solo songs include the euphonious "Wrong is never right," sung by Treemonisha's tenor beau, Remus; the menacing bass song "When Villains Ramble Far and Near;" and the winsome Treemonisha solo "The Sacred Tree." An amusing "Frolic of the Bears" adds a bizarre bit of grotesquerie, and a droll "We Will Rest Awhile" allows some fine stop-and-go barber-shop quartet harmonization. At the close of the opera, the mesmerizing "A Real Slow Drag" ushers in all-cast festivity when it leads into a recapitulation of "Aunt Dinah Has Blowed de Horn." The finale's resolute "Marching Onward" choral number is also extremely effective.

When Joplin writes in the American styles he grew up with and knew thoroughly, he is without equal. When he tries consciously to emulate European practices, he appears less secure. Taken as a whole, *Treemonisha* is a successful national work, telling when staged and eminently worth hearing.

NOTES

1. Daniel Gregory Mason, *Music in My Time and Other Reminiscences* (New York: Macmillan, 1938), pp. 365–66.

2. Katherine Marie Eide Longyear, "Henry F. Gilbert, His Life and Works" (Ph.D. diss., University of Rochester, 1968), p. 11.

3. Ibid., pp. 43–44.

4. Clifton Joseph Furness, in *D. A. B.*, s.v. "Gilbert, Henry Franklin Belknap."

5. H. G. Sear, "Henry Franklin Belknap Gilbert," *Music Review* 5 (1944), p. 251.

6. John Tasker Howard, *Our American Music*, 4th ed. (New York: Crowell, 1965), pp. 355–56.

7. Longyear, "Henry F. Gilbert," p. 40; Isaac Goldberg, "An American Composer," *The American Mercury* 15 (1928), p. 332.

8. Henry F. Gilbert, "The American Composer," *Musical Quarterly* 1 (1915), p. 171.

9. Henry F. Gilbert, "Composer Gilbert on American Music," *New York Times* (24 March 1918), section 4, p. 9.

10. Henry F. Gilbert, "Musical Hypocrites," *The New Music Review* 20 (1921), p. 238–39.

11. Henry F. Gilbert, "Humor in Music," *Musical Quarterly* 12 (1926), p. 40.

12. Clifton Joseph Furness, in *D. A. B.*, s.v. "Gilbert, Henry Franklin Belknap."

13. See Farwell's estimate of Gilbert in *Music in America*, eds. Arthur Farwell and W. Dermot Darby, The Art of Music 4 (New York: National Society of Music, 1915), p. 410.

14. Longyear reaches similar conclusions, in "Henry F. Gilbert," pp. 69, 131, 218.

15. The MacDowell melody sounds very much like that of "Danny Boy," which Fred E. Weatherly had published in 1913.

16. The program notes of the MacDowell Festival concert, which contain the Gilbert explanation of the work's inception and moods, are quoted in the Program Book for the concert of the Boston Symphony Orchestra, on 21–22 February 1919, pp. 804, 808.

17. Henry F. Gilbert, Symphonic Prologue to J. M. Synge's Drama *Riders to the Sea* (New York: Schirmer, 1919).

18. Clipping from the *Boston Herald* (21 February 1919), in the Boston Public Library, see Microfilm No. ML 40.H3, roll 5.

19. Henry F. Gilbert, "Folk-Music in Art-Music—A Discussion and a Theory," *Musical Quarterly* 3 (1917), p. 577.

20. Henry F. Gilbert, *Two Episodes* for Orchestra, opus 2 (Boston: H. F. Gilbert, 161 Tremont Street, n.d.). He presented a copy to Harvard College, signed by him and dated 3 May 1897; now in the Music Library, Shelf No. Mus 687.2.225.

21. Henry F. Gilbert, *Humoresque on Negro-Minstrel Tunes* (New York: Gray, 1913).

22. Olin Downes, "An American Composer (Henry F. Gilbert)," *Musical Quarterly* 4 (1918), p. 30.

23. Mason, *Music in My Time*, p. 372.

24. Johnston had also directed Gilbert's attention to Celtic literature and music.

25. Henry F. Gilbert, *Comedy Overture on Negro Themes* (New York: Gray, 1912).

26. Downes, "An American Composer," p. 24; the Hale quotation is from a clipping from the *Boston Herald* (14 April 1911), in the Boston Public Library: see Microfilm No. ML 40.H3, roll 4.

27. *Musical America* (3 October 1914), p. 17.

28. Ivan Narodny, "An American Composer's Success in Russia," *Musical America* (17 October 1914), p. 61.

29. Eliot Carter, "American Figure, with Landscape," *Modern Music* 20 (1943), p. 223.

30. Henry F. Gilbert, "Note" before the score of *The Dance in Place Congo*, Symphonic Poem (after George W. Cable), opus 15 (New York: Gray, 1922). The "Note" also is found in the Program Book for the concert of the Boston Symphony Orchestra, on 20-21 February 1920, pp. 1086–87.

31. The quotation may be found in the "Note" preceding the score.

32. This spiritual is identified as "You may bury me in the East," by H. F. P., in *Musical America* (20 December 1913), p. 21; and by Sear, "Henry Franklin Belknap Gilbert," p. 255.

33. See the Program Book for the concert of the Boston Symphony Orchestra, on 4–5 March 1921, pp. 1072–75.

34. Longyear, "Henry F. Gilbert," p. 31.

35. See, for example, Edward Ellsworth Hipsher, *American Opera and Its Composers* (Philadelphia: Presser, 1927), p. 200; Otto Luening, *Odyssey of an American Composer* (New York: Scribner's Sons, 1980), p. 240.

36. Luening, *Odyssey*, p. 240.

37. Gilbert's comments are contained in the Program Book for the concert of the Boston Symphony Orchestra, on 26–27 February 1926, pp. 1356, 1358, 1360.

38. Mason, *Music in My Time*, p. 373.

39. Quoted by Karl Krueger, in the jacket notes to MIA 141, Krueger's recording of the work for The Society for the Preservation of the American Musical Heritage.

40. Ibid.

41. Evelyn Davis Culbertson, "Arthur Farwell's Early Efforts on Behalf of American Music, 1899–1921," *American Music* 5 (1987), pp. 158–59.

42. Arthur Farwell, "Pioneering for American Music," *Modern Music* 12 (1935), p. 118.

43. *Musical America* (February 1952), p. 274.

44. See Edgar Lee Kirk, "Toward American Music; a study of the life and music of Arthur George Farwell" (Ph.D. diss., University of Rochester, 1958), p. 86.

45. Untitled front matter, in *A Guide to the Music of Arthur Farwell and to the Microfilm Collection of His Work*, ed. Brice Farwell, prepared by his children (New York: Briarcliff Manor, 1972).

46. Arthur Farwell, "Individual Advancement," *Musical America* (3 January 1914), p. 32.

47. Arthur Farwell, "Individual Advancement," *Musical America* (27 December 1913), p. 32.

48. Arthur Farwell, "The Heart of the Artist," *Musical America* (7 February 1914), p. 41.

49. Nicholas E. Tawa, *Serenading the Reluctant Eagle* (New York: Schirmer, 1984), pp. 1–19.

50. Farwell, "Introduction" to *Music in America*, pp. viii, xx–xxi.

51. Matthew Baigell, *Dictionary of American Art* (New York: Harper & Row, 1979), s.v. "Dallin, Cyrus Edwin."

52. Culbertson, "Arthur Farwell's Early Efforts," pp. 166–67.

53. Kirk, "Toward American Music," p. 180.

54. He drew material from Alice C. Fletcher's *Indian Story and Song from North America* (Boston: Small, Maynard, 1900).

55. Arthur Farwell, *Three Indian Songs* (New York: Schirmer, 1912). Gilbert Chase provides an excellent discussion of these pieces and reproduces Farwell's comments in his album notes to New World Records NW 213.

56. William Treat Upton, *Art-Song in America* (Boston: Ditson, 1930), p. 156.

57. The Farwell quotations and other information about the pieces may be found in Chase's album notes to NW 213.

58. Gilbert Chase and Neely Bruce, in *The New Grove Dictionary of American Music*, eds. H. Wiley Hitchcock and Stanley Sadie (New York: Grove's Dictionaries of Music Inc., 1986), s.v. "Farwell, Arthur."

59. The best guide to Farwell's symbolistic thinking is found in *A Guide to the Music of Arthur Farwell*.

60. Ibid., pp. 34–35.

61. Ibid., pp. 37–38.

62. Ibid., pp. 39–41.

63. Ronald David Ward, "The Life and Works of John Powell (1882–1963)" (Ph.D. diss., Catholic University of America, 1973), pp. 15, 22–25.

64. Harold Schonberg, *Facing the Music* (New York: Summit, 1981), p. 161.

65. Roy Hamlin Johnson has prepared a shortened performing edition of the sonata. It still sounds dull. See John Powell, *Sonata Teutonica*, opus 24, for Piano. Performance Edition with biographical and editorial notes by Roy Hamlin Johnson (New York: Oxford University Press, 1983).

66. Mason, *Music in My Time*, p. 299; Irving Lowens, review of CRI 368, in *High Fidelity* (December 1977), pp. 94–95.

67. I did ask Irving Lowens about his review, and he replied that he felt it necessary to give Powell's music the benefit of the doubt since so few other critics would.

68. Ward, "The Life and Works of John Powell," pp. 166–69.

69. The program notes of the original concert are reproduced in the Program Book for the concert of the Boston Symphony Orchestra, on 29–30 December 1922, pp. 653, 654, 656, 658, 660, 662.

70. Ibid., p. 664.

71. Ward, "The Life and Works of John Powell," pp. 70–72.

72. Frederick J. Hoffman, *The Twenties* (New York: Free Press, 1962), pp. 173–75.

73. John Peale Bishop, *The Collected Essays*, ed. Edmund Wilson (New York: Scribner's Sons, 1948), pp. 12–13.

74. John Powell, *Natchez-on-the-Hill*, Three Virginian Country Dances, opus 30 (New York: Schirmer, 1932).

75. Richard Loucks, *Arthur Shepherd, American Composer* (Provo, Utah: Brigham Young University Press, 1980), pp. 16, 19.

76. Ibid., pp. 30, 32, 33.

77. William S. Newman, "Arthur Shepherd," *Musical Quarterly* 36 (1950), p. 160.

78. Loucks claims Shepherd heard the tune as part of the incidental music to a play, *The Virginian*, whose pit orchestra the composer directed; see Loucks, *Arthur Shepherd*, p. 33.

79. Clipping from the *Boston Herald* (16 April 1921), in the Boston Public Library, see Microfilm No. ML 40.H3, roll 5.

80. Loucks, *Arthur Shepherd*, p. 54.

81. Arthur Shepherd, *Horizons*: Four Western Pieces for Symphony Orchestra (Boston: C.C. Birchard for the Juilliard Musical Foundation, 1929).

82. Olin Downes, "Music," *New York Times* (10 February 1933), p. 13.

83. Newman, "Arthur Shepherd," pp. 172–73.

84. Aaron Copland, "Scores and Records," *Modern Music* 15 (1938), p. 111.

85. For a summary of Joplin's life and music, see Edward A. Berlin, *The New Grove Dictionary of American Music*, ed. H. Wiley Hitchcock and Stanley Sadie (New York: Grove Dictionaries of Music, 1986), s. v. "Joplin, Scott.".

Chapter Six

Charles Tomlinson Griffes and Marion Bauer

Of all the composers taken up in this study, Charles Griffes (1884-1920) was the one most susceptible to the impress of nature and poetry. That is to say, not so much the nature seen in reality but more the one filtered through the sensibilities of poets and painters; not so much the poetry on any subject but more that with mystic connotations. He wished to capture the moods engendered by his sense perceptions, within compositions that sounded intuitive, soft-edged, and subtly tinted. He grew up in Elmira, New York, and studied piano with Mary Broughton. From an early age, he was reserved and introverted. He would make few friendships. Along with poetry, travel books attracted him, especially those on exotic lands. In addition, when not involved in music-making, he occupied himself with rendering drawings in pen-and-ink and landscapes in watercolor.

Convinced of his musical talents, Broughton persuaded Griffes to travel to Berlin, in 1903, where he remained for four years in order to study music. His Berlin teachers in composition were Philippe Rüfer and Engelbert Humperdinck. Most significantly, when Marion Bauer asked Griffes how he became interested in musical impressionism, he replied that one day in his Berlin pension, he heard Rudolph Ganz in another apartment playing Ravel's *Jeux d'Eau*, and the pleasure the piano piece gave him then caused him to study the music of Ravel and Debussy.[1]

On his return to the United States in 1907, he chose to teach music at the Hackley School, in Tarrytown, New York, where he remained until his death. The school assured him a living, allowed some leisure time for composing, and offered a refuge from the bustle of the outside world. Bauer writes that Griffes never had any intention of giving up his teaching position, saying: "I don't believe in the 'starving in the garret' type of artist. I could not do good work if I had a constant worry over finances or a struggle with poverty."[2]

No two more contrary artistic temperaments can be conceived than those of Griffes and Henry Gilbert. In 1917, Arthur Shepherd took Griffes to meet Gilbert. Griffes played selections from his *Fantasy Pieces*, opus 6, for Gilbert. Shepherd stated: "One could easily discern the Gilbertian reaction: first an astonishment at the fastidiousness, refinement, and maturity of craftsmanship, then a characteristic grin of resentment and dissent from the aesthetic underlying this music. How could such hypersensitive art and technique subsist in an American carcass?" After the meeting was over, Griffes complained about having "got dragged out" to see Gilbert, in Cambridge, wishing he had never gone to meet a musician whom he referred to sarcastically as "one of the really famous Boston composers."[3]

THE MUSICAL STYLE OF GRIFFES

In an America where other composers were making a tremendous effort to create a national music, Griffes took the stance of a composer devoted to the cultivation of an art not beholden to any national idiom. No wonder he disturbed Gilbert. His music sounded not American, in the Gilbertian sense. Still and all, it was inarguably not European. He inclined toward depicting scenes and emotions by means of evocative musical colors, yet he was not an impressionist after the current French fashion. Griffes the composer was engrossed in an intense absorption of atmosphere, of what the subject matter he contemplated implied. One has to become commensurably absorbed in order to catch his thought. He is an exceptional composer not simply because of his urbanity, his enthusiasm for recondite expression, or his innate acuteness of perception. He is exceptional because of his inviolable yet deceptive fervor and his ability to find the right sound for the emotive embodiment of any illustrative composition he happened to be working on. He was always alive to the many conceivable hues, gradations, and effects of his tonal art. He had a singular facility for immersing himself into the intricacies of psychological and spiritual sensation that characterized each of his works.

The music of Griffes's maturity is some of the boldest written by the mainstream composers and shows affinities to other works—first, of Debussy and Ravel; afterwards, of late Scriabin and Stravinsky. However, his earliest works, composed during his student days and for a brief period after his return to America, were Germanic, conservative, and certainly not unprecedented. About 1910, he began shaking off his

Germanic dependence, aided by the fresher sounds coming from France (Debussy, Ravel) and Russia (Mussorgsky, Scriabin). Throughout his brief life, he grew more venturesome, individualistic, and willing to test new ideas. Yet, he was never a radical experimenter. He built on his past and labored to extend his modes for musical discourse. He was what Irving Babbitt would have called a "true modern, in contradiction to the modernist," because he did not reject tradition. Modernism for him was not a "dogma" of the present time alone, but also "a completion and enrichment of present experience by that of the past."[4] The miniature, especially the solo song and the characteristic piano piece, was almost always the musical metiér he chose to write in. He rarely craved to achieve anything more monumental. Many of his orchestral works were originally conceived as piano pieces.

Some compositions are ternary in structure. Others are strung out as a free fantasy, although usually an echo of the beginning appears at the end. Still others may reveal a mirror arrangement, with the first portions of a piece recurring in reverse sequence after a middle section. Rarely encountered are the remaining traditional forms like sonata-allegro. Abstract works are few. Most compositions bear descriptive titles. However, his biographer Edward Maisel tells us that oftentimes it was after he completed a composition that he cast about for a fitting title or motto with which to preface it—a procedure also seen in Schumann and Liszt. The music came before the titles in the *Three Tone-Pictures*, opus 5, and the *Fantasy Pieces*, opus 6. On the other hand, a poem by Fiona MacLeod (William Sharp) was the original inspiration for *The White Peacock*.[5]

Around 1910, Griffes left behind him the German romanticism acquired from his mentors in Berlin, with its tonal plateaus relieved by temporary secondary-key references, enriched triadic harmony progressing in more or less customary manner, and heated emotional context. His music strikes the ear as more suggestive of a time and place, recreating an atmosphere with some delicacy, and less a dramatic personal statement. Tonality grows more elusive. Neomodality now mingles with the normal major-minor alignment. Ninth and eleventh harmonies enter with frequency. They are not subject to the expected functional logic but are in resonance with the mood being established. Several of them may closely follow each other in a parallel chordal stream. The simultaneous sounding of two different chords may occur, as also may samplings of bitonality. The seventh tone leading into the tonic makes fewer appearances. Melodic lines increase their chromaticism and gain in flexibility—flowing over the bar lines, less bound by the rule of meter. The change in style is heard early on, in the *Three Tone-Pictures* for piano (1910-12) and *Tone-Images*, three songs written between 1912 and 1914.

His music has obviously become impressionistic in style, yet individual as well. It apprehends the passing impression that remains for an instant but contains more than a second of meaning. Whatever the sensory stimulation, it has metamorphosed into feeling. However, the impressionism is not that of the French. The outline of Griffes's music is firmer than Debussy's; musical substance is more emphatic, less nebulous; rhythm is more plainly stated. The music's handling eschews Ravel's brilliance and his customary love of Spanish rhythm, harmony, and melody.

Exotic peoples, places, and cultures also fascinated Griffes. He was an avid reader of Lafcadio Hearn's vivid descriptions of travel in Eastern Asia. Friendship with the singer Eva Gauthier, who enjoyed Far-Eastern melodies, and with Michio Itow, a Japanese dancer, fostered this interest. The gapped scales peculiar to Eastern Asia and their characteristic usage attracted him, as also the novel sonorities produced by non-Western instrumental ensembles. *Five Poems of Ancient China and Japan* (1916-17), *Sho-jo* (1917), and *Sakura-Sakura* (1917) are three of several works that resulted from this influence.

About three years before he died, Griffes, in works like the Sonata for Piano, expanded his musical resources to include an array of non-triadic harmonies, synthetic scales of his own manufacture, and increased linear over vertical thinking. He seemed to be preparing to occupy a stylistic and expressive territory strictly his own. The music lover concerned with the fate of American music must deplore his untimely death.

THE SONGS OF GRIFFES

Griffes composed more songs than any other sort of composition. For the most part they tend away from the strophic and toward the through-composed. On occasion, a sort of freely realized ABA structure prevails, as in two songs from opus 11: "Thy Dark Eyes to Mine" and "The Rose of the Night." Coherence of the parts and unity of the whole are aided by the persistent accompaniment patterns, the recurring melodic phrases, and the controlled ebb and surge of tension. Everything irrelevant to the interpretation of the subject is excluded from the music. The vocalist sings melodies congenial to the voice. Harmonies, however complicated, support the singer. Rhythms, however diverse, commingle to give direction to every passage.

The American art song was an established genre by the turn of the century, with superb contributions from Chadwick, Foote, MacDowell, and Beach. Most examples are in a romantic vein, owing much to the Central Europeans, less to the French, and a little to British-American and American popular ballad styles. Not surprisingly, Griffes's early songs reveal a similar ambience. His five songs to German texts (ca.

1903-09) illustrate his youthful leanings. Aspects of the outdoors were fused to personal emotion in the poems by Lenau, Heine, Mosen, and Geibel. In his settings, Griffes's craftsmanship is excellent; his models are apparently the songs of Brahms, Strauss, and Wolf. He makes himself painstakingly receptive to the images in the texts and skillfully invents vocal lines and pianistic figuration sympathetic to the tonal pictures he wishes to draw. In songs like "Auf gehiemen Waldespfade" (one of the finest of the *Lieder*), we find triads with added sixths, chromatic harmonic motion, and the emphasizing of musical peaks through enharmonic changes and chords in second inversion. These first songs are lovely, but one also recalls Griffes's own comment that they were more the result of his studies than his own musical expression.[6] Nevertheless, they do make statements identifiable with Griffes rather than just Germany. We should keep in mind the observation of the anthropologist Wilson Wallis that culture does "not travel *in toto*" from one cultural area to another. It "is modified; it does not remain identical with its old self. . . . No cultural area of the New World, therefore, is an exact duplicate of one in the Old World."[7]

Stylistic change, however, is in the air with the *Tone Images*, opus 3: the "La Fuite de la Lune" and "Symphony in Yellow" (both from 1912) on poems of Wilde, and the "We'll to the Woods and Gather May" (1914) on a poem of Henley. German texts are abandoned; German thought is notably modified. The first song evokes a quiet, mist-laden atmosphere of "a dreamy place," until "suddenly the moon withdraws" and we sense a deft transformation of mood. The song ends in a hush of sound. The third song stands in stark contrast: insouciant, ingenuous, and simply conceived. "Symphony in Yellow" is the gem of the set. The poem sketches a fogbound scene. The music magically invokes a singular, odd, even alien aura that is entirely of Griffes's own invention and one that haunts the mind.

The *Two Rondels* (1914), opus 4, show further exploration of new ways of expression. "This Book of Hours" (Crane) and "Come, Love, Across the Sunlit Land" (Scollard) explore a detached sort of feeling, create a milieu of the long ago through modal harmonization, and unfold in lithe and elegant musical lines.

In *Four Impressions* (1915-16), Griffes has obviously turned to an individualistic impressionism. This set contains four of his most convincing and pleasing songs. Wilde wrote the poems: "Le Jardin (The Garden)," "Impression du Matin (Early Morning in London)," "La Mer (The Sea)," "Le Réveillon (Dawn)."[8] All four songs are through-composed. The first song reflects on a deserted and gloomy garden of dead vegetation and on the call of a lone wood-pigeon. An exquisite melancholy infiltrates the music, except for one swell of intensity where the singer reaches for a high note and the texture thickens. During this passage, the text tells of a black and barren sunflower and a windy garden walk. Then the delicacy of the opening returns. The piece closes as it began, despondently. The second song is the one that most approximates Debussy's style. Tolling chords in the piano blur one into another by means of the pedal. Tonality remains obscure from beginning to end. The delineation of waking life in the city is especially effective, with the clanging piano harmonies crescendoing to *ff*. A sudden quiet depicts a bird on a roof, after which the reiterated harmonies are heard in syncopation. Forlornness takes over on glimpsing a "pale woman all alone"; the voice now declaims; tunefulness has gone. A very soft dissonant chord ends the piece. Dreaminess disappears and excitement takes over in "The Sea." As usual in all of these songs, the beginning and the end of this one are the most tonally oriented. The middle, which describes a ship's steersman and a throbbing engine room, grows in excitement and chromaticism—at this point, the alteration of the music's course surprises the listener. The final song opens *mysterioso*, on an extremely low single line of music. In the fifth measure, the right hand commences to sound chords that steadily rise higher and higher until the voice enters on "The sky is laced with fitful red." A cogent tone painting continues throughout the composition.

That Griffes did not come completely under the sway of impressionism is established in the "Song of the Dagger," begun in 1912 and completed in 1916. The poem, translated from the Rumanian, is meant to be a fierce, acrid eruption of one seeking revenge for rejected love, symbolized by the bloodthirsty dagger. It has moments of theatrical punch, although the troubled, sensuous atmosphere essential for the depiction of this derangement is not always evident.[9] For example, the 5/4–4/4 dancing accompaniment in G Minor of the beginning seems an inappropriate way to interpret the thirsty dagger. The music is almost comforting in another section, which speaks of the maid finding the dagger sweet when it has quenched its thirst. Here, bare-bone octaves in the piano scarcely hint at the underlying disarray in the speaker's mind. Yet the work does have a severe attractiveness about it.

The *Three Poems* (1916), opus 9—"In a Myrtle Shade" (Blake), "Waikiki" (Brooke), "Phantoms" (Giovannitti) further reveal Griffes's not-so-predictable new style. The tired abstraction of the mind conveyed in the music of the first and the evasive dreamlike mood of the third are foils to "Waikiki." Rupert Brooke's poem is given a strange, and even a rude, setting that hints at Hawaiian music. William Treat Upton finds its harmony to be repellent, the voice's part, unvocal and unmelodic. He also discovers sinister beauty in the music for "The dark scents whisper and dim waves creep to me?" and intense passion in that for "Two that loved or did not love, and one whose perplexed heart did evil, foolishly."[10]

Griffes the researcher is very much to the fore in *Five Poems of Ancient*

China and Japan (1916-17), opus 10. It was about this time that he met Eva Gauthier after she returned from the Far East and listened to her praise the poetry and music of these distant lands. Five- and six-tone scales, harmonization in open fourths and fifths, few alterations in dynamics, and the reiteration of a limited number of brief musical ideas aim to capture an Oriental ambience. The music ends up sounding both quaint and immobile, as if fixated on one image and on one point in time.

Of the *Two Poems by John Masefield* (1918)—"An Old Song Re-Sung" and "Sorrow of Mydath"—the first is a powerful composition and one of his best; the second, one difficult to interpret and to like from start to finish. The brawny vigor and forthrightness of "An Old Song Re-Sung," which begins "I saw a ship a-sailing," leaves no room for impressionism.[11] Echoing the idiom of the traditional sea chanty, the tune is in three strains, each beginning similarly but ending differently. The third describes a sinking ship and the seamen drinking and singing as they go to their death. Here, the music grows louder, more animated, more dissonant, and more tonally inconclusive until a climax is achieved with the voice in a high range and the piano sounding a tonic seventh chord with a raised fifth tone and a lowered seventh tone. Then motion slows, dynamics soften, on "The broken glass was chinking as she sank among the wrecks." The home key is solidly reinstated but with the lowered supertonic tone persistently sounded by the pianist's left hand.

The finest set of songs is *Three Poems by Fiona MacLeod* (1918), opus 11.[12] The poems of William Sharp, who used the pseudonym Fiona MacLeod, project a Celtic romantic mysticism that Griffes found especially congenial: "The Lament of Ian the Proud," "Thy Dark Eyes to Mine," "The Rose of the Night." The combination of world-weariness and stern gravity is a dominant feature of the music in the first song. The scale employed emphasizes the raised sixth tone and avoids the seventh tone or lowers it. Moments of utmost poignancy are achieved on the words "the old grief" and "O blown, whirling leaf." The intensity of the sorrowing music is unallayed throughout; it is never sentimental. It ranks with "Symphony in Yellow" and "An Old Song Re-Sung" as one of the finest songs written by any American.

The second song centers on the emotions called forth by the beloved "Eilidh." A fluent vocal melody and opulent harmony, gentle cross-rhythms, and attractive countermelodies in the piano contribute to the allure of the music. It has an air of dreaming, of suspension from reality, brought about, in part, by the use of mildly discordant nondominant seventh chords. The last song is troublesome to describe. The text has a dead soul wooing a living soul, in order that both may be reborn—a concept difficult to digest. Musical expression achieves a singular emotionality, especially in the extraordinary climax of the piece. "The Rose of Night" is the most impressionistic, dissonant, and tonally elusive of the three songs.

The singer never finds it easy to translate a Griffes song into sound. The music taxes musicianship. However idiomatically vocal the melodies, they require careful study and alert rendering, for they abound in subtleties. More than in most songs by other Americans, the singer finds it imperative to listen to the implications of the piano's music and integrate this added enrichment of expression into his or her interpretation of the text. More than with the songs of any other composer, the vocalist must project in his or her delivery the sense of unremitting sincerity that the music manifests, in order to achieve a successful performance.

THE INSTRUMENTAL MUSIC OF GRIFFES

The *Three Tone-Pictures* (1910-12), opus 5, started life as piano pieces, but then were arranged for woodwinds with optional harp (1915), and for woodwind quintet, string quintet, and piano (1919). They comprise *The Lake at Evening*, *The Vale of Dreams*, and *the Night Winds*. In them we encounter Griffes's first significant shift to impressionism—the whole-tone formations, shifting tonalities, unresolved harmonies stressing the augmented fifth tone, series of parallel chords, careful regulation of sonorities, and figures that recur with some persistence. Form is more or less ternary. *The Lake* contains insistent pedal points and exploits repeated rhythmic patterns everywhere. The first section's pedal on *A* supports the principal key. The music moves to a new section, essentially an expansion of ideas already stated, with the pedal on *B*. The final section returns to the first section's music and pedal on *A*. Garry Clarke perceptively observes that the unresolved chords and rhythmic ostinatos suspend the work in a strange unmoving musical world, creating the effect of stillness, "not unlike that of Ravel's *Le Gibet* from *Gaspard de la Nuit*."[13] The next piece, *The Vale* contains dissonances throughout that veil harmonic differences. They produce the effect of resonances that harbor a private secret and intimate a meaning both inexplicable and profound in character. (The *De Profundis* for piano, of 1915, gives off a similar meaning.) The final tone picture is equally telling in its somber colorations for nocturnal breezes sensed but not seen.

The *Fantasy Pieces* for piano (1912-13), opus 6, include a *Barcarolle*, *Notturno*, and *Scherzo*. The first, a reflection on a poem by Sharp, introduces engaging water music and realizes a first-rate climax. The second piece pleased Griffes's friend, Marion Bauer, who praised its long melodic line based on the whole tone scale, which unfolds slowly over an accompaniment of even eighth notes, then triplets, then sextuplets.[14] Griffes's explanation of the *Scherzo* (the later orchestrated version is entitled *Bacchanale*) has links to *The Pleasure-Dome of Kubla Khan*: "From the Palace of Enchantment there issued into the night sounds of un-earthly revelry. Troops of genii and other fantastic spirits danced gro-tesquely to a music now weird and mysterious, now wild and joyous."[15]

A dance-drama, *The Kairn of Koridwen*, for flute, two clarinets, two horns, harp, celesta, and piano, was completed in 1916. Nikolai Sokoloff conducted its premiere in February 1917, with Griffes as pianist. The composer admitted that the plot was undramatic but found "some nice chances for descriptive music." He also saw the composition as "con-tinuous symphonic music in two movements or scenes," that could be performed as an independent concert piece. Scarcely any critics took notice of its performance, and those that did agreed it was in an advanced idiom: one that was adventurous in nature, requiring close attention, and with hardly any melody. Only Paul Rosenfeld, a champion of avant-garde music, was enthusiastic.[16]

Roman Sketches, opus 7, four piano pieces written between 1915 and 1916, includes *The White Peacock* (later orchestrated), *Nightfall*, *The Foun-tain of the Acqua Paola*, and *Clouds* (later orchestrated). All four of them are joined to verses by Sharp.[17] An impressionistic style prevails. Deli-cateness approaching affectedness threatens to invade the fabric of sound. Yet, the scope and potency of the whole excuses the occasionally overripe harmonies. In addition, the distinct sculpting of the melodic lines proves stimulating and rescues the music from the accusation of frailty. Finally, a welcome pungency cleanses the sweetness from the ear.[18]

The first, one of the most well received compositions that Griffes composed, is prefaced by the following verse:

Here where the sunlight
Floodeth the garden . . .
Moves the white peacock, as tho' through the noontide
A dream of the moonlight were real for a moment. . . .

Its start, *languidamente e molto rubato*, is Debussian; the mood, exotic and ethereal. Meter is flexible. Melody is one long line exposing two principal ideas, with the end returning to the music of the beginning. The initial idea features a chromatic descent in quarter and dotted-eight notes. The second is more lyric and in longer notes. Harmony is not always triadic, and major and minor constructions of the same chord may sound simultaneously.

Nightfall, in an arch structure, opens *lento misterioso, una corda*. The music is very soft, in a low range, and based on a G-sharp Minor har-mony, against which we hear a subdued clash of notes sounding *D-natural* and *E*. Soon, a barcarolle-like passage begins. The work builds up to a hefty *ff*. Then the bacarolle idea and the mysterious opening return.

The Fountain of the Acqua Paola, ternary in form, is mostly in constant sixteenth-note motion, *allegro moderato*, with a melody in longer notes. Nicely descriptive of the cascading water of a fountain, the composition may owe a debt to Liszt's *Jeux d'eau à la Villa d'Este*, and possibly to Ravel's *Jeux d'eau*.

The tranquil *Clouds* introduces several parallel chord streams by the two hands, which often go in opposite directions. Bichordal harmony occurs; or the conflict of different tonalities. Sharp's poem "*Agro Romano*" stimulated Griffes to compose the piece.

Without question, *The Pleasure-Dome of Kubla Khan*, opus 8, brought Griffes his first widespread recognition as a composer. It began life as a piano piece in 1912, was clothed in orchestral garb in 1917, and was premiered by Monteux and the Boston Symphony in November 1919. The audience acclaimed the music. A jubilant Griffes stated: "As I left the hall that evening I met my friend Dr. F. Morris Class. He sang out to me with great enthusiasm that an American had written a piece that had that evening stood out as a finer thing than Balakireff's 'Thamar,' which followed it on the program. I felt so, too."[19] Six months later Griffes was dead.

The music's inspiration was a poem published in 1816, "Kubla Khan: a Vision in a Dream," by Samuel Taylor Coleridge. This antecedent to symbolism and surrealism came to Coleridge during an opium-induced sleep and consists of a string of striking pictures drawn from imagination: the eternally flowing sacred river Alph, the Khan's pleasure-palace, the revelry within its walls, its bright gardens, the caves of ice, and the sunless sea.

When he first decided to realize the poem in music, Griffes searched in a New York library for Arabian music to use directly or to guide his own melodies. Gauthier told Bauer that Griffes eventually employed some Javanese melodies that she supplied in *The Pleasure-Dome of Kubla Khan*.[20] Nevertheless, the music of Asia is more felt than actually expressed in the score. All of the stale musical formulae meant to impart an Eastern flavor are avoided. What the final form should be proved a poser. The completed piano version was tried out on Farwell. Both he and Griffes agreed the work did not suit the piano. Yet, revision proved no easy thing. Griffes struggled with the nature of his new arrangement for several years before completing the orchestral score.[21]

In the program book for the concert of the Boston Symphony in November 1919, Griffes said:

As to argument, I have given my imagination free rein in the description of this strange place as well as of purely imaginary revelry which might take place there. The vague, foggy beginning suggests the sacred river running "through caverns measureless to man down to a sunless sea." Then gradually rise the outlines of the palace, "with walls and towers girdled round." The gardens with fountains and "sunny spots of greenery" are next suggested. From inside come sounds of dancing and revelry which increase to a wild climax and then suddenly break off. There is a return to the original mood suggesting the sacred river and the "caves of ice."[22]

The music begins *lento misterioso* on a low pedal chord in the strings, played *tremolo* and *sul ponticello*.[23] A gong is kept vibrating by applying friction to its edges. Piano chords enter, sounding mysteriously, softly, as if from a distance. One listens with more or less of an unidentifiable apprehension, a particular feeling that is unique to this work, while contemplating this vision of the endlessly flowing waters of the sacred river Alph coursing through immeasurable caverns down to a sunless sea. Now, the brasses enter. A harp is heard. Oboe melody, *espressivo*, and flute countermelody sound together, the flute's faster line mostly stepwise and descending chromatically. Other woodwinds join in. The piano reenters; tempo and dynamics increase; chromatic woodwinds play sixteenth-note triplets on thirds. It is as if a veil is lifting.

A new theme begins, played by flutes and violins. The music accelerates; a huge crescendo goes to *ff*. Now there is even faster movement. A languorous orientalized oboe melody, with the second tone missing, starts up. A flute enters, and tempo quickens again. However, the oboe tune returns, played even more languorously. The flute continues the melody. A still faster pace ensues and a cello soloist plays an augmented version of the tune; next, a variant of it is heard in the clarinet. The orchestra builds in force and a very prolonged climax is heard.

The tempo becomes lively. Fragments of dance, with rhythmic punctuations from the percussion group, float in and out. After this idea is worked up for a time, the music quietens. The last 11 measures look back to the piece's opening.

Contemporary reviewers loved the splendor of the music, the unusual imagination it revealed, the original use of harmony, and the fanciful orchestration. For several years the composition received frequent performances. Owing to the rejection of romanticism and the dominance of neo-classicism after the mid 1920s, Griffes's *Kubla Khan* was shunted to one side. David Diamond gave the new evaluation of the music as follows: "This much over-estimated score has a great deal of fake program atmosphere and very little actual music."[24] The judgment was both prejudiced and unfair. Taste changes, usually in pendulum swings. A work showing the quality of this one deserves to live.

Sho-jo, a Japanese pantomime in one scene, composed in 1917 and revised in 1919, is explicitly indebted to Far-Eastern musical idioms.

Gauthier, on her return from Japan, had given Griffes Japanese melodies that she had written down. Three of them he used in *Sho-jo*, a work that Adolph Bohm had requested for the Ballet Intime. The company, in 1917, included Michio Itow, the Japanese dancer, among its 40 members. The opening performance, under the direction of Marcel Ansotti, was scheduled for August 1917, in Atlantic City.[25]

Sho-jo, the spirit of wine, symbolizes happiness. The dance is of an ever-smiling and wine-imbibing young man who desires a lovely young woman he has envisioned. But her form eludes him and he eventually drops from exhaustion. Griffes's original instrumentation called for three solo woodwinds, harp, percussion, and four strings with mutes. This limited force, he thought, had a kinship to Japanese ensembles. When revised, the scoring was for orchestra. He described what he did as "*developed* Japanese music." He purposely did not "use the term 'idealized.' " Cadman, he said, had not developed his Amerindian tunes, but used them just as themes with harmonizations à la Broadway. Furthermore, modern music tended "more and more toward the archaic, especially the archaism of the East. The ancient Greek modes, the pentatonic scales of China and Japan are much used." He saw "a striving for harmonies which suggest the quarter-tones of Oriental music, and the frequent employ of the characteristic augmented second, as well as of" organ point. He also saw "the Oriental" as more at home with dissonance than consonance. "And all this I have borne in mind in the development of the *Sho-jo* music."[26]

He employs harmonizations in octaves, fifths, fourths, and seconds as more in accord with the East; thirds and sixths are omitted. The instrumentation is laid out so as to sound spare and fragile. The strings give impersonal backing to the tunes played by the woodwinds. The work was a novelty for Americans. No significant portion of the public took the music to heart.

The *Poem* for Flute and Orchestra, of 1918, was far more successful than *Sho-jo*, and is one of Griffes's finest compositions. It was written with the flautist Georges Barrère in mind and premiered in November 1919 by Barrère with the New York Symphony Orchestra. The scoring requires a solo flute, two horns, harp, percussion and strings.[27] An arch structure embraces the music. The quiet melody impresses the ear as an air retrieved from antiquity. At measure 30 a new theme sounds, an augmented inversion of the first tune but much varied. Later we hear an *accelerando* and persistent string chords reiterated in eighth-note triplets. The flute plays agitatedly and high up. Then the tranquil melody returns.

After a recapitulation of the first theme, an *allegro scherzando* ensues and a third theme sounds. Soon the tempo lessens; loudness and speed increase. A hint of the first theme occurs. Stabilization comes with the return of the second theme. Eventually the first theme returns, played by solo viola then the flute. The piece closes very softly.

The music is airy and lovely. Impressionism is on the wane. The shifting moods command attention: for example, the staid unfrivolous beginning contrasted with the spirited dance rhythms suggestive of the East in the middle section. As they were with *Kubla Khan*, contemporary critics were impressed. Richard Aldrich finds it original, indicative of "a true creative impulse," and skillfully crafted. The *Poem* had "real charm and individuality." He finds the mood "grey at the outset, and the orchestration corresponds in color; there is then a dance-like movement of an unusual tonality, with the suggestion of Oriental rhythm and Oriental coloring in the orchestra, delicately scored."[28]

Another composition, a mighty one, was completed the same year as *Poem*: the Sonata for Piano, in three movements, which was revised in 1919. In it, impressionism is nowhere to be found. No verses or descriptive titles preface the movements. However, it is not Bauer's "neoclassic work of austere idiom,"[29] despite the fairly explicit motives, lucid and uncluttered fabric, ordered structures, and economy of means. On the contrary, it evidences considerable feeling, including ardor and ferociousness, rather than detached or reined-in expression, and is not predicated upon eighteenth-century stylistic exemplars. In addition, it is the converse of Gilbert's vernacular idiom. The composition requires concentrated attention from the listener; only then will it disclose the extreme depth of feeling encompassed by its lyricism. The music is taut, arresting, brimming with ideas, and frequently jarring in comparison with the burnished contours of his impressionistic works. The musical language is muscular, surprising, a bit strained perhaps, yet invariably telling. The melodic lines and harmonies are based on an artificial scale that generates tritones and augmented intervals. Unprepared and unresolved dissonances abound.[30] A probable influence was the music of Scriabin. Griffes did hear Katherine Ruth Heyman play the Piano Sonata No. 8 and other pieces by Scriabin and did observe that she gave him "interesting information about exotic scales."[31]

The chromatic first movement is in a sonata form whose sections are articulated more by thematic treatment than key areas. It opens *feroce*, before the restless first theme, *allegretto con moto*, is heard. This theme dominates the measures that follow until the thunderous close of the first section. A contrasting theme, derived from the second half of the first theme, begins, marked *expressivo* and *legato*. Texture thickens; the music makes a big statement before the exposition of ideas ends. The development is on the first theme and continues *agitato molto* until the recapitulation of the two themes. After the coda, the second movement is entered into without any pause.

The eloquent slow movement, opens *molto tranquillo*. The melody is solemn and chantlike. A more agitated second section ensues that makes reference to the conflict of tones heard with the initial theme of the first movement. This is followed by a quiet and altogether lovely contrasting passage. Next comes a return to the opening melody. The movement closes with a clanging *accelerando* that leaves everything up in the air.

The last movement is in modified sonata form. For the most part, the first theme sounds nervous and unsettled. A new, richer textured idea enters after a few measures. Next, the first theme is developed. Then we hear a lengthy slower section. A *presto* coda ends the movement.

At least three more pieces were composed just before the composer's death. One of them, Three Preludes for piano, takes less than five minutes to perform, omits indications for dynamics and expression, and goes from sounding unsettled, to music of some delicacy, and ends up implying an expression both abstracted and rather urgent. The musical idiom concurs with that of the sonata.

The second composition, *Salut au Monde*, is music intended for a festival drama based on texts by Whitman. Here, Griffes employs several untraditional procedures, including the outright use of chords built on open fifths and choral parts without exact pitch designations. He blocked out an instrumentation for a chamber ensemble that includes woodwinds, brass, percussion, harps, and piano, which Edmond Rickett utilized in order to complete the score.[32]

The third composition, *Two Sketches for String Quartet*, based on Indian themes is unusual for Griffes, since it is based on Amerindian melodies.[33] The inward looking first sketch, *lento e mesto*, features warm pensive lyricism and draws on a "farewell song of the Chippewa Indians," according to the published score. The five-tone scale that Griffes employs, the modal flavor of the passages, and the treatment of the tune do not sound particularly "Indian." The first violin plays an ethereal first theme high in its range; the viola introduces a ruminative second theme (the Chippewa-Indian one) in its lower range; and all four instruments intone a third theme loudly and passionately. After some working out in imitation, the second theme returns strongly accented and very loud to close the first section. All three themes sound related to each other. A second section starts off with a new melodic idea, and after a dozen measures employs some striking colorings as the cello plays pizzicato and the viola plays a thirty-second-note rhythmic pattern *sul ponticello*. Eventually the first theme returns to end the movement. The more extroverted second sketch, *allegro giocoso*, is a rhythmic dance that tries to sound "Indian" but ends up sounding a bit commonplace, especially in its first half. The second half of the movement grows more chromatic and shifts its style: to one directly beholden to Debussy's string quartet. No specific Amerindian tune is cited for the movement.

Audiences found the piece most enjoyable. When the Flonzaly Quartet performed it in Boston, Philip Hale wrote:

The first Sketch, based on a mournful theme, is singularly beautiful in the poetic treatment, in the dexterous employment of the instruments without a vain attempt to procure orchestral color. There is no anxious striving after effects, no desire to straighten the drowsy bourgeois in his seat, no effort to be original at any cost. The music is of a strange beauty, yet not remote, but warmly human. The other Sketch, ingenious and entertaining, was written, no doubt appropriately, in more realistic fashion; one might say more in the spirit of George Catlin. . . . "[34]

As should be clear, Griffes was an tireless investigator of widely different modes of musical expression, whether in melody, harmony, rhythm, or instrumentation. Germany, Russia, France, the United States, and the Far East provided a continuous input of disparate approaches to music that stimulated his own creativity. Fortunately, Griffes was able to assimilate these diverse influences into his own works so as to retain his own identity. He was blessed with an innate musical gift which he united to workmanship of significant quality. His extraordinary talent for programmatic composition stressing mood rather than description and his responsiveness to unusual tonal colorations of utmost subtlety set him apart from most of his peers. For the reasons just cited, his music retains its vitality and commands attention to this day. Yet, he worked as an artist for barely more than a dozen years before he died. What he might have become is, of course, a matter that must be left to conjecture. What he left us are several masterworks that remain as significant now as in the years they were created.

MARION BAUER

Of French descent, Bauer (1887-1955) met Griffes in 1917, befriended him, and became a champion of his music.[35] Born in Walla Walla, Washington, she demonstrated early musical gifts. For this reason, her father, an amateur musician, commenced her musical education. Later she traveled to Paris, where she studied piano with Raoul Pugno and theory with Nadia Boulanger and André Gédalge. Her instructors also included Henry Holden Huss, Eugene Hefley, Walter Henry Rothwell, and Jean Paul Ertel. She herself became an important figure in the advancement of music in the United States. She taught at New York University and the Juilliard School, and lectured annually at the summer Chautauqua Institute. Her books and articles won her a good-sized following among the general music public. An active abettor of American music, she helped start the American Music Guild and served on the board of the League of Composers.

Although her musical works are not in the same league as those of Griffes, several of them deserve more than the neglect they are accorded today. Many of her compositions are short—songs and piano pieces. A lesser number are for orchestra (some of these are orchestrations of piano pieces) or for chorus and orchestra. In one, the romanticism learned from her Central-European teachers may come to the fore; in another, the impressionism that she heard in Paris and encountered in the music of Griffes prevails. Most compositions integrate both approaches, with the latter usually predominating. Significantly, the chapter on "Impressionistic Methods," in her book *Twentieth Century Music*, contains musical examples from the works of Debussy, Ravel, and Griffes, and from her own works.[36]

Although not averse to using folk material in some of her compositions, she showed annoyance at the European attitude that "considers jazz the one original contribution that America has made to modern music. And to Europeans, music is not typically American unless it reflects the Negro or the Indian."[37] Although she did not hesitate to introduce posttraidic harmonies into her music and never tried to incorporate intense emotion within any piece, she never repudiated the triadic tradition, nor accepted Stravinsky's neoclassic strictures against music indicative of mood or feeling:

The artist of today [1933] has a phobia against any display of feeling. In the fear of being sentimental he has sacrificed sentiment. He rationalizes to the point of revolting against the nineteenth century, the epoch of romantic thinking and belief in a soul, and of establishing an affinity with the eighteenth century, when art and thought were intellectual, classic, and "pure." To my way of thinking, however, our artist is building a false foundation for his declaration of faith . . . Bach, Mozart, or Haydn were [not] coldly classical and chastely intellectual! They were expressing emotions in the means at their command. . . .[38]

When she wrote of the attempt by contemporary composers to escape the obvious, avoid time-worn combinations, utilize medieval modes in place of major-minor scales, explore new ways of cadencing other than dominant to tonic progressions, and novel harmonizations (like chords with added seconds, others sounding unresolved appogiatura tones simultaneous with a base triad, and still others built on intervals of the fourth or fifth rather than the third,) she was referring not only to the propensities of several of the bolder contemporary composers but also those of herself.[39]

Her songs won praise in her day for their ability to reveal the pervasive moods of the verse and for the sometimes exceptional yet discreet procedures employed to underline these moods. The music always expressed feeling; but also apparent was control over strong emotion. Frequently mentioned among her songs are the *Four Poems*, opus 16 (1916), settings of verse by John Gould Fletcher, which Goddard Lieberson finds commanding in structure, engrossing in harmony, and subdued in emotional expression. William Treat Upton praises opus 16 without reservation: "We see it made perfectly clear that the freest possible use of modern color and effect is entirely compatible with an underlying sense of form and a very real appreciation of the value of an expressive melodic line, as we have already seen it so abundantly proved in the songs of Griffes. Indeed, in easy command of modern technique, in rich pictorial quality, in vivid play of the imagination and sustained dramatic interest, these songs may worthily take their place beside Griffes' own." Upton also thinks highly of "Roses Breathe in the Night" (1921), which he finds similar to Duparc's "Chanson Triste." When, in 1944, Charles Mills heard her song "The Harp," he described it as a impressive composition and one of the finest contemporary American songs that he had heard.[40]

In a handful of works, Marion Bauer circumspectly put borrowed materials into service: for example, Amerindian in *Sun Splendor* (1926) and *Indian Pipes* (1927), both of them originally for piano but later orchestrated; and African in *Lament on African Themes* (1928) for chamber orchestra. Among her well-received chamber works were the Violin Sonata, opus 14 (1922), the *Fantasia quasi una Sonata* for violin and piano, opus 18 (1928), the String Quartet, opus 20 (1928), and the Viola/Clarinet Sonata, opus 22 (1935).

When the League of Composers sponsored a concert in 1928, where Bauer's music was heard alongside music by Marc Blizstein and Roy Harris, Henrietta Strauss noted in her review that Bauer was the solitary abstainer from absurd explanations of what her music was all about. Strauss added: "Her string quartet, while neither as finely conceived nor as moving as her sonata for violin and piano, was invested with the only sincere emotion manifested."[41] For the most part, late works, like the Concertino for Oboe, Clarinet, and String Quartet, opus 32 (1943) and the Trio Sonata for Flute, Piano, and Cello, opus 40 (1944), were regarded as slight, attractive, straightforward compositions whose antecedents were French.[42]

We cannot help but wonder why Marion Bauer has been excluded from most recent histories and encyclopedias on American music, given her talent as a composer and her importance as an educator, writer on musical subjects, promoter of American music, and service to the American musical community. We also wonder why her music is neither performed or recorded. It is superior to many a contemporary European piece that easily wins a hearing.

NOTES

1. Marion Bauer, "Charles T. Griffes as I Remember Him," *Musical Quarterly* 29 (1943), p. 363.

2. Bauer, "Charles T. Griffes," p. 356.

3. Edward Maisel, *Charles T. Griffes*, updated ed. (New York: Knopf, 1984), p. 216.

4. Irving Babbitt, *On Being Creative* (Boston: Houghton Mifflin, 1932), p. 27.

5. Maisel, *Charles T. Griffes*, p. 153.

6. A Walter Kramer, "Charles Tomlinson Griffes: Cut Down in His Prime, a Victim of Our Barbarous Neglect of Genius," *Musical America*, 22 May 1930, reprinted in the Program Book for the concert of the Boston Symphony Orchestra, on 15–16 January 1932, p. 732.

7. Wilson D. Wallis, *Culture and Progress* (New York: Whittlesey House, 1930), p. 10.

8. Charles T. Griffes, *Four Impressions*, ed. Donna K. Anderson (New York: Peters, 1970).

9. Charles T. Griffes, *Song of the Dagger* (New York: Peters, for Henmar Press, 1983).

10. William Treat Upton, *Art-Song in America* (Boston: Ditson, 1930), p. 257; "The Songs of C. T. Griffes," *Musical Quarterly* 9 (1923), p. 320.

11. Charles T. Griffes, "An Old Song Re-Sung" (New York: Schirmer, 1920).

12. Charles T. Griffes, *Three Poems by Fiona MacLeod* (New York: Schirmer, 1918).

13. Garry E. Clarke, *Essays on American Music* (Westport, Connecticut: Greenwood, 1977), p. 94.

14. Bauer, "Charles T. Griffes," p. 365.

15. Ibid., p. 365.

16. Maisel, *Charles T. Griffes*, pp. 185, 187–88.

17. Charles T. Griffes, *Roman Sketches* for the piano (New York: Schirmer, 1917).

18. In this regard, see the remarks of Norman Peterkin, in "Charles T. Griffes," *Chesterian*, New Series No. 30 (1923), p. 163.

19. A. Walter Kramer, "Charles T. Griffes: Cut Down in His Prime, a Victim of Our Barbarous Neglect of Genius," *Musical America* (22 May 1920), p. 39.

20. Bauer, "Charles T. Griffes," p. 370.

21. Maisel, *Charles T. Griffes*, pp. 194, 197–98.

22. See the book of clippings in the Boston Public Library, Shelf No. **M.460.122.

23. Charles T. Griffes, *The Pleasure-Dome of Kubla Khan*, Symphonic Poem for Grand Orchestra (New York: Schirmer, 1920).

24. David Diamond, in *Modern Music* 16 (1939), p. 275.

25. *New York Times* (5 August 1917), section 8, p. 5.

26. Maisel, *Charles T. Griffes*, p. 205.

27. Charles T. Griffes, *Poem* for Flute and Orchestra (New York: Schirmer, 1951).

28. Richard Aldrich, "Music," *New York Times* (17 November 1919), p. 20.

29. Bauer, "Charles T. Griffes," p. 376.

30. Charles T. Griffes, Sonata for Piano (New York: Schirmer, 1921).

31. Maisel, *Charles T. Griffes*, p. 179.

32. Bauer, "Charles T. Griffes," p. 374.

33. Charles T. Griffes, *Two Sketches for String Quartet*, based on Indian themes (New York: Schirmer, 1922).

34. Quoted in John Tasker Howard, *Charles Tomlinson Griffes* (New York: Schirmer, 1923), p. 20.

35. Bauer, "Charles T. Griffes," p. 366.

36. Marion Bauer, *Twentieth Century Music* (New York: Putnam's Sons, 1933), pp. 131–159.

37. Ibid., p. 270.

38. Ibid., p. 294.

39. Ibid., pp. 128, 142, 157, 236.

40. Goddard Lieberson, "More One-Man Shows," *Modern Music* 14 (1937), p. 93; William Treat Upton, *Art-Song in America* (Boston: Ditson, 1930), p. 15; Charles Mills, in *Modern Music* 21 (1944), p. 191.

41. Henrietta Strauss, in *Modern Music* 5 (March/April 1928), p. 28; paginated by issue rather than by volume.

42. Donald Fuller, in *Modern Music* 21 (1944), p. 238–39; see also Charles Mills, in *Modern Music* 22 (1946), p. 144.

Chapter Seven

John Alden Carpenter

Carpenter was born (1876) in Park Ridge, Illinois, and died (1951) in Chicago. His mother, a trained but amateur singer, stimulated his interest in music. The German-educated Amy Fay and the Viennese musician Ernest Seeboeck, both resident in Chicago, were his first music teachers. He would graduate from Harvard College in 1897, after having studied there with John Knowles Paine. Unlike Daniel Gregory Mason, Carpenter always admired Paine, thinking himself "fortunate to be under his guidance." He spoke of his "deep affection and . . . lasting debt" to Paine, who made time for him even while in the throes of composing the opera *Azara*.[1] He would also study briefly, in Rome, with Edward Elgar, the noted English composer, and at greater length with Bernard Ziehn, in Chicago, a fairly advanced music theorist.

For much of his life (1909-36) he worked in his father's firm, George B. Carpenter & Co., a Chicago enterprise dealing in mill, railroad, and vessel supplies.[2] Carpenter always resented being called a businessman composer, insisting that when he gave his attention to music he was a composer and nothing else.[3] His teachers' precepts and various contemporary compositions that he heard influenced his musical thinking. The style that he evolved was a compendium of everything he had experienced, which he digested and shaped into a manner of expression all his own. Although he would not jettison musical tradition, he left himself open to contemporary trends: those from France (Debussy, Ravel, Stravinsky) and those on home soil (jazz, popular music). After he heard Stravinsky's Symphony in C, he wrote a letter to Alice James, dated 21 January 1941, stating: "I was fascinated by its workmanship, but sadly missed the old Russian 'oomph' which seems now to be permanently watered out of his native blood. But he is a great man anyway, and I love him." Five years later, he heard Benjamin Britten's tradition-linked opera *Peter Grimes*, and described it as a "striking and important new work."[4] Carpenter believed that he could not afford to overlook any contemporary music or to brush off jazz and popular music. He found Amerindian music elemental; but when removed from its native environment, it was deprived of its natural traits and strength. African-American music was likewise elemental, but if used artistically, care had to be taken not to lose the "felicitous sense of harmony and . . . lilt in rhythm that's irresistible."[5]

Almost from the beginning of his creative career, he specialized in pictured fantasy, urbane moods, delightful whimsy, lively wit, and sentiment—now tender, delicate, or restrained, and now assertively rhythmic or raffish. Carpenter, who held to firm standards of propriety, would rarely allow his music to sound coarse or ill-mannered. Nor would it harbor measures that were overly emotional. Neither Wagner's transcendent visions, nor Tchaikovsky's passionate subjectivity, nor Strauss's overripe textures found a place in his scores. He shared with Chadwick, Hill, Farwell, Gilbert, and Griffes the desire to escape from the established German way of thinking and writing that had both stimulated the development of music in America and drained the vitality from too much American music. Some degree of circumspection guided his pen when he worked on a composition, however much it leaned toward the vernacular. Still and all, he was capable of compassion conveyed poetically, as in *The Birthday of the Infanta*; of empathy with the human condition, as in *Krazt Kat* and *Skyscrapers*; and of an absorbed observation of the flow of existence, as in *Sea Drift*. "The role of music and art," Carpenter said, "is to nourish and sustain people."[6]

CARPENTER'S MUSICAL LANGUAGE

Carpenter composed quite a few programmatic compositions, some given titles only, others provided with a detailed description. He confirmed that his music was normally inspired by outside sources, stating: "With only a few exceptions [notably the two symphonies and his chamber music] everything that I have written has started from a non-musical basis." That non-musical basis had to give outlet to a special mood or emotion: "All music that lives is based on a mood, whether directly or indirectly."[7]

The attributes belonging to most of his works are not difficult to detect. The listener can ordinarily understand and enjoy the music directly, without elaborate preparation prior to a concert. Tunes are clearcut, harmonies appropriate to the tunes, and textures mostly homophonic. Many works move with a pulsing swing. When contemporary writers pointed out the "jazz" elements in several of his compositions, they were referring to rhythms and tone production connected with ragtime, blues, and the styles associated with American marches and Broadway shows.

Exact reiteration of brief melodic phrases, harmonic-rhythmic patterns, and, sometimes, larger sections assist in comprehension. In most instances, Carpenter intends his musical diction to be affable and accessible. Indeed, sportiveness is a captivating attribute of some compositions, an attribute found in works written throughout his career. From less capable hands, such compositions may emerge sounding half-finished and extemporaneous, progressing capriciously, like preliminary studies. The composer may lack the adroit judgment and attention to the means for synthesizing tonal quality, melodic figures, and form that he needs in order to endow the music with artistry. These virtues, fortunately, Carpenter does have. He succeeds in offering sophisticated and satisfying recreation.

Yet, his music contains surprises, as well as jolts; how a piece will unfold cannot always be foretold. He does not invariably offer immunity from incertitude and stress. In addition, quite a few works pesistently veer toward the melancholic. On occasion, gloom can permeate the final measures or his music glimmers darkly and enigmatically, as in *Sea Drift*.

Although one hesitates to call Carpenter an impressionist after the French fashion,[8] he does use the paraphernalia of impressionism: modal and whole-tone alongside major-minor scales, evasive tonality often the result of altered triadic intervals, unresolved dissonance, sweeps of parallel harmonies, and coloristic and non-functional chords. On the other hand, rhythm, especially when syncopated, declares itself American. Melody proceeds in pliable fashion, now and again sounding Spanish, or suggesting African-American blues or songs of Tin Pan Alley. Harmony can turn percussive, harsh, repudiating the triad for vertical constructions in seconds and fourths. In short, during a great deal of Carpenter's life, his musical style remains pliant, the idiom, variable, in order to accommodate whatever the desired expression. This is in contrast to most of the other composers taken up in this study, the majority of whose works show greater stylistic consistency.

PIANO PIECES AND SONGS

Carpenter was an able pianist. Yet, there is scarcely anything major among Carpenter's compositions for piano. *Minuet* and *Twilight Reverie*, both published in 1894, are agreeable, cautious, and proficiently written pieces from his student years at Harvard. The more substantial Piano Sonata in G Minor, written during his senior year, was offered as a graduation exercise in 1897. Paine undoubtedly guided its composition.

Its solemn first movement, in sonata-allegro form, opens with a big, nicely sculpted, declarative first subject that is not too distanced from the idiom of Edward MacDowell's first two piano sonatas (1893, 1895). After a softer repetition of it, a heavier and tenser transitional passage leads to a calm, clearly expressed second subject, which is then nicely expanded upon. The development section and recapitulation are as regularly and lucidly set forth as the exposition. The continual rhythmic flow never experiences a stoppage from beginning to end. The second movement, *adagio con moto*, is in ternary form. Its chordally-inspired first theme projects melancholy very well but undergoes too many repetitions. The Finale, *allegro con brio, feroce*, is a rondo whose music develops a great deal of drive and impresses the listener with its urgent stress, save for the quiet lyrical second subordinate theme. It is altogether an admirable accomplishment for a young musician but hardly indicative of the music still to come.

A *Nocturne* from 1898 reveals him trying out barbershop-like downward-sliding chromatic harmonies and a top line that evolves as if sung by a vocalist. A *Polonaise Américaine* (1912) hints at the "Spanish" Carpenter of later works. Harmony is bolder, more assertive; melody not as fetching as one might wish. An *Impromptu* (1913) shows him inclined towards French music with its clever rhythms and modal harmonies. Other brief characteristic pieces for piano followed: *Little Indian* (1916), *Little Dancer* (1917), *Tango Américain* (1920), five *Diversions* (1922). Each is pleasant to hear; none pursues new pathways.

Carpenter's songs are far more consequential than the piano pieces. Even the earlier ones show him less timid and conventional. By 1914, an unnamed writer in *Musical America* was describing him as a well-known "composer of art-songs of a peculiarly modern type." Songs like "The Green River," "The Cock Shall Crow," and "Don't Ceäre," the writer said, were "decidedly fine pieces of work." The 17 songlets comprising *Improving Songs for Anxious Children* came in for praise: "There are many harmonic touches in these songs of Mr. Carpenter's which are individually conceived and which have been ingeneously written down within technical limitations. For the piano accompaniments have been kept as simple as possible so that they may be played as well as sung by juveniles."[9]

Three years later, writes Thomas Pierson in his study of Carpenter, prominent singers (Kirsten Flagstad, Marion Anderson, Gladys Swarthout, Maggie Teyete) included his songs in their repertoires. Alma Gluck was quoted in a *New York Times* interview, 7 October 1914, as saying that she found him a serious song writer and an outstanding composer: "He has the force and originality of Strauss and the refinement and charm of Chausson. But more than that, he is himself."[10]

Carefully considered harmonies, transparent textures, refined techniques akin to those found in French music, and an occasional folklike tone somewhat reminiscent of that heard in a few songs by George Chadwick and Arthur Foote occur in the 12 songs published in 1912 and 1913.[11] For example, the through-composed song "The Green River" (1912), text by Lord Alfred Douglas, starts slowly, with its opening measure sounding the mediant-seventh chord of B Major. Tonic chords are avoided. Spare single-tone lines, half-step chromaticism, and elusive tonality produce a dreamlike background to the words "I know a green grass path that leaves the field/And, like a running river,—winds along/ Into a leafy wood, where no throng/Of birds at noon-day." The loneliness of the scene is enhanced by the declaiming voice, which descends monotonously by half-steps. The vocal line grows more lyrical and at last, on the last word of "and no soft throats yield/Their music to the moon," the listener hears a tonic chord for the first time. Yet, tonality constantly remains unsettled, nicely limning the unease and longing of the speaker. Later, the unexpected outburst of feeling on the words "Let it be shape of sorrow with wan face./Or love" is extremely effective after all of the suppressed feeling that has gone before. Loudness grows and a telling addition of a treble countermelody in the piano heightens the expression.

To cite a second example, "Don't Ceäre" was also published in 1912. The poem by William Barnes is in a Dorsetshire dialect. Carpenter's music is meant to sound animated and jocose. The setting is strophic. The music remains simple and mostly diatonic. The melodic structure is in four parts: AABC, and the first two sections resemble the Scottish air associated with Burns's *Comin' Thro' the Rye*. At the end of the last stanza, the melody indulges in skips of the fifth rather than the previous conjunct motion, and the accompaniment executes a delightfully jaunty high-treble countermelody.

Two song cycles contain his most highly praised songs: the six songs of *Gitanjali* (Song Offerings") to words by the Bengali poet Rabindranath Tagore (1913) and the four of *Water Colors* to words by various Chinese poets (1916). Speaking of the former, Felix Borowski parallels the remarks of other writers on music when he commends their comeliness, honest melodiousness, harmonic resourcefulness, and distinctiveness when compared with the usual American song-compositions. In the latter, he finds "an irresistible combination of whimsicality and expressiveness" that was typical of Carpenter's music in general.[12]

Tagore's *Gitanjali*, published in 1912 and awarded the Nobel Prize (1913), harbors brief, earnest statements in free verse. Modeled on ancient devotional poetry, they veer between moments of rapture and others of self-possession. Direct and oblique meanings emerge from the words. The settings by Carpenter capture atmosphere and feeling. The music owes a debt to Debussy's impressionism; but fully developed individuality predominates, not slavish imitation. Each poem receives a treatment all its own. The winsome "When I Bring You Colour'd Toys," one of the most admired songs of the lot, moves briskly. Sentimentality never mars its measures. Texture remains airy and open. The accompaniment produces a *fauxbourdon* effect with fourths by the right hand going back and forth on adjacent intervals, and the thirds supplied by the left hand. Also much admired, "The Sleep that Flits on Baby's Eyes" derives much of its effect from chords kept in root position and from the use of a tonic-ninth chord, with its fifth augmented to close two of the phrases. A third outstanding piece, "Light, My Light" is in praise of the light that brings joy. Streams of harmony over a pedal, nondominant seventh chords, and chords emphasizing the augmented fifth prevail. Otherwise harmonic change is slow, even though the music goes at a good clip. The low-pitched, sonorous, minor-key seriousness of "On the Day When Death Will Knock at the Door," and the slowly clanging toll of bells, with high treble and low bass chords alternating of "I Am Like a Reminant of a Cloud of Autumn" are other high points of this set. The music of *Water Colors* intimates, rather than duplicates, Chinese music. Arpeggiated figures give delicacy and impart gracefulness to "On a Screen" (text by Li-Po), and "The Odalisque" (text by Yü-hsi). "Highwayman" (text by Li-Shê) has fuller textures and admits many chords constructed on fourths rather than thirds. The coquettish playfulness of "To a Young Gentleman" (poem collected by Confucius) features dainty clashes of a major second. The sensitivity of the composer to the spirit of the poems is everywhere apparent.

If the listener can accept that Carpenter is not trying to don an African-American mantle, then the infectious jazz-derived accentuation in *Four Negro Songs* (1926), to poems of Langston Hughes, can also become quite enjoyable.

CHAMBER MUSIC

Carpenter wrote little chamber music. A Violin Sonata, String Quartet, and Piano Quintet comprise most of it. His Sonata for Violin and Piano was completed in 1911 and published by Schirmer in 1913. Several writers have spoken of its Frenchness, in particular the debt it owes to Franck's Violin Sonata. However, except for mention of the cyclical return of musical ideas, the writers remain vague about the connection between the two works and to some extent disagree with each other. Borowski declares the first movement has a poetic atmosphere akin to Franck's; Pierson speaks of the work's cyclical form and the Franckian atmosphere of the slow movement; Carl Engel believes the third movement reminiscent of Grieg and Franck; and John Tasker Howard finds a Franckian spirit in the entire work. They do agree that Carpenter does not merely parrot Franck, that he reveals his proper person.[13] Yet, whatever Franckisms there are appear on the surface, and Franck's manner of building up passages to peaks of intense emotion is not Carpenter's. Instead, suavity and sophistication predominate. Moreover, the cyclical idea was already old when Franck and d'Indy applied it—works by Beethoven, Schumann, and Berlioz, among others, had already evidenced it.

Admittedly, the work leans more to the Gallic than the German, except for the *poco meno mosso* in 3/4 time of the second movement, where for a short while artlessness replaces the supremely cultivated sound. In all four movements, one hears diverse non-dominant harmonies with added seconds, sixths, or sevenths that produce intriguing resonances. The first movement, a *larghetto*, concentrates on two thematic ideas, the second redeploying elements of the principal theme. The working-out of the two themes is expert, and, except for a couple of quivers of passion, controlled in expression. The principal feeling is one of a rather deceptive tranquility, of the sort imparted in French pastoral paintings of the eighteenth century.

The second movement begins with a very loud, boldly stated first theme, and moves on to the less speedy, Schubertian contrasting melody already mentioned. A sort of development ensues, with the two ideas more ruminated on than altered in any structural fashion. Both themes are recapitulated, with the second freely varied in its restatement.

The third movement, *largo mistico*, begins with a muted violin playing a subdued melody. The slightly faster contrasting melody refers back to the opening idea of the first movement, though quite altered. (It is heard again in the Finale.) A brief return to the first tune, the violin now sans mute, concludes the movement.

Fast and jocose are the directions for the Finale, whose principal theme is clearly based on that of the first movement. A cadenza occurring later in the violin also alludes to the first movement's principal theme. The violin engages in brilliant passage work throughout the movement. Eventually there is a grand peroration, with the principal theme stated in longer notes and slower tempo. This is by far the most impressive of the four movements, its measures filled with happily invented sounds and forming a fitting conclusion to the whole.

The sonata was much admired in its time. After hearing it, John McCormack wrote in the *Musical Leader*, 26 December 1916: "If this was the work of any but an American, it would be one of the sensations. Every musician would be raving about it. It is immense in its bigness of thought and working out."[14]

In 1927, Carpenter completed a Quartet for Stringed Instruments, and had it premiered and published the next year.[15] The fast first movement is in A Minor and common time mostly. The vigorous and loudly-exposed principal theme exploits a rhythmic pattern consisting of eighth notes grouped 3 + 3 + 2 in a measure. The violin both skips over wide intervals and glides through half-step chromatics. A slower moving, pensive contrasting theme, marked *rubato*, sounds later against harmonies featuring the augmented fourth (or diminshed fifth). One hears no clear tonality, although the beginning points to E-flat Minor. Interestingly, the first unequivocally triadic harmony without a seventh, a C-Minor chord, is not heard until measure 155, at which point the viola introduces a new, Spanish-sounding section that persists until the violin recapitulates the first theme. Yet, the Spanish flavoring soon returns and continues until the close. The next movement begins without pause.

The *adagio* second movement has a ternary form and progressive tonality. The opening idea, *con sordino*, is based on constantly reiterated melodic rhythmic patterns of one-measure length. Its middle portion goes faster. The return of the first melody is marked *lento*. The next and final movement is also to begin without pause. The Finale, moderate in speed, opens on a Spanish-like dance tune. An Appalachian-folk type of melody succeeds. Eventually a lengthy slow section, with melody in the cello, is heard. Here, the American popular-ballad idiom is vaguely called to mind. Later, thematic references are made to the first theme of the first movement before the piece ends with a return of the Finale's opening tune.

The similarity of expression that prevails in all three movements makes for some monotony. However warm and expressive the music seems, it does cut back on the seriousness and moments of deep reflection that attended the Violin Sonata. There is greater indulgence in the sheer sensuousness of the sound. On balance the quartet strikes the ear as offering a congenial, inviting, and undemanding experience.

The Quintet for Piano and Strings, like the String Quartet, carries its weight lightly. Composed in Algiers in 1934, it introduces melodic material heard in this North African country. Some elements from this composition later found their way into the Second Symphony.[16]

WORKS FOR LARGE ENSEMBLES

Gitanjali won Carpenter acclaim as an American song composer possessing fine creative and artistic ability. The suite *Adventures in a Perambulator* (1914) was the first of a series of compositions that won him fame as a gifted American composer whose orchestral voice was new, assured, and unique. He had written two earlier orchestral works, a *Berceuse* (1908) and a Suite for Orchestra (1909), without attracting widespread attention. Those two works, however, had given him valuable experience in handling the orchestral medium. *Adventures in a Perambulator* also benefited from the many days of inquiry that Carpenter devoted to the sound of individual instruments and of instrumental combinations while attending rehearsals of the Chicago Symphony.[17] The Chicago Symphony premiered the work in 1915. Shortly thereafter, even as singers performed his songs far and wide, orchestral conductors of major ensembles included his suite in their programs. Marion Bauer spoke of the "new American impressionism" that she detected in *Adventures* and in the Concertino that came out in 1915. Paul Rosenfeld, who had a few reservations about the piece, commented on Carpenter's charm, his adult commentary on a child's world, and his pseudo-realistic impressionism, quite unlike what was heard in Debussy's *The Children's Corner* and Ravel's *Ma Mère L'Oye*. Mason said *Adventures* was essentially Gallic in economy of means, distinctive color, and ironic wit.[18]

Carpenter had already indicated his interest in children by composing the *Improving Songs for Anxious Children* in 1901-02. *Adventures in a Perambulator* came into existence 12 years later. The composition is based on an ingenious program told from the standpoint of a baby who is being wheeled about, and is in six divisions.[19] It is scored for a large orchestra, used discreetly. The percussion group includes xylophone, glockenspiel, bells, and celesta. The harmony remains predominantly triadic, though sequences of parallel fourths and fifths are occasionally heard. Textures are clear. Feeling is held carefully within bounds. Orchestration sounds French. Americanisms are few. Intellectualization is kept at a minimum. From beginning to end, Carpenter's imagination mixes drollness and whimsy with fantasy and poetic expression. The listener is invited to relax and enjoy.

The first section, *"En Voiture,"* is a *larghetto* in 3/4 meter: "I go out;" "I am placed in my perambulator . . . and we are off!" It briefly introduces the recurring motives that depict the nurse (in two cellos), the perambulator (in celesta and strings), and the baby ("almost immediately [and over the perambulator idea], the first flute announces the ingenuous idea, a descending scale, which stands for 'Myself' ").[20] A limited amount of parallel diatonic chord movement occurs.

Next comes the persuasively funny "The Policeman," whose motive sounds in the woodwinds against strings playing *pizzicato*: "Round like a ball; taller than my Father. Blue—fearful—fascinating." The policeman's lumbering gait is nicely sketched out. After a bit of elaboration on the motive, the policeman (solo bassoon) and the nurse (solo violins) indulge in a musical flirtation until a muted trumpet and also a hint of the perambulator theme cut in. The first part is now recapitulated.

"The Hurdy-Gurdy" is livelier than the previous section: "Absorbing noise . . . so gay!" It introduces intriguing allusions to popular music and a snatch of Verdi sounding in two xylophones and harp, and then features a modest waltz based on the perambulator theme with some interpolations of the nurse and baby motives. Nurse and baby sway to the hurdy-gurdy man's playing until the policeman arrives to chase him away. The section ends very quietly, with the hurdy-gurdy man playing in the distance.

"The Lake" has a flute suggest lightly ruffled water; and strings and horns, waves: "Waves and sunbeams . . . dancing, swinging." The music shows the composer indulging in sentiment rather than humor, and is slow and quiescent. Brief lyric phrases drift in and out of the harmony.

In "Dogs," tunes like "Ach Du Lieber Augustin" and "Where, Oh, Where Has My Little Dog Gone?" enter the woodwinds. The latter tune forms the basis of a short preposterous fugue, to suggest "dogs playing 'Follow the Leader.' " The animals, "lots of them," are projected as cordial and well-behaved creatures.

Finally, one hears "Dreams," an august restatement of the main motives, especially a broad version of the theme identified with the nurse, but in no definite key. At the end, the music consists of a lullaby based on the baby and nurse themes. Now the baby feels contentment, finds pleasure in lying still with closed eyes, just listening to the wheels of the perambulator.

Philip Hale heard *Adventures* in Boston, in 1915. He chides the composer for a few musical mannerisms but endorses the whole as pleasingly whimsical. "The Lake" and "Dreams," he says, are filled with sentiment, "at times emotion," and therefore contribute "plausible contrast." "Dogs" is "well expressed," but Hale finds it foolish and recommends cutting it out. His conclusion is that Carpenter had "delicate fancy," "vivid imagination," "surprising facility and ingenuity," and "truly individual expression." The numerous harmonic effects are attractive and original. The writing for orchestra is "singularly effective, by felicitous combinations of timbres, by the peculiar use of instruments, and especially by the daring and successful treatment of the pulsatile section." He describes the music as "ultra-modern with a respect for flowing lines," but "not a new chapter in the gospel of deliberate and sensational ugliness." Humor is genuine in the policeman episode. "The Hurdy-Gurdy" is a daring "tour de force with an intoxicating use of xylophones." Hale mentions the influence of French composers and possibly Strauss, but he feels that Carpenter thinks for himself and has "his own manner of expression. This music would command respect and admiration in any country."[21]

A year after the completion of *Adventures*, Carpenter offered the public a second work that would be much talked about, the Concertino for Piano and Orchestra. It was given a first performance in Chicago, in 1916, with Percy Grainger at the piano. In the program notes for that concert, Carpenter stated:

Not to impose upon it a definite 'program' but merely to establish the mood of the piece, it may be suggested that the Concertino is, in effect, a light-hearted conversation between piano and orchestra—as between two friends who have traveled different paths and become a little garrulous over their separate experiences. The conversation is mostly of rhythms—American, oriental and otherwise. . . . In form, the Concertino is in three short movements . . . the last two separated by an almost imperceptible pause. Each movement is in the simplest song form—first subject, second subject, and repetition—except the last movement, which has a short coda based on the first subject in the first movement.[22]

The first movement, *allegro con moto*, opens on a syncopated one-measure melodic-rhythmic pattern, which is heard six times in the low strings; then the piano enters with its own syncopated subject, a Latin-Americanish march-like tune.[23] Soon, the violins join the piano on the subject. Variants on the ideas heard in this opening will be sprinkled throughout the Concertino. The middle section introduces a somewhat broader subject (a ragtime ballad), first heard in the violins, next picked up by the piano, then played by oboes, clarinets, and piano and violins— as the music becomes increasingly animated and sharply accentuated. Eventually a recapitulation of the first section ensues. The movement dallies on exposed intervals of the fourth and fifth. Harmonic motion toward a reposeful perfect cadence is avoided. Cross-rhythms abound. Clusters of tones are stressed percussively. The measures are gathered into loosely joined episodes.[24]

The slow movement, a *lento grazioso*, contains a graceful, yet sadly expressive first subject, the piano playing a one-measure melodic-rhythmic pattern and muted cellos playing a *legato* melody with seventh tone absent and fourth tone scarcely used. It sounds like an impressive syncopated spiritual. The middle section provides a fine contrast. At one point the piano is made to imitate chimes. After the recapitulation of the opening, the piano and cellos hold their final notes, and immediately the Finale follows.

The Finale, in 5/8 meter, has a theme organized in irregular patterns of two quarter notes and one eighth note or a half note and an eighth note. The measures are charged with a hard, percussive fervor. In the middle, a curious waltz breaks out and features the tinsely sound of harp and glockenspiel. One is reminded of the hurdy-gurdy waltz in *Adventures*. After the return of the opening, the syncopated ideas from the beginning of the first movement give a potent finish to the composition.

All three movements revel in a jazz-like and popular music atmosphere, one also with a Latin tinge. It is a composition of boundless imagination and vivid and showy conceits, full of unexpected changes and enticing resonances. A bold venture for its time, the Concertino was an experiment in bringing the rhythmic vitality and unique instrumental combinations of the American dance-band idiom into the symphonic concert hall, several years before George Gershwin would do the same with the *Rhapsody in Blue* and before the "jazz" experiments of Milhaud and Stravinsky. The public loved the work as did many concert reviewers. Some critics, who equated artistry with high-toned earnestness, thought it too frivolous to be taken seriously and took exception especially to what they considered the banal waltz of the last movement. Rosenfeld, who thought *Adventures* lacked "the terror, the buzz and glow of the universe of the nursery," declared that the Concertino was an artistic failure because it avoided deep involvement with "the load of the beauty and awfulness of life."[25]

Perhaps to prove that he could write serious symphonic music, Carpenter completed a First Symphony in 1917, and supplied it with the motto "Sermon in Stones," which makes reference to the duke's speech in Shakespeare's *As You Like It*:

Sweet are the uses of adversity;
Which like the toad, ugly and venomous,
Wears yet a precious jewel in his head.
And this our life, exempt from public haunt,
Finds tongues in trees, books in the running brooks,
Sermons in stones and good in everything.

The work was first heard at the 1917 Festival of the Litchfield County Choral Union, in Norfolk, Connecticut. Carpenter offered no explanation for the relation between motto and music, save to say that the symphony went in the direction of optimism. The composition's first movement is a somber *largo* that achieves considerable strength, although relieved by a livelier, more heartening contrasting section. The main subject is stated first in the strings, next in the oboe. The fleeter second subject is first heard in solo violin and horn. Both ideas undergo development. The second movement, a Scherzo, has a main melody in the strings that is derived from the opening of the previous movement. The music then proceeds to a waltz-related passage for cellos. The slow middle section deviates starkly from the dancing rhythms of the opening and close. The last movement starts off at moderate speed, but later introduces a more leisurely section. Its coda speeds up to a climactic *allegro*, where one hears themes from the first movement repeated.

Throughout the composition, the music lurches back and forth between different musical treatments and moods, reducing the sense of coherency. One hears arresting passages and attractive melodies, but misses the pungency and natural ease of the Concertino. Yet, all in all, the work is first-rate. When first heard, it aroused public interest. However its stay in the concert repertoire was short-lived.

Carpenter completed *The Birthday of the Infanta* in the same year as the symphony. This work, a ballet-pantomime, had a story line adapted from Oscar Wilde that allowed the composer to indulge his proclivity for Spanish music. However, whatever the Spanishisms, they are more subtle than blatant. The Chicago Opera gave the ballet an initial performance in 1919. Carpenter arranged a concert suite in three movements from the music, which version the Chicago Symphony presented in 1920. The first, "Introduction," contains four of these scenes: Entrance of the Infanta, Children's Dance, Arrival of the Guests, and The Gypsy Dance. The second, "The Bull Fight," is only an imagined contest in which boys ride hobby horses. The third, "Entrance of the Dwarf," concentrates on a woeful figure, Pedro, with The Fatal Dance, The Tragedy, and The End.

The music associated with the several striking scenes is handled adroitly. Carpenter retains the listener's attention through his splendid display of phantasy—diverting, bizarre, colorful, and sad—and his inventive handling of the orchestra. The distinctly sectional divisions of the musical structure, the articulation of melody in short phrases, the pictorial function of harmony, and the firm management of rhythm have their parallels in Stravinsky's early ballets, although certainly nothing imitative is at all apparent. The outrageous tone of the whole work corresponds to the anything-but-noble-and-exalted compositions of France's Eric Satie and Les Six. Richard Aldrich reviews the work quite favorably. Hale, who heard it as a concert suite, criticizes the music as usually "disjointed, scrappy, rather common," but praises the emotional appeal of the ending, where Pedro dies and the Infanta exits. Percy M. Young gives his view in the August 1927 issue of the English publication *Musical Opinion*: "A young friend who happened to overhear the music [*The Birthday of the Infanta*] expressed surprise . . . that such pleasure-giving music (without rhythmic idiosyncrasy) could be American. Thereby she supported the two main points of my thesis,—that prejudice acts against American music, which is commonly and fallaciously supposed to be nothing if not syncopated, and that the musician most qualified to introduce his country's music to the British is Carpenter."[26]

Carpenter wrote *Krazy Kat* in 1921, and Americans heard it first in 1922. Its fame was instantaneous; audiences loved it; many American and European performances ensued. The music public found in *Krazy Kat* a delightful entertainment and the peak of up-to-date stylishness. This "Jazz-Pantomime,"[27] based on George Herriman's cartoon character, explains Bauer, was an American impressionistic caricature. The democratically-oriented composer employed "commonplace" material, including burlesque harmonic turns and jazz rhythms, with expertise and artistry: "Frankly experimental, it helped to develop a new style of 'showing up' American life to ourselves without *apologia*, an expressionism or realism which has developed in the last decade."[28]

Krazy Kat is the anti-hero, a term first employed in 1897 by W. P. Kerr for a character that poetry, plays, and novels had lampooned over the centuries—one who is awkward, sappy, and prone to foolish blunders; one without the customary grandness and heroic attributes. The anti-hero had occupied the ancient Greek comedies written by Aristophenes. Contemporary with Carpenter, Edward Arlington Cheever was portraying him as "Minniver Cheever." Carpenter had already suggested the anti-hero in *Adventures in a Perambulator*, where everything is told from the point-of-view of a baby, who is helpless, naïve, and nonetheless a little sardonic.

Carpenter's composition evokes that kind of half-sleep where peculiar, ludicrous images dart through one's mind. By means of strange, outwardly trivial allusions, the music tries to evoke that ephemeral atmosphere of trance-like absorption which ceases to exist upon awakening. The cartoon characters—the cat, mouse, and canine cop—are thriftily presented in brief, ever-changing situations. These are thoughtfully depicted in the music. The gaucheness of Herriman's Krazy Kat is made more tolerable through the composer's conscientious and compassionate craftwork. Though charmingly comic, the music may possibly also suggest our own hidden feelings of defenselessness and susceptibility to attack, thus communicating an intimate pathos that moves us to pity.

No episode is prolonged; nothing continues longer than a minute or two. The "Foreword" to the score describes Krazy Kat as the world's greatest optimist, a Don Quixote and Parsifal, whose dreams are shattered by Ignatz Mouse. The piece begins with an Introduction. Passages in parallel fourths, and with mock-seriousness, proclaim the pantomime to come. Soon the fourths make a chromatic movement downward and grow softer and slower. Portamento slides between notes convey an impression of lazy sleep. The curtain rises. Krazy Kat is discovered asleep. A lovely expressive motive in the bass resembles breathing and a faster moving flute mimics a wheeze. Offisa Pup goes by swinging his club to a moderately paced marching theme. The "sleep" motive returns. Bill Postem enters on a perky staccato figure, and pastes up an announcement of a Grand Ball, to the accompaniment of a waltz. Krazy rises from sleep to poignant lyricism. He notices the poster announcing the ball and also a ballet skirt hanging from a clothes line. Ignatz Mouse (a jaunty idea in the piccolo) readies a brick to throw at Krazy's head, but Offisa Pup frightens him away. Krazy puts on the skirt and executes a "zippy but languorous Spanish dance, complete with castanets." He has a bouquet of katnip handed to him by a mysterious stranger (the piccolo discloses he is the disguised mouse). The doped Krazy Kat loosens his inhibitions and dances the Katnip Blues, stated in an attractive fox-trot rhythm. Ignatz Mouse beans him with a brick, which makes his dancing grow more delirious. Finally worn-out, Krazy staggers back to his tree and sinks down. Offisa Pup goes by. The moon rises and Krazy dreams. At the end the opening theme returns.

Howard says that Krazy Kat is an intensely human figure who mirrored the weaknesses and vanity shared by all men, and Ignatz Mouse the agent through whom we are brought down to earth from our dreams: "The score sharpens the elemental nature of these conflicting passions, and intensifies the fundamentally American quality of exaggeration in symbolism. Jazz rhythms, fox trots, quasi-Broadway tunes, and even the Spanish atmosphere of Krazy's dance, are highly appropriate; but it is a more subtle, intangible quality that gives this music its authentic American flavor."[29]

Carpenter gives a more explicitly American flavor to his ballet *Sky-scrapers*, completed in 1924 after Sergei Diaghilev, who had noted the great success of *Krazy Kat*, solicited a work for the Ballet Russes from Carpenter. Carpenter originally composed the piece, states Thomas Pierson, without any clear guidance from a libretto, plot, or locale.[30] The composer and Robert Edmond Jones then planned the stage scenario and Samuel Lee assisted with the dances during the summer of 1925. When Diaghilev failed to follow through with a production, it was premiered at the Metropolitan Opera House in February 1926.

The first three decades or so of the twentieth century was the era of the American skyscraper, three of the most famous being New York City's Woolworth Building (1913) and Empire State Building (1931), and Chicago's Tribune Tower (1925). It was also an era when machinery and robotic work practices came to the fore, whether in factories, mines, or construction, and could not help but influence the handiwork of novelists, dramatists, painters, and composers. The oppressiveness of the machine and the dreary repetitiveness of labor helped determine the mode of expression for a great deal of the burgeoning realism in the arts, and the harsh metallic clang of the workplace strengthened the musical drive toward disjointed melody, cacophonous harmony, and jagged rhythm. The Italian F. T. Marinetti issued his "Futurist Manifesto" in February 1909, in which he denounced the past and praised the new dynamism of the machine. Francesco Pratella and Luigi Russolo, turning to music, elaborated the principle of bruitisme: that contemporary musical language should replicate industrial noises. Then came the wild, pounding, aggressive sounds of Stravinsky's fauvist composition *Le Sacre du printemps* (1913), which many soon took as the musical counterpart to the barbarism of World War I. Presently, in the United States, Henry Cowell's experiments with disharmonious tone clusters brought him notoriety. Around the same time, George Antheil's music interpreted the tyranny of the machine and the disposition toward barbarism in works like *Sonata Sauvage, Mechanisms,* and *Ballet Mécanique.*

Jazz, growing out of ragtime and blues, was coming into its own in the second and third decades of the century. Jazz players were traveling to Europe and capturing the fancy of prominent European composers like Stravinsky, Milhaud, Honegger, and Poulenc. Some musicians, particularly European ones, believed that jazz was the perfect expression of the bruitisme principle and embodied the spirit of modern life. Several of the American mainstream composers have already been cited as flirting with sounds approximating either ragtime or jazz, although bruitisme scarcely figured in their calculations. Gershwin's *Rhapsody in Blue* was heard in December 1925. Louis Gruenberg was issuing his jazz-inspired works: *Daniel Jazz* in 1923; *Jazz Suite, Jazzettes,* and *Jazzberries* in 1925; and his masterwork, the opera *The Emperor Jones* in 1933. The 1920s were soon called The Jazz Age.

Carpenter himself had already introduced sounds and rhythms close to jazz into his Concertino and *Krazy Kat*. Now came *Skyscrapers*, without doubt his most talked-about composition. Bauer declared it to be the quintessence of the newfound American realism. Fifteen years after its completion, the young composer Elliot Carter interpreted it as a "directly pictorial" work in the spirit of Reginald Marsh and Dos Passos: "It evokes just as keenly as they do that boisterous, brutal era of the mechanical heart."[31] As for the elements borrowed from jazz, Carpenter himself said to a reporter on the *New York Herald Tribune* (14 February 1926) that the symphony orchestra was inimical to true jazz; what he wrote was "jazz filtered through an orchestra of that sort. It is jazz once removed. Jazz depends on the sonority of the jazz band. To get something of this sonorous jazz effect we have used the saxophones and a banjo." Oscar Thompson, in *Musical America*, quoted him as stating the music in *Skyscrapers* was "semi-jazz" and in some places remote from jazz. The composer had not interpolated cabaret tunes outrightly into his score. Nevertheless, he had made use of a few phrases from "Massa's in the Cold, Cold Ground," momentary allusions to "Yankee Doodle" and "Dem Goo-Goo Eyes," and given some intimations of the blues.[32]

An examination of the score[33] shows an instrumentation for a large orchestra, including a compressed air whistle tuned to F natural, tenor banjo, three saxophones, celesta, xylophone, glockenspiel, cylinder bells, thunder machine, and two pianos. There is provision for an optional chorus of six tenors and six sopranos. Carpenter wants strict observance of all accent marks and dynamics. By *fp* and *ffp*, he intends sharp crisp attacks, then an immediate release of pressure. The piece alternates between work and play, and tries "to reflect some of the many rhythmic movements and sounds of modern American life."

The curtain rises with the first measure of the music. The audience sees converging black and white stripes on the backdrop, symbols of danger, and two blinking red traffic lights. The meter is an off-center 5/4, then 2/2. The sound is rhythmic, non-melodic. Brittle, ringing passages are dominated by reverberating cylinder bells, percussive pianos, and plucked strings. In the second scene, the first backdrop lifts on a "huge and sinister skyscraper in the course of construction." The orchestra produces an impression of frenzied labor, that of riveters and other steelworkers at their jobs. Meter is mostly 5/4. The passages are still mostly rhythmic. The influence of Stravinsky's *Petrouchka* and *Le Sacre du printemps* is clear. There is an increase in non-jazz syncopations and cross accentuation. Brief melodic-rhythmic motives penetrate the musical fabric. Parallel-motion, chromatically-sliding chords, with a great deal of minor second and major seventh clashes, deviate from the traditional triadic harmonies. Bichordal or bitonal intrusions occur.

The third scene shows the transition from work to play. Laborers enter from the right, their steps stiff and mechanical, and exit on the left gay and relaxed. The processional music, moderate in speed, gradually takes on a jazzy tone, especially when the tenor banjo enters. Dissonance becomes less strident, more bouncy in its impact.

Scene four is an exaggeration of the Coney Island type of amusement park. The workers are at play. Snatches of march-songs are heard. A jovial, gaudy German street-band enters. A lightening flash freezes the dancers; thunder; the stage darkens. The piece briefly reflects on work, making references to the music of scene two. Then the playing resumes with a series of dances. Hints at popular tunes commence: "Old Folks at Home," a tango, fox trot, blues, cowboy ditty, *La Cucaracha*, "Yankee Doodle." Scene five shows the return to work and gradually the mechanical processional takes over. Scene six opens with the blast of a factory whistle. The workers labor at their jobs to "mechanical" sounds reminiscent of the composition's opening. *Skyscrapers* now ends.

Harmony is chiefly triadic, not necessarily functional, and with many altered intervals including diminished fifths and augmented fourths. No overall tonality integrates the scenes, but rather the recurrence of music previously presented. The orchestration is brilliant. Strings prominently playing *legato* melodies, which is not characteristic of Carpenter's style in general, are even less in evidence here. The episodes are concise and cogent. The composer is serious. He intends neither drollery nor parody. On the other hand, his music has undertones of compassion for the barrenness in the toil and struggle permeating contemporary human life. The result is a candid and exhilarating work, a major effort by a major composer. The discounting of the cultural past (a permanent fixture in American criticism) that calls *Skyscrapers* dated is a subjective verdict levied most often by advocates promulgating different musical agendas, not necessarily the judgment of the musical public. One must keep in mind that oftentimes a composition becomes outmoded owing only to a few influential skeptics.[34] Later events and experiences have not inevitably rendered *Skyscrapers*'s music worthless or at best quaint—

that is to say, pleasant but old-fashioned—at least, not for all listeners. Hearing it today for some may be rewarding indeed.

Compassion changed to steadfast belief in country and humanity in the *Song of Faith* (1931) for speaker, chorus, and orchestra, written for the United States Bicenntenial Commission in order to honor the two-hundreth anniversary of the birth of George Washington. The Great Depression was then in full swing. The composition's motto is a stanza from Whitman's *Calamus*, retitled "For you, O Democracy," which tells of the permanence of America, of comradely love, of cities inseparably linked together. The text, written by the composer, recalls our ideals and the message of Washington, who gave the country its freedom. Recollections of "Yankee Doodle," Amerindian music, an old family lullaby, and "the invigorating music of the 'Yankee band' " are heard.[35] The music stops, a gong resonates mysteriously, then a speaker delivers words by Washington alongside a musical commentary. The *Song of Faith* ends affirmatively, voicing trust in what the future will bring. It is an occasional, though timely, piece—simple, sincere, and strong. Its depth of human feeling and hope for mankind are welcome. Moreover, it surely had an input into Copland's thinking when he composed the *Lincoln Portrait*. However, *Song of Faith* cannot be considered one of Carpenter's most outstanding works. Of it, Carpenter modestly said: "If my *Song of Faith* can succeed in lighting a single candle of reaffirmation, I shall be content."[36]

A second, certainly more minor, composition, *Patterns* for piano and orchestra, was commissioned by Serge Koussevitzky and performed by the Boston Symphony in 1932. Carpenter attached no program to it. In one movement and 18 minutes long, it contains, according to Carpenter, "a highly sentimental waltz bit, and short fleeting passages with jazz implications, as well as an absurd bubbling up of my concealed Spanish blood."[37] *Patterns* is a pleasant diversion. The American musical vernacular rarely appeared again in any of the works he wrote after 1932.

After *Patterns* came a surprise. In 1933, Carpenter completed *Sea Drift*, a symphonic poem for full orchestra that neither exploits nor hints at any Americanisms or Spanishisms in its title or music. The composer supplies no program for the music.[38] The source of inspiration was a group of intensely personal poems about the sea that Whitman collected under the common title *Sea Drift* in *Leaves of Grass*. One of these poems is the noted lament about disconnection and the pain of losing a loved one, "Out of the Cradle Endlessly Rocking."

Carpenter's *Sea Drift* is without doubt an impressionistic piece, but far more individual than French. Tune fragments, played by solo instruments, are layered onto the harmony like smidgens of unmixed colors on a canvas. Carefully calculated orchestral resonances operate like pigmentation built up to represent the ever-changing light reflected from expanses of water. *Sea Drift* retains utmost flexibility through malleable motives and subtle nuances. At the same time, motivic melodies and harmonies blend together, from first measure to last, into a whole that is more meaningful than its parts. He was aware of Debussy's *La Mer*, Delius's *Sea-Drift*, and Vaughn Williams's *Sea Symphony*. Nevertheless, one has the conviction that he hardly glanced at any other work for guidance, not even Debussy's *La Mer*; he wished to fashion his own sounds.[39]

Bauer was quoted earlier as referring to Carpenter's American impressionism and realism. One detects in *Sea Drift* the desire to formulate anew the meaning of musical realism so that the composer can go beyond mere picturesqueness, penetrate below surface emotions, and arrive at a core of genuine experience, the deeply felt experience of Whitman. The music does capture the sea's eternal motion. Yet more importantly, it shows what the sea really signifies and how its massiveness and movements release deep subjective responses in onlookers. He tells us how the water looks and, what is more, how its sight touches our inmost feelings. He therefore investigates and expresses the shifting conditions of the sea as if it were a vital force, allowing *Sea Drift* to gain a wealth of significance.

The music took almost 20 years to become a reality. He explains: "I have often found, in the case of my compositions, that the germ of an idea may become implanted and then lie dormant for a long period, only to be stirred into active life, after perhaps a considerable interval by influences outside myself and not always recognizable." Around 1915, he experienced his "first acute Whitman excitment and for some time, then, studied the problem of setting to music in vocal form excerpts from some of the 'Sea-Drift' poems." Nothing satisfactory resulted from the excitement. Eventually, in 1933, while sojourning at Eze,[40] a village on the Mediterranean, he discarded the notion of a vocal piece and opted for orchestra alone to record "the imprint upon me of these poems. . . . My work represents an effort to transcribe my impressions derived from these magnificent poems."[41]

The central musical concept is the unremitting ebb and flow of sound, of two notes against three. Wavelike one-measure crescendos and diminuendos are frequent. The lowered seventh tone gives off strong modal signals, at the same time contributing to the consciousness of an elusive tonality. Significant melodic motives occur at the beginning, in the violins, then English horn and violins. They recur throughout the work as first stated or in variation, some quite free. They may appear in inversion, retrograde, or retrograde inversion. In place of a purely musical development, metamorphoses of these motives give them varying expressive implications. The initial impress that the piece leaves is of an almost unvaryingly slow, melancholic, moody, vaguely defined "drift" from first sound to last. Occasional climaxes well up like giant waves.

Sea Drift opens *lento tranquillo*, with timpani and string basses playing eighth notes in triplets, while the violas and cellos play chromatic figures in eighth notes in a two-to-a-beat division. The first motive enters, and the music picks up a little speed. To be noted is the three-note motive's characteristically wide upward skip then stepwise descent to the next note. After the violins introduce the motive, wisps of it return in the oboe and clarinet. The music speeds up a bit more. A second and longer motive, a smooth rocking phrase of two-measure length, enters. From the start of the composition, a slowly increasing number of instruments has articulated the continuous flux of eighth notes, rising and falling like ocean swells. Strings, woodwinds, and brasses achieve a first climax.

The middle of the work, which begins *con bravura*, is marked off by more open harmonies, harp and piano arpeggios, and very freely altered representations of the motives. For a while the flow of undulating eighth notes ceases. Lyricism becomes more prominent. The solos for English horn are especially affecting. Then what sounds like a new idea starts up, but soon an allusion to the first motive is made.

Later, the continuous flow of notes heard at the beginning resumes, only the motion is that of quarter notes, not eighth notes. After a last climax in the full orchestra, indicated by *lento trionfalmente*, the sound subsides. English horn and vibraphone enter alternately for brief evocative recollections of the main motivic material; then the music dies to complete silence. *Sea Drift* exposes a progressive tonality of fourths: from D-flat to A-flat (=G-sharp) to E-flat.

When the Chicago Symphony premiered it, a critic or two grumbled about the lack of strong contrasts, failing to see that Carpenter wanted to maintain a single governing ambience. Others found the textures altogether convincing, the "close-woven" variations and metamorphoses drenched in rich colors, and the total effect not *La Mer*'s sunny day and brilliant sunshine but something more profound, tragic, and mysterious.[42] Incontestably, *Sea Drift* is a major composition conceived on a grand plan. Nothing else in his music is more weighty and more recognizably impressionistic.

The works composed after Carpenter reached the age of 60 are neither as bold as *Skyscrapers*, nor as highly concentrated as *Sea Drift*. The orchestral *Danza*, first heard in Chicago in 1935, is brief and bewitching in its tangy rhythms and Spanish-American seasoning. Carpenter said that the opening theme in 5/4 meter is based on three tones, E-F-G, "an offshoot from a larger work based on Oriental musical idioms on which I have been engaged ever since a visit to China last spring. In the course of the larger work I found myself toying with the following idea, which seemed to set up such a persistent irritation of its own, that I finally gave it its head and used it as the principal rhythmic germ of *Danza*."[43]

Premiered by the violinist Zlatko Balokovic with the Chicago Symphony conducted by Frederick Stock, in 1937, the Violin Concerto is less adventurous than *Skyscrapers* and diffuses more heterogeneous moods and materials throughout its length than does *Sea Drift*. In one movement, with four clear-cut divisions, it requires a large orchestra.[44] The violin sounds sparklingly, the antitheses of solo instrument and orchestra are persuasively managed, and the total effect is warm and rhapsodic. After a brief introduction, the fast first section focuses mainly on one motive introduced lustily by the orchestra. The violin takes it up and shares it with other instruments in passages that go from humorous, to graceful, to pointedly rhythmic, to vehement. Without pause, the music enters the slow and sad second section, where the composer apportions out an expressive melody among first violins, solo violin, and French horn. A violin cadenza interrupts the proceedings to lead into the third section, which is light and sprightly, and points up the soloist by means of accented triplet figurations. The slow end-section ruminates on the material of the opening section and ends quietly—the violin poised on a high E, while bells chime a last reference to the opening motive. The Concerto is by no means a negligible work.

A respectable one-movement Symphony in C, written for the fiftieth anniversary of the Chicago Symphony, was heard in 1940. Concise, calm, melodious, it was based on a theme previously heard in his first symphony of 1917. A Symphony No. 2, in three movements (*Allegro, Andante, Allegro*), appeared at the 1942 concerts of the New York Philharmonic. Knowledgeably written, well-ordered, romantic, and with some muscle and more charm, it borrows some ideas from the Quintet of 1934. Similar virtues are contained in *The Anxious Bugler*, a symphonic poem (1943), *The Seven Ages* Suite for Orchestra, after Shakespeare (1945), and the *Carmel* Concerto for Piano and Orchestra (1948). Carpenter was never capable of writing truly inferior music!

Carpenter is without question one of the first composers to write music on and of the American urban scene, mining the riches in jazz, dance music, and popular balladry to do so. In their time *Krazy Kat* and *Skyscrapers* provoked heated discussion but were deemed to successfully represent a newfangled American civilization distinct from that of Europe. The witty and whimsical note he struck in *Adventures in a Perambulator* was all his own and welcomed enthusiastically by audiences. Few composers of his time could match the spontaneity and immediacy of human experience captured in the song cycle *Gitanjali*. Never a garrulous composer, his works say concisely what they have to say then are silent. He did like to introduce Spanishisms into compositions. More often than not firm rhythms give backbone to the sound that he dispenses. Finally, *Sea Drift*, so impeccable in its evocation of mood and emotion, stands singular in the musical literature. The Gold Medal that Carpenter received in 1947 from the National Institute of Arts and Letters was a fitting cap to the many years he toiled on behalf of American music.

NOTES

1. Letter from New York City, dated 25 April 1939, to M. A. DeWolfe Howe, now in Harvard University's Houghton Library, shelf No. bMS AM 1524 (206).

2. John Tasker Howard, *Our American Music*, 4th ed. (New York: Crowell, 1965), p. 371.

3. John Tasker Howard, "John Alden Carpenter," *Modern Music* 9 (1931), p. 8.

4. John Alden Carpenter, letter dated 21 January 1941, to Alice (Runnells) James, in the Houghton Library of Harvard University, Shelf No. bMS Am 1938 (160); letter dated 7 August 1946, to Alice (Runnells) James, also contained in Shelf No. bMS Am 1938 (160).

5. Carpenter, in the *Christian Science Monitor* (30 October 1915) and quoted in Thomas C. Pierson, "The Life and Music of John Alden Carpenter" (Ph.D. diss., University of Rochester, 1952), pp. 13–14.

6. Quoted in David Ewen, *American Composers* (New York: Putnam's Sons, 1982), s.v. "Carpenter, John Alden."

7. Carpenter is quoted in Madeleine Goss, *Modern Music Makers* (New York: Dutton, 1952), p. 44.

8. Daniel Gregory Mason, in *The Dilemma of American Music* (New York: Macmillan, 1928), pp. 6–7, did believe that "many of Carpenter's clever and refined—almost too refined—songs and piano pieces might have been written by Debussy, while his Suite for orchestra, 'Adventures in a Perambulator,' is essentially Gallic in its economy of means, its distinctiveness of color, and its ironic wit."

9. "New Music," *Musical America* (10 January 1914), p. 12.

10. Pierson, "The Life and Music of John Alden Carpenter," p. 8.

11. *Eight Songs for a Medium Voice* (New York: Schirmer, 1912); *Four Songs for a Medium Voice* (New York: Schirmer, 1913). Hans Nathan, in "United States of America," *A History of Song*, ed. Denis Stevens (New York: Norton, 1970), p. 426, finds a connection with Mahler's folk-style.

12. Felix Borowski, "John Alden Carpenter," *Musical Quarterly* 16 (1930), p. 456.

13. Borowski, "John Alden Carpenter," p. 457; Pierson, "The Life and Music of John Alden Carpenter," p. 20; Carl Engel, in *Cobbett's Cyclopedic Survey of Chamber Music*, 2nd ed., ed. Walter Willson Cobbett (London: Oxford, 1963), s.v. "Carpenter, John Alden"; John Tasker Howard, *Our Contemporary Music* (New York: Crowell, 1941), p. 36.

14. Quoted in Pierson, "The Life and Music of John Alden Carpenter," p. 20.

15. John Alden Carpenter, *Quartet for Stringed Instruments* (New York: Schirmer, 1928).

16. Pierson, "The Life and Music of John Alden Carpenter," p. 34.

17. Ibid., p. 7.

18. Marion Bauer, "Impressionism in America," *Modern Music* (January/February 1927), p. 17 (the pagination is by issue, not by volume); Paul Rosenfeld, *Musical Chronicle (1917-1923)* (New York: Harcourt, Brace, 1923), pp. 169–70; Mason, *The Dilemma of American Music*, pp. 6–7.

19. John Alden Carpenter, *Adventures in a Perambulator* (New York: Schirmer, 1917).

20. The quotations here and later are from the program book of the Chicago concert, reproduced in the Program Book for the concert of the Boston Symphony Orchestra, on 24–25 December 1915, pp. 536–38; also see Philip Hale, *Philip Hale's Boston Symphony Programme Notes*, ed. John N. Burk (Garden City, New York: Doubleday, Doran, 1935), p. 114.

21. Clipping from the *Boston Herald* (25 December 1915), in the Boston Public Library; see Microfilm No. ML 46.H3, roll 4.

22. Carpenter's comments were reproduced in the program notes of the Chicago Symphony, for the concert of 12 December 1939; see the book of clippings in the Boston Public Library, Shelf No. **M.410.17.

23. The subject sounds like a conga, a dance that would be popularized by Desi Arnaz, among others, in the late 1930s.

24. John Alden Carpenter, Concertino for Piano and Orchestra (New York: Schirmer, 1920).

25. Rosenfeld, *Musical Chronicle*, pp. 170, 172.

26. The Aldrich commentary is from the *New York Times* (24 February 1920), and is contained in a book of clippings in the Boston Public Library, Shelf No. **M.483.209; Hale's, from the *Boston Herald*, (26 February 1921) may be found in the Boston Public Library, Micro ML 46.H3, roll 5; Young's is quoted in Pierson, "The Life and Music of John Alden Carpenter," p. 9.

27. John Alden Carpenter, *Krazy Kat*, A Jazz-Pantomime (New York: Schirmer, 1922).

28. Marion Bauer, *Twentieth Century Music* (New York: Putnam's Sons, 1933), pp. 167–68.

29. Howard, *Our American Music*, p. 37.

30. Pierson, "The Life and Music of John Alden Carpenter," pp. 28–29.

31. Bauer, *Twentieth Century Music*, p. 168; Elliot Carter, in *Modern Music* 17 (1940), p. 96. In the same volume of *Modern Music*, p. 256, Arthur Cohn, an advocate for the music of his own day, dismissed *Skyscrapers* ("Carpenter's noisy and dated *Skyscrapers* with all its bombastic trivialities and 'super-corny' orchestration") as a trifling effort.

32. Both of Carpenter's statements may be found in Philip Hale's notes on the work, in the Program Book for the Concert of the Boston Symphony Orchestra, on 9–10 December 1927, pp. 592, 593, 596.

33. John Alden Carpenter, *Skyscrapers*, A Ballet of Modern American Life (New York: Schirmer, 1927).

34. For a detailed discussion of this problem in American criticism, see Nicholas E. Tawa, *The Coming of Age of American Art Music* (Westport, Connecticut: Greenwood, 1991), pp. 191-201.

35. Philip Hale in the *Boston Herald* (24 February 1932); the clipping is reproduced on microfilm, Shelf No. ML 46.H3, roll 7, in the Boston Public Library.

36. He is quoted by Lawrence Gilman, in the *New York Herald Tribune* (1 May 1932), the quotation reproduced in Goss, *Modern Music-Makers*, p. 41.

37. Program Book for the concert of the Boston Symphony Orchestra, on 21–22 October 1932, p. 118.

38. John Alden Carpenter, *Sea Drift*, Symphonic Poem (New York: Schirmer, 1934). The music was revised in the early 1940s.

39. Alfred Frankenstein, writing in *Modern Music* 11 (1934), p. 104, thought the music was reminiscent of Delius; Olin Downes, writing in the *New York Times* (6 October 1944), p. 18, said that despite traces of Debussy, the music was not imitative.

40. The work was completed in Pride's Crossing, Beverly, Massachusetts. At the end of the score, Carpenter writes: "Éze-Pride's Crossing, Feb.-Sep. 1933."

41. Lawrence Gilman, "Novelties," *New York Herald Tribune* (4 November 1934), section 5, p. 8.

42. See respectively, Frankenstein, op. cit., p. 104; Downes, op. cit., p. 18; Hanson, in the *Saturday Review of Literature* (24 February 1951), his remark reproduced in Pierson, "The Life and Music of John Alden Carpenter," p. 33.

43. Quoted by John N. Burk, in notes provided for the Program Book, for the concert of the Boston Symphony Orchestra, 17–18 November 1936, p. 561.

44. John Alden Carpenter, Concerto for Violin and Orchestra (New York: Schirmer, 1939). At the end of the score appears: "*Éze Village* and *Beverly*, March to September 1936."

Chapter Eight

An Added Note

After a detailed examination of the music of the mainstream composers, one can see that these musicians gave appropriate weight, each after his or her own fashion, to an extension of handed-down usages, and to at least some trial of the new. Every one of them thought that the traditions with which they had grown up needed refurbishing and acted accordingly. The evolution away from past practices was an additive procedure. Fresh ideas and materials were tried out and, if proved to be congenial, incorporated into more familiar ways of thinking and into a long-standing musical framework. If inconsonant with a composer's disposition, they were dropped. We found that the composers, except for Marion Bauer, started from a German-oriented pedagogical and stylistic base before exploring other possibilities. Not a single one maintained a static style; not a single one thought his or her practices were old hat, or in any way inferior to the most modern compositional methods of the time. Each one was capable of surprises. Each one zigged and zagged along his or her own creative road. What surprises us is that with every zigzag, one after another of the composers created music that represented his or her own individual personality.

For example, we watched Griffes with breathtaking interest as he swiftly veered away from his teachers Rüfer and Humperdinck and the Lieder-styles of Brahms and Strauss toward French impressionism, then toward Chinese and Japanese musical idioms—from the student songs, to *The Roman Sketches, Five Poems of Ancient China and Japan,* and *The Pleasure Dome of Kubla Khan.* The process was one of continuous enrichment, not revolutionary rejection, of a previous mode of expression. There was no standing still for Griffes. He flirted with Amerindian tunes

(*Two Sketches on Indian Themes*) but found no abiding comfort in them. Anglo-Celtic mysticism and an attendant modal thinking proved more congenial (*Three Poems by Fiona MacLeod*). Just before his untimely death, a grand synthesis of all that he had musically experienced and a further step toward posttriadic musical practices were realized in the movements of his Piano Sonata, fitting last words from an exceptional composer.

We observed Mason coming away from the teaching of Paine as a young, dedicated Brahmsian (the Violin Sonata and Clarinet Sonata) and carrying the burden of the Mason family musical tradition and of Anglo-Saxon Americanism. Study with the French composer Vincent d'Indy produced a modification of the prevalent Brahmsianisms in several of his works (Symphony No. 1 and No. 2). Both works are romantic in conception, melodious yet muscular, and beautifully crafted. Nevertheless, we felt rather impatient with the ruling caution with which he tried out anything new. Could it be possible that, unlike Griffes, he was content with the status quo? Fortunately, it soon became apparent that he was seeking a way out. In the excellent song cycle *Russians*, he suddenly swerved toward a rawboned realism, but then retreated. His *String Quartet on Negro Themes* revealed him toying with African-American tunes and rhythms and Debussian harmonies. Again, he backed away. On the other hand, works like the *Suite after English Folk-Songs* were a happy outlet for his bent toward British-American traditional music. Only twice after completing *Russians* did he truly cast off self-restraint and give untrammeled expression to feelings usually kept in abeyance— the uninhibited joyousness of *Chanticleer* and the deeply personal *A Lincoln Symphony*. A fusion of everything that was best in the Mason approach to creativity was achieved. In addition, a bracing American spirit breathes in the music, although that spirit is difficult to relate to anything in particular in the music. On balance, Mason's music cannot be confused with that of Brahms or Paine. It is itself. On the whole, he strikes us as a master who allowed his individuality to develop without special cultivation on his part. He joined himself to past masters in essential ways by means of an unostentatious command of his métier and of an expression, however indebted to others, that he himself had sincerely felt.

To give a last example, Gilbert, a New Englander, had studied with Whiting and MacDowell, two American composers educated in Germany. From the beginning, a certain restlessness governed his life. He began his adulthood in Bohemian fashion, playing violin in dance bands, doing a stint in a real estate agency and a music publishing firm, cutting pies and cultivating silkworms for a living. After an introduction to recent Russian music and to the Dvořák compositions with an American provenance, he conducted his own investigation into folk music and its artistic possibilities. He also traveled in Europe and found the music-making in Paris especially congenial. Gilbert felt encouraged to try his own hand at composition. At the same time, he took up the cause for a national music. As he composed his first pieces, the restlessness already noted, the unwillingness to accept things as they are, governed his creative direction.

His *Humoresque on Negro-Minstrel Tunes* showed him boldly asserting the artistic worthiness of nineteenth-century popular music in which African-American and backwoods idioms were inextricably entwined. The musical vehicle that contained them, however, was predominantly of European origin, the procedures similar to that of Grieg and Norwegian folk music (or so Gilbert claimed). More clearly African-American in melody and rhythm was the *Comedy Overture on Negro Themes, Dance in Place Congo* (where even harmony makes a tentative attempt at breaking away from common European usage), and *Negro Rhapsody*. All four creative attempts give the impression of rough-and-ready, emphatic pieces. *Two South American Gypsy Songs* and *Indian Sketches* communicate further explorations of folk sources, while *A Rag Bag, Negro Dances, American Dances*, and *Dance* for jazz band reveal his steady inquiry into American popular music.

Gilbert also had a constant interest in Celtic music, witness his *Symphonic Prologue for Riders to the Sea* and the *Celtic Studies*. Yet, toward the end of his life, he took his lead from Whitman and tried to comprehend the several-sided spirit of his native land in three works, his musical contributions to the *Pilgrim Tercentenary Pageant*, and the *Symphonic Piece* and *Nocturne, after Walt Whitman*, the last two mature and convincing creations. Clearly, Gilbert was a composer always on the move. Just as clearly, whatever he might have said about the need for striking out on a different course, he proved himself a humanist, a reformer seeking to increase the compass of the artistic vision that he had inherited from older American composers like MacDowell and Chadwick.

In the descriptions of these three Americans, we can see that the composers of the early third of the century, though writing music quite different from each other, thought of change as an essential concomitant to continuity. As far as we can discover, they mouthed no sophisms about the death of music as the Western world had known it. They did not speak of history's inevitable advance away from tonality and triadic harmony toward an obscure future destination. They did believe that, as they set forth their own adaptations of past conventions, they could express a fresh distinctiveness that excluded disdain for their forebears and did not resort to a revolutionary manner for manner's sake. Their music reminds us of a statement by Edith Wharton, in *The Writing of Fiction* (1925), that "true originality consists not in a new manner but in a new vision. That new, that personal, vision is attained only by looking long enough at the object represented to make it the writer's own; and the mind which would bring this secret germ to fruition must be able to nourish it with an accumulated wealth of knowledge and experience."

Predicting what style or genre a transitional composer might try next was not always an infallible exercise. Radical change could take place abruptly. This is another conclusion that one can reach. To all intents and purposes, Converse was working steadfastly to introduce the religious faith of his New England, the symbolism of the transcendentalists, and the optimistic universalism of Whitman into his works. Engrossing compositions like *The Mystic Trumpeter*, *The Pipe of Desire*, and *Job* were the result. Then without warning, the joyous, colloquial, and very much-of-this-world *Flivver Ten Million* appeared. Shortly thereafter he composed the festive scenes of *California*, in which he kept the content light, entertaining, and free of heavy-handedness. Cadman, ambitious for popularity, won fame for his Amerindian songs, instrumental pieces, and opera *Shanewis*. Also well received were his *Dark Dancers of the Mardi Gras* and the *Pennsylvania Symphony*. Nevertheless, nobody anticipated that in his middle 60s and months before his death, this essentially lyrical composer would produce his deliriously intoxicated *A Mad Empress Remembers* and a thumbs-up frolic, *Huckleberry Finn Goes Fishing*. Color, fantasy, and picturesqueness had been Taylor's forte when he wrote *Through the Looking Glass*, *Circus Days*, and *Jurgen*. Soon after the premier of the last composition and seemingly out of the blue, he collaborated with Edna St. Vincent Millay on an opera, *The King's Henchman*, a medieval drama that caught fire from its first presentation owing to its fascinating theatricals, fetching vocal writing, and satisfying musical portrayal of human conflict.

The first 30 years of the century also saw, as never before or after, a large American production of descriptive music, both in the shape of a personal contemplation of a mind-picture, to which the composer gave an emotional musical characterization, or of a realization in quasi-pictorial and expressive musical terms of a program supplied by the composer and made available to an audience. Griffes's *Three Tone Pictures* and Carpenter's *Sea Drift* are examples of the former type; Gilbert's *Dance in Place Congo*, a tragicomic day passed among old New Orleans's slaves, and Converse's *Ormazd*, where good and evil, the givers of light and denizens of darkness, war against each other, are examples of the latter.

The most dedicated musical painter of all was Hadley. His expertise was manifold: an orchestrator par excellence, an adroit conjurer of atmosphere and mood, a lyricist prolific in contagious melodies to fit any situation. No other American composer of his time showed as keen a relish for the sheer sensuousness of sound itself. Herein lies a large measure of his distinctiveness. The Second Symphony, *The Four Seasons*; symphonic poem, *Salome*; orchestral rhapsody, *The Culprit Fay*; and musical joyride, *Scherzo Diabolique*, are examples of American program music conveyed vividly to the listener. The same facility was applied to his operas, like the fun-and-games *Bianca* and impassioned *Cleopatra's Night*. Their success with audiences of his day was amazing. He added nothing new to the musical vocabulary. He did use the language in which he had grown adept to describe, with a great deal of vitality, the changing seasons, the sound and sense of different parts of the world, events in history, and the terrain of feeling. In doing so, he delighted the ear and stimulated the imagination. His was not a fly-by-night art—facile perhaps, but one to be reckoned with.

We continue this postscript with a mention of Carpenter and his dance-stage compositions: *Birthday of the Infanta, Krazy Kat*, and *Skyscrapers*. Almost singlehandedly he raised American ballet to a position of importance. In the last two works, he pioneered the musical delineation of the contemporary American urban scene, elevating it into something universal. Krazy Kat is Everyman at his myopic extreme, barely coping in a zany world. Skyscrapers are the monstrous structures ready to overwhelm what humanity still survives in ordinary men and women. Old and contemporary popular songs, jazz, blues, and dances current in the United States are employed to drive the message home. Some later critics have asserted that Carpenter's approach to the vernacular was too well mannered and "gentlemanly." On the contrary, propriety and correct behavior have less to do with his treatment of the vernacular than the desire to put his material into some order and thus render it amenable to artistic handling beyond itself. We have noted, in Chapter 7, that he once said that he wished to nourish and sustain people with his art. This he did and at the same time gave pleasure to whoever would listen.

We join to the virtues of the music just described those of Hill's compositions with their polish, lucidity, and grace; and Farwell's music that insisted on the worthiness for inclusion of indigenous, especially Amerindian, sounds. Add also Shepherd's staunch musical feeling for the American West, Daniels's sensitively realized vocal works, and Bauer's brief and perfectly sculpted piano pieces. Then again, there was Scott Joplin's unique and exciting venture into operatic writing based on ragtime, *Treemonisha*. The patent sincerity and honesty in all of these efforts to create a viable American music also characterizes this generation of artists and enhances the virtues described. Not least, the composers wished to contribute works to satisfy the inchoate yearnings in their listeners, to offer honest re-creation. If at the same time, a preponderance of their works were seen to possess the human values that upgraded and separated men and women from the animalism in modern life, then so much the better.

Several of these composers were also the teachers of the next generation and provided musical exemplars for the younger composers, in styles they could try to emulate, modify, or even reject. Kelley instructed Wallingford Riegger. Converse taught Alan Hovhaness. Farwell worked with Roy Harris and Bernard Rogers; Hill, with Virgil Thomson, Walter Piston, Roger Sessions, Elliott Carter, Irving Fine, Ross Lee Finney, and Leonard Bernstein. Chadwick and Gilbert helped William Grant Still realize his African-American style. Hill gave direction to his students and sent most of them off, not to Germany, but to Paris and Nadia Boulanger. Shepherd aided Roy Harris in his look westward. Griffes's experimentation with the musical styles of Asia preluded the endeavors of Colin McPhee and Lou Harrison. Carpenter had some input into Copland's jazz-blues style of the 1920s, and any number of the mainstream composers into Copland's "American" style of the late 1930s and 1940s. From Hadley and Taylor to Hanson and Barber is but a small step.

These composers supplied the bridge between the older New England-centered musicians—Paine, Chadwick, Parker, MacDowell, Foote, and Beach—and the later composers of the twentieth century. They deserve to be taken seriously. Their music merits a new hearing.

Selected List of Recordings

Bauer, Marion

From New Hampshire Woods for Piano	LP Northeastern 204
Prelude and Fugue for Flute and Strings	LP CRI SD 101
Sonata for Viola and Piano	LP Northeastern NR 222
Symphonic Suite for Strings	LP CRI SD 101
Turbulence for Piano	LP Northeastern 204

Cadman, Charles Wakefield

"At Dawning"	LP New World NW 247
Dark Dancers of The Mardi Gras for Two Pianos	LP Cambria C 1017
Four American Indian Songs	LP New World NW 213
A Mad Empress Remembers for Cello and Piano	LP Musical Heritage Society MHS 4348
Piano Music	LP Cambria C 1017
Trio in D Major for Piano, Violin, and Cello	LP Cambria C 1017

Carpenter, John Alden

Adventures in a Perambulator	LP ERA 1009
Concertino for Piano and Orchestra	LP CRI 180

Diversions for Piano	CD New World NW 328/329–2
Gitanjali	LP Orion 77272
Krazy Kat	LP New World NW 228
Nine Piano Pieces	CD New World NW 382/329–2
Quartet for Strings	78 Schirmer 2513–15
Sea Drift	CD New World NW 321–2
Skyscrapers	CD EMI/Angel CDC 7 49263–2
Sonata in G Minor for Piano	CD New World NW 328/329–2
Sonata for Violin and Piano	LP Orion ORS 76243
Song of Faith	78 Victor 26529–30

Converse, Frederick Shepherd

"Chorista's Prayer," from *The Sacrifice*	78 Columbia A 5298
Endymion's Narrative	CD Albany TROY 030–2
Flivver Ten Million: A Joyous Epic	CD Albany TROY 030–2
The Mystic Trumpeter	LP Desto DST 6407

Daniels, Mabel

Deep Forest	LP CRI SD 145
Three Observations for Oboe, Flute, Clarinet, and Bassoon	LP Desto DC 7117

Farwell, Arthur

The Gods of the Mountain	LP SPAMH MIA 128
Land of Luthany for Cello and Piano	LP Musical Heritage Society MHS 4348
Navajo War Dance for Piano	LP New World NW 213
Pawnee Horses for Piano	LP New World NW 213
Quintet in E Minor for Piano and Strings	LP Musical Heritage Society MHS 3827
"The Old Man's Love Song"	LP New World NW 213
Sonata for Cello and Piano	LP Musical Heritage Society MHS 4348

| *Three Indian Songs* | LP New World NW 213 |
| Twelve Songs | CD Albany TROY 043 |

Gilbert, Henry

Americanesque	LP SPAMH MIA 128
The Dance in Place Congo	LP New World NW 228
	LP Everest 3118
Humoresque on Negro-Minstrel Tunes	LP SPAMH MIA 128
Mazurka for Piano	LP New World NW 206
Nocturne for Orchestra	LP SPAMH MIA 141
Suite for Chamber Orchestra	CD Albany TROY 033–2

Griffes, Charles Tomlinson

Bacchanale for Orchestra	CD Delos DE 3099
De Profundis for Piano	CD Gasparo GSCD 233
Fantasy Pieces for Piano	CD Gasparo GSCD 232
Four German Songs	CD New World NW 273–2
Four Impressions	CD New World NW 273–2
Four Roman Sketches for Piano	CD Gasparo GSCD 231
Legend for Piano	CD Gasparo GSCD 234
Notturno for Orchestra	LP SPAMH MIA 104
Notturno for Piano	LP Delos DCD 3030
The Pleasure Dome of Kubla Khan for Piano	CD Gasparo GSCD 234
The Pleasure Dome of Kubla Khan for Orchestra	CD New World NW 273-2
	CD Delos DE 3099
Poem for Flute and Orchestra	CD Delos DE 3099
Rhapsody in B Minor for Piano	CD Gasparo GSCD 232
Roman Sketches for Piano	CD Delos DCD 3006
Sonata for Piano	CD Gasparo GSCD 233
Song of the Dagger	CD New World NW 273–2
Symphonische Fantasie	LP SPAMH MIA 125
"Symphony in Yellow"	LP EMS 501
Three Poems of Fiona MacLeod	CD New World NW 273–2
Three Preludes for Piano	CD Gasparo GSCD 231

Three Tone-Pictures for Piano	CD Gasparo GSCD 234
Three Tone-Pictures arr. for Ensemble	CD New World NW 273–2
	CD Delos DE 3099
Two Sketches based on Indian Themes for String Quartet	LP Vox SVBX 5301
	LP SPAMH MIA 117

Hadley, Henry

Concertino for Piano and Orchestra	78 Victor 12599–600 in Set M 634
The Culprit Fay	LP Interlochen National Music Camp NMC 1957–79
One Morning in Spring, Rhapsody for Orchestra	LP Lyrita SRCS 106
Quintet for Piano and Strings	LP Vox SVBX 5301
Salome	CD Library of Congress OMP 106
Scherzo Diabolique	CD New World NW 321–2
Symphony No. 2, *The Four Seasons*,	LP SPAMH MIA 145
The Trees So High for Baritone, Chorus, and Orchestra	LP Lyrita SRCS 106

Hill, Edward Burlingame

Sextet for Piano and Winds	LP Columbia ML 4846
Stevensoniana Suite No. 1	LP SPAMH MIA 142

Joplin, Scott

Treemonisha	LP Deutsche Grammophon 2707083

Mason, Daniel Gregory

Chanticleer Festival Overture	CD New World NW 321–2
Country Pictures for Piano	LP Grenadilla 1026
Pastorale for Clarinet, Violin, and Piano	Musical Heritage Society MHS 3143
Prelude and Fugue for Piano and Orchestra	LP Turnabout GTVS 34665
Quartet on Negro Themes	LP Vox SVBX 5301

Sonata for Clarinet and Piano	CD Centaur CRC 2067
Three Pieces for Flute, Harp, and String Quartet	78 Royale 1867–68

Powell, John

In Old Virginia	78 Music Sound Books 78158–59
Rhapsodie Nègre	LP New World NW 228
Sonata Noble for Piano	LP Golden Age GAR 1003
Sonata Psychologique for Piano	LP CRI SD 505
Sonata Teutonica for Piano	LP CRI S368
	LP CRI SD 368
Sonata Virginianesque for Violin and Piano	78 Royale 29
Variations and Double Fugue on a Theme of F. C. Hahr for Piano	LP CRI SD 505

Shepherd, Arthur

The Old Chisholm Trail, from Symphony No. 1, "Horizons"	LP Epic BC 1154
Piano Music	LP CRI S 383
Quartet for Strings No. 2	78 Yaddo 113–114
Sonata for Piano No. 2	LP Western Reserve Univ. WRUD M 1
Sonata for Violin and Piano	LP Golden Crest GC 201
Three Songs	LP New World NW 327
Triptych for Soprano and String Quartet	LP New World NW 218

Taylor, Deems

Ballet from *Casanova*	LP Allegro AL 3150
"Oh! Caesar, Great Wert Thou!," from *The King's Henchman*	LP New World NW 241
Peter Ibbetson Suite	78 Columbia 71204–05D in Set X 204
Portrait of a Lady	LP Desto 6417E
Through the Looking Glass	CD Delos DE 3099

Selected Bibliography

Aldrich, Richard. *Concert Life in New York, 1902–1923*. New York: Putnam's Sons, 1941.

Ammer, Christine. *Unsung*. Westport, Connecticut: Greenwood, 1980.

Anderson, Donna K. *The New Grove Dictionary of American Music*, eds. H. Wiley Hitchcock and Stanley Sadie. London: Macmillan, 1986, s.v. "Griffes, Charles, T(omlinson)."

Anon. "Charles Wakefield Cadman." *The Musician* 20 (1915), 687–88, 738.

Bauer, Marion. "Charles T. Griffes as I Remember Him." *Musical Quarterly* 29 (1943), 355–80.

———. *Twentieth Century Music*. New York: Putnam's Sons, 1933.

Boda, Daniel. "The Music of Charles T. Griffes." Ph.D. diss., Florida State University, 1962.

Borowski, Felix. "John Alden Carpenter." *Musical Quarterly* 16 (1930), 449–68.

Canfield, Jr., John Clair. "Henry Kimball Hadley: His Life and Works (1871–1937)." Ed.D. diss., Florida State University, 1960.

Carter, Elliott. "American Figure with Landscape." *Modern Music* 20 (1943), 219–25.

Chase, Gilbert and Bruce, Neely. *The New Grove Dictionary of American Music*, eds. H. Wiley Hitchcock and Stanley Sadie. New York: Grove's Dictionaries of Music Inc., 1986, s.v. "Farwell, Arthur."

Clarke, Garry E. *Essays on American Music*. Westport, Connecticut: Greenwood, 1977.

Cobbett, Walter Willson, ed. *Cobbett's Cyclopedic Survey of Chamber Music*, 2nd ed., 2 vols. London: Oxford, 1963.

Copland, Aaron. *Music and Imagination*. New York: Mentor, 1959.

Culbertson, Evelyn Davis. "Arthur Farwell's Early Efforts on Behalf of American Music, 1889–1921." *American Music* 5 (1987), 156–75.

Daniels, Mabel Wheeler. *An American Girl in Munich: Impressions of a Music Student*. Boston: Little, Brown, 1905.

Downes, Olin. *Cobbett's Cyclopedic Survey of Chamber Music*, 2nd ed., ed. Walter Willson Cobbett. London: Oxford, 1963, s.v. "American Chamber Music. I."

———. "An American Composer (Henry F. Gilbert)." *Musical Quarterly* 4 (1918), 23–36.

———. "Henry Gilbert: Nonconformist." *A Birthday Offering to Carl Engel*, ed. Gustave Reese. New York: Schirmer, 1943, pp. 88–94.

———. "J. A. Carpenter: American Craftsman." *Musical Quarterly* 16 (1930), 443–68.

———. *Analytical Notes* to Converse's "The Pipe of Desire." New York: Gray, n.d.

Elson, Louis C. *The History of American Music*, 1st ed. 1904, revised to 1925 by Arthur Elson. New York: Macmillan, 1925.

Engel, Carl. *Cobbett's Cyclopedic Survey of Chamber Music*, 2nd ed., ed. Walter Willson Cobbett. London: Oxford, 1963, s.v. "Shepherd, Arthur."

———. *Cobbett's Cyclopedic Survey of Chamber Music*, 2nd ed., ed. Walter Willson Cobbett. London: Oxford, 1963, s.v. "Carpenter, John Alden."

Engel, (A.) Lehman. *This Bright Day*. New York: Macmillan, 1974.

Ewen, David. *American Composers*. New York: Putnam's Sons, 1982.

———. *Composers of Today*, 2nd ed. New York: Wilson, 1934.

Farwell, Arthur. "Individual Advancement: II." *Musical America* (27 December 1913), p. 32.

———. "Pioneering for American Music." *Modern Music* 12 (1935), 116–22.

Farwell, Arthur, and Darby, W. Dermot, eds. *Music in America*. The Art of Music 4. New York: National Society of Music, 1915.

Farwell, Brice, ed. *A Guide to the Music of Arthur Farwell and to the Microfilm Collection of His Work*, prepared by his children. New York: Briarcliff Manor, 1972.

Frankenstein, Alfred. "Reviving Henry F. Gilbert." *Modern Music* 21 (1944), 173–75.

Garofalo, Robert Joseph. *The New Grove Dictionary of American Music*, eds. H. Wiley Hitchcock and Stanley Sadie. London: Macmillan, 1986, s.v. "Converse, Frederick Shepherd."

———. "The Life and Works of Frederick Shepherd Converse (1871–1940)." Ph.D. diss., Catholic University of America, 1969.

Gilbert, Henry F. "The American Composer." *Musical Quarterly* 1 (1915), 169–86.

———. "Folk-Music in Art-Music—A Discussion and a Theory." *Musical Quarterly* 3 (1917), 577–99.

———. "Humor in Music." *Musical Quarterly* 12 (1926), 40–55.

———. "Music After the War." *The New Music Review* 19 (1920), 44–48.

———. "Musical Hypocrites." *The New Music Review* 20 (1921), 238–39.

———. "Notes on a Trip to Frankfurt in the Summer of 1927." *Musical Quarterly* 16 (1930), 21–37.

———. "Originality." *Musical Quarterly* (1919), 1–9.

Gilman, Lawrence. *Stories of Symphonic Music*. New York: Harper & Brothers, 1908.

Goldberg, Isaac. "An American Composer." *The American Mercury* 15 (1928), 331–35.

Goss, Madeline. *Modern Music-Makers*. New York: Dutton, 1952.

Hale, Philip. "Musical and Dramatic Criticism." Clippings of newspaper reviews, in the Boston Public Library. Microfilm, rolls 1–8, Shelf No. Micro ML 46.H3.

————*Philip Hale's Boston Symphony Programme Notes*, ed. John N. Burk. Garden City, New York: Doubleday, Doran, 1935.

Hanson, Howard. *Music in Contemporary American Civilization*. Lincoln, Nebraska: University of Nebraska Press, 1951.

Haskins, James, with Kathleen Benson. *Scott Joplin*. Garden City, New York: Doubleday, 1978.

Hipsher, Edward Ellsworth. *American Opera and Its Composers*. Philadelphia: Presser, 1927.

Hoffman, Frederick J. *The Twenties*. New York: Free Press, 1962.

Homer, Sidney. *My Wife and I*. New York: Macmillan, 1939.

Howard, John Tasker. *Charles Tomlinson Griffes*. New York: Schirmer, 1923.

————. *Deems Taylor*. Studies in Contemporary Composers 5. New York: C. Fischer, 1927.

————. "John Alden Carpenter." *Modern Music* 9 (1931), 8–16.

————. *Our American Music*, 4th ed. New York: Crowell, 1965.

————. *Our Contemporary Music*. New York: Crowell, 1941.

Hubbard, W. L., ed. *The History of American Music*. The American History and Encyclopedia of Music 8. Toledo, Ohio: Squire, 1908.

Hughes, Rupert. *Contemporary American Composers*. Boston: Page, 1900.

King, Maurice R. "Edgar Stillman Kelley: American Composer, Author, and Teacher." Ph.D. diss., Florida State University, 1970.

Kirk, Edgar Lee. "Toward American Music; a study of the life and music of Arthur George Farwell." Ph.D. diss., University of Rochester, 1958.

Klein, Sister Mary Justina. *The Contributions of Daniel Gregory Mason to American Music*. Washington: Catholic University of America Press, 1957.

Kramer, A. Walter. "Charles Tomlinson Griffes: Cut Down in His Prime, a Victim of Our Barbarous Neglect of Genius." *Musical America* (22 May 1920), pp. 39–40.

Krueger, Karl. *The Musical Heritage of the United States: The Unknown Portion*. New York: Society for the Preservation of the American Musical Heritage, 1973.

Leedy, Denoe. "Arthur Shepherd." *Modern Music* 16 (1939), 87–93.

Leichtentritt, Hugo. *Serge Koussevitsky. The Boston Symphony Orchestra and the New American Music*. Cambridge, Massachusetts: Harvard University Press, 1946.

Levy, Alan Howard. *Musical Nationalism*. Westport, Connecticut: Greenwood, 1983.

Lewis, Ralph B. "The Life and Music of Daniel Gregory Mason." Ph.D. diss., University of Rochester, 1957.

Longyear, Katherine E. *The New Grove Dictionary of American Music*, eds. H. Wiley

Hitchcock and Stanley Sadie. London: Macmillan, 1986, s.v. "Gilbert, Henry F(ranklin Belknap)."

———. "Henry F. Gilbert, His Life and Works." Ph.D. diss., University of Rochester, 1968.

———. "Henry F. Gilbert's Unfinshed 'Uncle Remus' Opera." *Yearbook for Inter-American Musical Research* 10 (1974), 50–67.

Loucks, Richard. *Arthur Shepherd, American Composer.* Provo, Utah: Brigham Young University Press, 1980.

Luening, Otto. *The Odyssey of an American Composer.* New York: Scribner's Sons, 1980.

MacArthur, Pauline A. "Henry Hadley's Place in American Music." *Musical America* (29 October 1921), 21, 24.

Maisel, Edward. *Charles T. Griffes,* updated ed. New York: Knopf, 1984.

Mason, Daniel Gregory. *Contemporary Composers.* New York: Macmillan, 1918.

———. "Democracy and Music." *Musical Quarterly* 3 (1917), 641–57.

———. *The Dilemma of American Music.* New York: Macmillan, 1928.

———. *Music as a Humanity.* New York: Gray, 1921.

———. *Music in My Time and Other Reminiscences.* New York: Macmillan, 1938.

———. *Tune in, America.* New York: Knopf, 1931.

Moore, Douglas. *From Madrigal to Modern Music.* New York: Norton, 1942.

Moore, MacDonald. *Yankee Blues: Musical Culture and American Identity.* Bloomington: Indian University Press, 1985.

Nathan, Hans. "United States of America." *A History of Song,* ed. Denis Stevens. New York: Norton, 1970, 408–60.

Newman, William S. "Arthur Shepherd." *Musical Quarterly* 36 (1950), 159–79.

Perison, Harry D. "Charles Wakefield Cadman: His Life and Works." Ph.D. diss., University of Rochester, 1978.

Peterkin, Norman. "Charles T. Griffes." *Chesterian.* New Series No. 30 (1923), 161–69.

Pierson, Thomas C. "The Life and Music of John Alden Carpenter." Ph.D. diss., University of Rochester, 1952.

Porte, John F. "Charles Wakefield Cadman, an American Nationalist." *Chesterian.* New Series, No. 39 (1924), 223–26.

Rosenfeld, Paul. *An Hour with American Music.* Philadelphia; Lippincott, 1929.

———. *Musical Chronicle (1917–1923).* New York: Harcourt, Brace, 1923.

Sear, H. G. "Henry Franklin Belknap Gilbert." *Music Review* 5 (1944), 250–59.

Severance, Ruth. "The Life and Work of Frederick Shepherd Converse." M.A. thesis, Boston Unversity, 1932.

Shepherd, Arthur. *Cobbett's Cyclopedic Survey of Chamber Music,* vol. 2, 2nd ed., ed. Walter Willson Cobbett. London: Oxford University Press, 1963, s.v. "Converse, Frederick, Shepherd."

———. *Cobbett's Cyclopedic Survey of Chamber Music,* 2nd ed., ed. Walter Willson Cobbett. London: Oxford, 1963, s.v. "Hadley, Henry Kimball."

———. *Cobbett's Cyclopedic Survey of Chamber Music,* 2nd ed., ed. Walter Wilson Cobbett. London: Oxford, 1963, s.v. "Stillman-Kelley, Edgar."

———. *Cobbett's Cyclopedic Survey of Chamber Music,* 2nd ed., ed. Walter Willson Cobbett. London: Oxford, 1963, s.v. "Mason, Daniel Gregory."

Slonimsky, Nicolas. "Composers of New England." *Modern Music* (February/ March 1930), 24–27. Paginated by number, not by volume.

Smith, George Henry Lovett. "Edward Burlingame Hill." *Modern Music* 16 (1938), 11–16.

Sonneck, Oscar. *A Survey of Music in America.* Washington: McQueen, 1913.

Taylor, Deems. *Of Men and Music.* New York: Simon & Schuster, 1937.

Thompson, Randall. "The Contemporary Scene in American Music." *Musical Quarterly* 18 (1932), 9–17.

Thomson, Virgil. *American Music Since 1910.* New York: Hilt, Rinehart & Winston, 1971.

Tuthill, Burnett C. "Daniel Gregory Mason." *Musical Quarterly* 34 (1948), 46–60.

Tyler, Linda L. *Edward Burlingame Hill.* Westport, Connecticut: Greenwood, 1989.

Upton, William Treat. *Art-Song in America* with *A Supplement to Art-Song in America.* Philadelphia: Ditson, 1938.

———. "The Songs of C. T. Griffes." *Musical Quarterly* 9 (1923), 314–28.

Ward, Ronald David. "The Life and Works of John Powell (1882–1963)." Ph.D. diss., Catholic Unversity of America, 1973.

Wu, Arlouine G. *Constance Eberhart: A Musical Career in the Age of Cadman,* ed. Leland Fox. n.p. University of Mississippi Press, 1983.

Index

About the Author

NICHOLAS E. TAWA is Professor of Music at the University of Massachusetts, Boston. A specialist in American musical history, his books include *Sweet Sounds for Gentle People*, *Serenading the Reluctant Eagle*, *A Most Wondrous Babble* (Greenwood Press, 1987), *The Way to Tin Pan Alley*, and *The Coming of Age of American Art Music* (Greenwood Press, 1991).